THE

DIVORCE
SOURCEBOOK

Third Edition

THE
DIVORCE
SOURCEBOOK

Third Edition

DAWN BRADLEY BERRY, J.D.

New York Chicago San Francisco Lisbon London Madrid Mexico City
Milan New Delhi San Juan Seoul Singapore Sydney Toronto

The *McGraw·Hill* Companies

Library of Congress Cataloging-in-Publication Data

Berry, Dawn Bradley.
    The divorce sourcebook / by Dawn Bradley Berry. —3rd ed.
       p.   cm.
    Includes index.
    ISBN 0-07-147686-5 (alk. paper)
    1. Divorce—Law and legislation—United States—Popular works.   I. Title.

KF535.Z9B379   2007
346.7301'66—dc22   2006022993

1 2 3 4 5 6 7 8 9 10 11 12 13 14 15 16 17 18 19   FGR/FGR   0 9 8 7 6

ISBN-13: 978-0-07-147686-7
ISBN-10:   0-07-147686-5

Credits for literary permissions can be found on page 299, which is to be considered an extension of this copyright page.

McGraw-Hill books are available at special quantity discounts to use as premiums and sales promotions, or for use in corporate training programs. For more information, please write to the Director of Special Sales, Professional Publishing, McGraw-Hill, Two Penn Plaza, New York, NY 10121-2298. Or contact your local bookstore.

This book is printed on acid-free paper.

Contents

Acknowledgments

SPECIAL THANKS TO those who helped to turn the idea for this book into a reality: Roberta Beyer, Clarette Bradley, Judith Finfrock, David B. Riggert, Kathleen Robertson, Nicky Whelan, Anne Kass, Cynde Goyen, Lee Ann Fisher, Steve Feher, Judy Lawrence, Kathy Potter, Becky Ralston, Patricia Murphy, Kathryn Lang, Sharon Newell, Cloyd Hinkle, Tony Kaye, Elle Kovak, Lynn Peters, Willy Berry, Clayta Spear, Jacque Moise, Laura Levin, John Kirby, and Laura Kirby; and to my unfailingly good-natured and supportive editors, Bud Sperry, Maria Magallanes, Natasha Graf, Sarah Pelz, and Craig Bolt.

The stories in this book are true; however, the names of several contributors have been changed at their request. My thanks to them for their willingness to share their experiences and insights.

Introduction

IN HER MEMOIR, *Fear of Fifty*, Erica Jong writes, "Divorce is my generation's coming of age ceremony—a ritual scarring that makes anything that happens afterward seem bearable." Most of those who have been through this "ceremony"—even one in which the participants tried to make the ordeal as civilized and painless as possible—would likely agree.

To echo the words of millions of other divorced people: I never thought it would happen to me. Not the divorce itself, not the emotional roller coaster, not the loneliness or sadness or fear. This was perhaps the greatest surprise of all—that even what my former husband and I called the "world's most amicable divorce" would nevertheless prove to be one of the most wrenching transitions of my life.

At times, I found myself utterly bereft and totally flummoxed. I made some of the exact mistakes I had warned others against. I did stupid things I knew were stupid. I ignored important things I knew were important. In the real dark nights of my soul, I even found myself reading my own self-help books—this one, along with the *Divorce Recovery Sourcebook*—in what felt like an exceedingly pathetic attempt to make sense of my bewilderment and conflicted feelings.

But reading helped, as did talking to friends, to a counselor, and to others who had survived a divorce. I was lucky. In the comments and shared wisdom of others, I found both solace and sense. I survived, I learned, and after a few years of flailing, I found some measure of equilibrium. I found love again. And I found a wealth of new insights into an experience I had formerly viewed only from the outside.

According to the most recent statistics, nearly 50 percent of all American marriages will end in divorce. What the statistics don't reflect, however, is the human suffering behind each and every divorce, no matter how friendly. In the words of one man, "It takes too long and costs too much." A friend of mine, having endured a miserable divorce from her first husband, warned her second husband that their marriage had better work, because she would rather face a murder trial than another divorce!

Divorce poses many legal, financial, and emotional challenges. On the positive side, people divorcing today have more choices and sources of support than ever before. As the divorce rate has increased, social stigmas condemning people who are divorced have all but disappeared. Innumerable books, websites, support groups, legal aid clinics, classes, counselors, church programs, and products are at hand to ease the pain, expense, and aftermath of this difficult transition. Other services and goods are becoming increasingly available to those seeking to build new lives after divorce, whether as singles, solo parents, or stepfamilies.

Yet despite all the developments, things can still go terribly wrong in a divorce. Children are taken away from loving mothers who have made their share of sacrifices and worked hard to support them, and are turned over to deadbeat fathers simply because these fathers are at home. Good fathers who have been devoted, attentive parents are denied not only custody of their children but visitation rights as well when a vindictive mother makes false accusations of abuse. Couples who can't agree to a division of property appear before an impatient judge who orders everything sold at a loss and the money divided. Wives who have been battered in body and spirit are bullied by their abusive husbands into signing away everything. Parents blinded by hate lose sight of their children's terror and agony as they go to war over custody.

Fortunately, such events in divorce are becoming more rare. Because they still do occur, however, it is essential for anyone dissolving a marriage to know his or her rights and responsibilities, as well as what to expect and how to plan for problems that may arise. The goal of this book is to provide an overview of the options available to those divorcing, and a guide to where more detailed information may be found.

I've included only the recommendations and advice I believe to be good, sound, and sensible. I've also endeavored to provide not only the what, but also the how, gleaned from professionals in various fields. At the back of this book you'll find an extensive list of sources of help, from books and websites to therapy groups, from hotlines to public agencies.

The Divorce Sourcebook is full of dos and don'ts, things the experts preach that you must always do or warn that you must never do. But it's equally important to remember that we are all fallible human beings. None of us behaves ideally or does everything right, even when life is running smoothly. In the midst of a divorce, you can't expect yourself to do everything perfectly. Divorce brings out the worst in people. You will make mistakes, do things you're not proud of, and act in ways you ordinarily would not. Don't beat yourself up over your goofs. Take note of what you learn and move on. Skipping a day of work to wallow in bed, get sloppy drunk, and sob all afternoon doesn't mean you're irresponsible or ready for rehab. One tactical error in financial planning is unlikely to doom you to a life of destitution. One nasty exchange with your spouse in front of the kids won't scar them for life. Do the best you can and then let it be.

Millions of people have survived the tempest of divorce at least once. Some of their stories are told in the pages that follow. Most have gone on to build better lives, knowing in retrospect that they are stronger and wiser for having lived through it. So will you.

1

The Development of Family Law and Social Attitudes

A Brief History and a Look at Where We Are Today

IN MANY WAYS, divorce is a complex, confusing, and difficult process. As a result, many people harbor misconceptions about what to expect when facing a divorce. A large part of this confusion can be attributed to the history of family law. Today's divorce experience has been shaped by legal, religious, psychological, and social forces. Theories and procedures have changed dramatically over the past hundred years, and they continue to evolve more rapidly than ever before. Understanding how we got to this point can provide a perspective on both the negative and positive aspects of divorcing today.

Divorce Before 1900

The first divorce in recorded American history occurred in a Massachusetts Puritan court in 1639. The decree was awarded to a woman who had learned that her husband was a bigamist and already had a wife. The husband was fined, imprisoned, and finally banished to England. Four years later, a woman was again granted the next American divorce, because her husband had deserted her and was living with another woman. These circumstances fit the strict requirements at that time, when adultery was the only ground for divorce. A man could divorce on the ground of adultery alone,

1

and his wife could be banished, put to death, or at the very least be publicly shamed. Adultery alone was not enough for a woman to divorce a man, however; additional grounds such as bigamy or desertion also had to be proved. Partial divorces were allowed for cruelty or desertion. These divorces often caused great hardship to women, who remained economically tied to absent husbands. A husband who deserted his family could show up later and claim control of all of the wife's earnings, even the money she had made after he abandoned her.

From the late 1700s until the mid-1800s, in many states, a divorce could be obtained only by petitioning the state legislature to pass a private legislative act ending the marriage. Not suprisingly, this process was lengthy and difficult. It was far more available to men, with the most common ground for divorce being an "immoral wife."

Yet by the late 1700s, divorce was common enough that scholars were criticizing the "high divorce rates." At that time, a study in Connecticut revealed that one in every hundred marriages ended in divorce. Andrew Jackson married a divorced woman, which created great scandal when he ran for president but didn't prevent his election in 1828.

Legal changes began in the early nineteenth century. Social reformers such as Elizabeth Cady Stanton, an early advocate of equality for women, had begun to speak out in favor of more liberal and egalitarian divorce laws. By the 1830s, women who were deserted by their husbands could get a divorce or at least regain the right to control their property and establish limited economic independence. During the 1840s, the process was simplified, and more women began petitioning for divorce. Historical reports indicate that then, as now, the most acrimonious battles were over child custody.

By the mid-nineteenth century, the courts had been given the authority to order divorces, including the power to award alimony to women whose husbands engaged in adultery or cruelty. However, many women did not seek a divorce until after a husband had deserted, so alimony was often impossible to collect. Divorce carried a heavy stigma at this time, too. Women were viewed as the guardians of decency and morality in the family and were often castigated for having "failed in the moral education" of a spouse who engaged in adultery or abandoned the family.

During the mid-1800s, progress in divorce laws tended to be restricted to the northern states, while the southern states remained loyal to the more strict English tradition. An especially ugly bit of hypocrisy also retarded the evolution of fair divorce laws in the south. Many men resisted making adultery an equally applied ground for divorce because of the long acceptance of liaisons between white men and female slaves. Yet husbands often used a wife's interracial encounter as grounds for immediate divorce, accompanied by harsh legal and public condemnation that precluded an award of alimony.

Early divorce laws were more liberal in many other countries. Under ancient Athenian law effective around AD 200, a Greek couple could go their separate ways after merely filing a notice with a magistrate. A husband or wife, under old Irish law, could end a marriage simply by walking away from it on the first of February. "Deadly and notorious hostility" was sufficient to gain a divorce in Prussia in the 1750s, while in enlightened France, couples could get a no-fault divorce by mutual consent as early as the 1790s, although they did have to show that they had gone through an extended process of attempted reconciliation involving both families. When the French monarchy was restored in 1816, however, divorce was completely abolished. In the 1830s, Swedish couples could divorce on grounds of incompatibility, ill treatment, drunkenness, or hatred and bitterness between spouses. Two years of separation was ground for divorce at the end of the eighteenth century in Denmark.

For centuries, divorce was unavailable or difficult to obtain in predominantly Catholic countries, but most allowed divorce in some cases by the turn of the twentieth century, with the exception of Spain, Italy, and Ireland. Ireland was the last country in the Western world to adopt modern laws permitting divorce, which became effective in 1996.

When and how easily divorce should be granted has always been a subject of considerable debate in the United States. In the 1820s, Robert Owen, a journalist, congressman, and social reformer, campaigned publicly for laws providing easier release for those trapped in an unhappy marriage. Indiana was one of the first states to enact liberal divorce statutes. Anyone meeting the residency requirement could obtain a divorce even if the other spouse had disappeared and could not be located. This sparked controversy between those who believed that easier divorce laws encouraged immorality and those who felt that harsh restrictions were more likely to cause hypocrisy, adultery, and domestic violence. Vestiges of this debate continue today.

The Married Women's Property Acts, first enacted in New York and Pennsylvania in 1848, protected the property rights of women who entered a marriage owning property of their own. However, they did not change the common-law rules that gave the husband full rights to all property acquired during the marriage, including the earnings of the wife. Perhaps the most important aspect of these acts was to recognize at least some rights of married women. At about the same time, organized groups began to work for greater rights and protection for working women, and for women's right to vote. Such efforts were often made with the support and assistance of those working for the abolition of slavery. Writer, speaker, civil rights leader, and former slave Frederick Douglass was one of the early advocates of equal rights for women.

The first self-help book on divorce, entitled *How to Get a Divorce*, was published in New York in 1859. After the Civil War, the divorce rate increased dramatically. Demographic changes occurring during the next twenty years also impacted divorce. The number of people who never married reached an all-time high in 1877. Everyday life began to take on more of the characteristics familiar today, such as fewer children and closer emotional ties between parents and children. Women became less involved in farming or other family business and occupied the position of homemaker and keeper of peace and morality in the family. The law slowly began to change in response to the dominant social trends. For example, awards of alimony to homemakers rewarded a woman's devotion to her family and placed the burden of support on the husband.

State laws governing divorce fluctuated during the latter half of the nineteenth century, with some becoming more liberal and others becoming more restrictive or abolishing divorce altogether.

Statistics from this period indicate that harsh divorce laws did little to preserve families. People simply went their separate ways and worked things out the best they could without the involvement of the legal system. Some of the family laws passed during this time were blatantly sexist or patently outrageous. For example, South Carolina laws set forth how much wealth a married man could bequeath in his will to his mistress at the expense of his wife. Not surprisingly, there was no comparable law for women.

The movement west during the late nineteenth century also affected divorce throughout America. Western states tended to have less restrictive grounds for divorce, shorter residency requirements, and laws that made the process easier. Some states, including Utah, North Dakota, South Dakota, and Indiana, viewed more liberal divorce laws as a business opportunity. Entire towns sprang up, often in areas where railroads converged, just to cater to people seeking a "migratory divorce." Lawyers, judges, hoteliers, and restaurateurs all profited from the so-called divorce trade. Of course, there was public outcry over the alleged immorality of such enterprises, but the nation was also forced to recognize that divorce had become a facet of modern society and was not going to go away.

National statistics on divorce were compiled by Congress for the first time in 1887. At about the same period, the social stigma surrounding divorce began to lift somewhat. Many social scientists shifted the blame for divorce from the individuals to society and proceeded to work toward social reform. Educational programs on how to create a sound family life began to emerge, and books on how to have a good marriage grew in popularity.

The philosophy and purpose of divorce laws also changed around this time. Although the marital partnership was not yet considered a union of equals, it was assumed that marriage was a joint economic enterprise. Each person was considered responsible for contributing to the prosperity of the home and was fairly entitled to share in the fruits of his or her labor. In community property states, each spouse became entitled to half of all the income and property the couple acquired during the marriage, based on the rationale that both spouses contributed equally to the economic assets of the home, whether by earning income or by maintaining the home and raising children.

Divorce in the Twentieth and Twenty-First Centuries

By 1900, most states had some system of divorce law in place, and while some significant variations remained, most shared similar elements. Virtually all were fault-based, using the rationale that a lifelong union should not be dissolved unless one spouse committed a serious wrong against the other. This caused obvious problems for people who simply did not get along, especially in states such as New York, where for many years the only ground for divorce was adultery. Individuals and their attorneys often went to ridiculous lengths to manufacture the evidence necessary to satisfy the legal requirements. People possessing dramatic abilities but few scruples actually made their livings as "professional witnesses." Proof-of-fault requirements often led to a tremendous waste of time, open perjury, and unnecessary hostility, especially since property awards were often based on fault. The cases were rampant with gender bias, too. Wives were frequently charged with "cruelty" for such acts as substandard housekeeping.

Changing Social Attitudes

Society changed more during the twentieth century than in the previous five hundred years. These rapid and extreme changes had a direct impact on the nature of family life. Industry brought people off the farm and into the city. Job opportunities for women increased, and women enjoyed greater career independence as well as more diversions in their leisure time. The balance of knowledge and social awareness expanded with the advent of radio, movies, and television. Mechanization freed both men and women from time spent on household chores. Dance halls and nightclubs, previously open only to men, began welcoming women and couples. The expectations of the average person rose considerably. People began to see happiness and excitement in a marriage as a necessity rather than a luxury. As early as 1910, alarmists railed against the feminist movement as a leading cause of the breakdown of the family, and the debate raged on over whether marriage should be viewed as a religious sacrament or a legal contract.

Marriage counseling was available by the turn of the century, and "visiting marriage," similar to today's commuter marriage, was accepted as an alternative for some couples. Advances in psychology, such as the embrace of Freud's theory that unhappy marriage and divorce was a result of childhood events, began to turn the focus toward children from divorced homes. In 1914, the first separate family court was established in Ohio. Courts devoted exclusively to family issues are the norm today.

Beginning in the 1920s, prevailing attitudes toward marriage and the family underwent drastic change. Couples began to experiment with alternatives to traditional marriage. Terms such as "trial marriage" or "setting up light housekeeping" were used by unmarried couples who lived together. There is some evidence that cohabitation remained fairly common throughout the century, even in more conservative times. "We did the same things then that you do now," one woman, now in her eighties, told me. "We were just more discreet."

Popular acceptance of the idea that women could—and should—enjoy sex just as much as men sparked a sexual revolution in the 1920s. An increase in the number of pregnant brides followed, as did an increase in the divorce rate. This era also saw a rise in "collusion" between spouses who mutually agreed to dissolve their marriage yet were still required to prove a fault-based ground for divorce in court. By the 1930s, "mental cruelty" was a legal ground for divorce in many states and served as a catch-all forerunner to today's no-fault statutes. Controversy over the issue of migratory divorce continued until 1942, when the U.S. Supreme Court ruled that Nevada's six-week residency requirement to obtain a divorce was valid.

By the mid-twentieth century, divorce was no longer an unusual event or a cause for whispering and gossip, yet a double standard remained. Although men who left their wives were often scorned as irresponsible gadabouts, women almost invariably received more harsh condemnation after a divorce. When my mother divorced her first husband after World War II, she says she was labeled a "man hater." (She jokes that this had its advantages, though, because she had plenty of dates with men who thought they were "safe" with her.) By this time, however, divorce was becoming commonplace enough that it was viewed as a reasonable choice. My aunt told me that in 1935, she approached her marriage with some trepidation but realized that divorce was at least a realistic option if the marriage didn't work out (fortunately, it did). She said the judge who performed the marriage commented that none of the couples he had ever married had been divorced. This statement was not as astounding then as it would be today, but it does show that the subject could be discussed freely in the 1930s.

The Divorce Revolution

Author Lenore Weitzman, Ph.D., describes the changes that took place during the late twentieth century as a "divorce revolution." In her book of the same name, she explains the revolution's three components:

- The soaring divorce rate
- The widespread adoption of no-fault divorce laws
- The changing social attitude toward divorce

The divorce rate in the United States increased gradually but slowly between 1860 and the early 1960s, except for a brief period of substantial increase immediately after World War II. Between 1966 and 1976, the divorce rate doubled, and each year between 1975 and 1981, the rate soared rapidly. There were approximately 1.2 million divorces in 1981, with a minuscule drop by 1985.

By 1973, more than 60 percent of divorcing couples had children. This led to changes in the law. "The best interest of the child" became the court's predominant concern when parents divorced. Controversy arose and continues today over such ideas as the "tender years" doctrine, which advocates a preference that a child stay with the mother until at least the age of seven or eight. Debate also persists over such issues as how closely visitation and custody rights should be tied to child support as well as discrimination against working mothers in custody decisions.

Married women were still considered subordinate by legal concepts that remained in place until the 1970s. Such laws included those permitting women to marry at a younger age without parental consent, requirements that the wife assume her husband's surname, power of the husband to determine the family domicile, the absolute right of the husband to his wife's sexual services without recognition of marital rape, and laws providing that only men may sue for loss of consortium (loss of love and sexual companionship) if a spouse was injured or killed.

Many other biases were subtle, and although the laws have changed, some remain in practice today. The exercise of basic rights, such as registration to vote, obtaining a driver's license, and buying insurance, can still be more difficult for women who do not take their husband's name or share the same domicile. In 1994, a friend of mine who had kept her maiden name through eleven years of marriage was told by her husband's insurance company that it would not issue her an insurance card under his policy in her own name. She was forced to use his last name—which she had never legally taken.

As late as the 1960s and 1970s, subtle social messages hinted that single adults, especially those who were divorced, were somehow not a normal part of society. In the book *Divorcing*, psychologist Mel Krantzler writes of the difficulty of even buying single-serving portions of packaged food after his own divorce in 1970. At that time, there were also no support groups or social events to provide the acceptance and help available to divorced people now. Television and movies universally portrayed the content nuclear family that never grappled with divorce.

Fortunately, the 1970s and 1980s were times of tremendous change in this regard. In 1980, Ronald Reagan, a divorced man, was elected president of the United States. Divorce had become a part of so many lives that it was no longer considered abnormal. As the 1980s progressed, divorce became increasingly viewed as a common life transition, not an aberration or personal failure.

No-Fault Divorce

Author Lenore Weitzman, Ph.D., describes the changes that occurred during the late twentieth century as a "divorce revolution." Undeniably, the advent of no-fault divorce reflected a major change in both the law and social attitudes. When California adopted its no-fault divorce law in 1970, it was the first time in the modern history of the Western world that a requirement of fault as the basis for a divorce was abolished completely. Under the new law, one party could obtain a divorce by asserting that irreconcilable differences had caused the irremediable breakdown of the marriage. Other states, as well as other countries, were quick to jump onto the no-fault bandwagon. All were eager to eliminate the hostility, sham testimony, and abuses common under the fault-based system. By 1985, all fifty states had some form of no-fault divorce in place.

Undeniably, the no-fault system has eliminated, or at least reduced, many of the evils of fault-based divorce. Under the old system, alimony was often used as a threat or weapon by one or both parties. Support was generally awarded only to the "innocent" spouse, so the party found "guilty" of adultery by the court typically was barred from receiving any alimony or was ordered to pay more than someone divorced on other grounds. Property awards also followed this trend, and in some states judges were required to award more than half the property to the "innocent" spouse. Thus, vicious battles and exaggerated claims were not uncommon. Unfair settlements were sometimes leveraged under the threat of personal humiliation, professional damage, or the financial risk of bringing a case to court (a practice that, unfortunately, persists today—but with less frequency).

The new laws brought radical changes in several areas of the divorce process. One spouse could unilaterally divorce the other without his or her agreement. Financial awards were based on needs and resources rather than on good or bad behavior. Alimony and property awards sought to treat men and women equally, and a forum was established in which amicable divorces could be legally encouraged. The goal behind the change was to make the laws more modern, civilized, and realistic.

Yet the new laws did not entirely eliminate the concept of fault from divorce cases. Fault may be considered in awarding alimony, according to the law in some states. Also, behavior that directly damages the other spouse may still be punished. A spouse who has committed "waste" (harm to the couple's financial property, such as that caused by gambling or buying elaborate gifts for a paramour) may be ordered to reimburse the estate. Likewise, virtually all states now allow one spouse to sue the other for torts (wrongful acts that cause injury), in the same way that strangers may sue one another. Domestic tort claims are often brought in cases in which one spouse has deliberately hurt the other by violence. Fault-based behavior also remains relevant in child custody cases in which abuse or parental fitness is an issue.

And this is the downside of the no-fault scheme. Areas in which fault is very much an issue, as in cases of spousal or child abuse, are sometimes either glossed over in an attempt to remove all aspects of fault from the process or exaggerated and misused, as when one partner falsely accuses the other of inappropriate behavior to try to gain leverage in unrelated matters, such as property division.

In addition to eliminating punishments, rewards have been abolished under the no-fault system. People who faithfully invested in the partnership by being an ambitious breadwinner or devoted homemaker in spite of mistreatment by a spouse receive no economic reward for their sacrifice.

Alimony awards were substantially restructured under the no-fault laws. The changes reflected the modern belief that women were or could become independent and self-sufficient after a divorce. In theory, exceptions to this assumption were made for women with custody of young children, women in need of transitional support for a period of education or job training, and older homemakers who could not be fairly expected to begin a new life or become completely self-supporting. Yet the general presumption against alimony has reduced the overall size, duration, and frequency of awards, sometimes with unfair results. For example, a woman is sometimes awarded an unrealistically short term of alimony, such as one year, in which she is expected to reconstruct her life, learn new work skills, and become entirely self-supporting after being out of the workforce for ten or twenty years. Whereas most states leave the amount and timing of alimony awards up to the judge, a few states have a fixed time limit of one to three years.

Thus, despite the noble goals and truly positive reforms, the new no-fault laws were soon found to have the potential to create a variety of unfair consequences. In some cases, they merely removed the hostility to an even more inappropriate arena, that of child custody. Disputes over custody and support have become the new emotional dumping ground, one in which children are the real victims.

The Backlash Against No-Fault Divorce

The past decade has seen a great deal of change in virtually all aspects of family law. A few states have begun to adopt measures allowing same-sex marriages or making registered domestic partnerships, similar to marriage, available to gay or older couples (who would lose social security or other benefits if they married). There also has been a growing nationwide trend toward the reform of no-fault divorce laws.

On Valentine's Day 1996, Michigan state representative Jessie F. Dalman led what has been termed "the divorce counter-revolution" when she introduced legislation designed to establish a two-tier divorce system. Under the proposed Michigan law, a childless couple could obtain a no-fault divorce upon mutual consent, but for those with minor children, or in cases in which one spouse opposed the divorce, the filing spouse would have to produce evidence of marital fault of the other—proving one of what Hofstra law professor J. Herbie DiFonzo calls "the unholy trinity": adultery, desertion, or extreme cruelty. By 1997, at least nine other states had introduced similar bills. The Michigan law never passed, but later that year, after heavy lobbying by conservative Christians, Louisiana adopted a new marriage law that allows couples to choose between two forms of marriage, "traditional" or "covenant." A Louisiana couple wed in a traditional marriage may divorce after a six-month separation, while those in a covenant marriage cannot divorce unless they have been separated for two years or prove egregious wrongdoing by one spouse—adultery, abandonment, or mental or physical abuse.

Numerous state legislatures have continued to consider bills proposing covenant marriage, but as of 2006, only three states (Arkansas, Arizona, and Louisiana) had adopted covenant marriage laws. Couples in these states may choose to enter into either a covenant marriage or the traditional form of marriage. All covenant marriage laws restrict the time frame and grounds for divorce, with immediate divorce granted only on fault-based grounds, and no-fault available only after a long period of separation (or, in Arizona, upon mutual consent). All require some form of premarital counseling, as well as counseling before divorce.

Laws such as the covenant marriage statutes, which make it harder for couples to divorce, are controversial. Some people feel that they help strengthen families and prevent hasty divorces—certainly a worthy goal, especially when children are involved. But others ask if government intervention is really an effective way to achieve this objective—whether such laws actually enhance marital commitment and family ties, or merely add to the expense and trauma of divorce for couples who have made up their minds to split. There is also growing concern about whether the laws may effectively trap women and children in violent homes.

From a constitutional perspective, such laws are troubling in their religious underpinnings and regulation of matters recognized as highly private and personal. And what about the problems that led to the proliferation of no-fault laws in the first place—the deception, the collusion, the perjury, the invention of damaging and humiliating stories of grievous wrongdoing by one spouse, when in reality the couple simply did not get along and desired to end the marriage? During the 1960s, 90 percent of divorces on fault grounds were granted without contest, after brief, perfunctory hearings in which one party appeared to jump through the required hoops. The other 10 percent involved a dismal public airing of a couple's dirtiest laundry. Was this era of dishonesty and false blame really more positive for a couple's children? As Professor DiFonzo wrote in the Idaho Law Review, "Bills to gut no-fault divorce and return to the scarlet-letter milieu of proving fault are nostalgic attempts to recapture what never was."

While few would disagree that marriage should not be viewed as a revolving door, especially by parents, it is also important to ask whether it is in the best interest of a child to grow up in a home in which one or both parents are miserably unhappy. Innumerable studies of the effect of divorce on children have concluded that children are damaged less by divorce than by exposure to intense conflict, whether their families are intact or divided. And one fact has been documented beyond question: children who live in a home in which one parent is brutally abusive to the other suffer horribly and face heightened risk for a host of problems, including academic failure, illness, suicide, and the inability to form healthy family relationships of their own. Any laws that make it harder for victims of family violence to escape their abusers should be viewed with grave concern.

It is also vital to remember that no-fault laws were adopted not only to make divorce faster and easier, but also to preserve the integrity of the law and to maintain the dignity of families enduring what was already a difficult and painful process. As stated by Professor DiFonzo in the *Idaho Law Review*, "In the face of overwhelming evidence presented of the farcical nature of American society's lengthy dalliance with fault-only divorce mechanisms, the conclusion that we should reinstall the unholy trinity of fault in our divorce pantheon is untenable. Conditioning a divorce upon one spouse's epitomizing the other as an adulterer, deserter, or beast provides not only a pathetic parody of the complex dynamic of intense psychological relationships, but also grossly overestimates the power of law over culture. The mightiest law is that of necessity: couples who desire to divorce will do so."

Experience bears out the truth of the professor's words. The reality is that nearly everyone who enters into a marriage expects, or at least hopes, that it will last a lifetime. Most divorces occur as the result of unanticipated change—in one's partner, outlook, circumstances, or other aspects of life. In reality, very few couples divorce impulsively, especially when children are involved. Even during the heyday of no-fault, most divorcing clients I encountered found the process emotionally taxing and practically arduous. Of all the many, many people with whom I spoke in preparing this book, only one stated the opinion that her divorce happened too quickly. The overwhelming majority of people who seek a divorce have given the matter months or even years of serious reflection before putting the legal wheels in motion.

Family law attorney David B. Riggert comments, "There is no sense in making it harder to get divorced." Instead, Riggert believes that if one spouse is ambivalent about the divorce, the couple should seek counseling before filing. "If someone comes to me for consultation about a divorce but makes a comment such as, 'This wasn't my idea,' I immediately ask if they have been to couples counseling. If they haven't, I suggest it would be to their advantage to try it before proceeding with the divorce—their money may be better spent on counseling instead of attorney's fees. Some couples I've sent to counseling have reconciled. I would much rather see them try this route first than invest a lot of effort and money—mine and theirs—in preparing for a divorce and then deciding they don't want to go through with it."

Many state legislatures agree with Riggert's perspective. While covenant marriage and legal recognition of same-sex unions have garnered the bulk of the media's attention, the divorce reform movement had a far broader effect in spawning laws that require or encourage some form of counseling before couples marry or divorce. A majority of the states now have some form of predivorce counseling laws. These laws vary widely, ranging from those that merely set up a state counseling agency for voluntary use by any troubled couple to those that permit a family court judge, or either party to a divorce, to request mandatory counseling. In other states, counseling may be required when minor children are involved or when a no-fault divorce is contested by one party.

Many people believe that the counseling laws are a wiser choice than covenant marriage laws, because of their constructive focus and wider application. In some states, divorce-related counseling programs deliberately take a two-tiered approach: first, to try to save the marriage, but also to give the parties and their children a realistic picture of what to expect and how to cope if the divorce proceeds. Such programs have been praised as minimally intrusive into the private sphere while also teaching skills that will prove useful, whatever course the family ultimately chooses.

The "divorce revolution" has also generated an opposite trend. At the same time some laws have been enacted to make divorce more difficult, others have been passed to simplify certain divorce proceedings, especially in cases in which the couple has no young children or high-value assets. In California, for example, a process called "summary dissolution" is available to couples who have been married five years or less, have no children from the relationship, do not own a home or other real estate, have marital property valued at less than $25,000 and combined debt not exceeding

$5,000, are not seeking spousal support, and have agreed in writing to a division of assets and debts and to other terms of the divorce. The paperwork to accomplish a summary dissolution is simplified, and no court appearance is required. Other states have similar provisions.

Changes in Child Custody Laws

As the divorce process has undergone significant changes over the past few decades, child custody laws have also changed in significant ways. First, in conjunction with the move toward equality between the sexes, the traditional idea that primary custody of young children should automatically go to the mother has been eliminated, at least on paper. All states are now legally mandated to give men and women equal rights to custody based on what is in the best interest of the child.

As a corollary, most states now have adopted a legal principle allowing, or in some cases preferring, joint custody. Joint custody does not mean that the children will automatically spend 50 percent of their time with each parent. Instead, it means that both parents have the right to "frequent and continuing contact" with the child, to participate fully in the child's life, and to share important decisions, such as those affecting the child's health, schooling, and religious upbringing. Most children continue to live primarily with one parent—still the mother in the majority of cases—after the divorce. In practice, joint custody is often similar to the shared parenting commonly found under sole custody arrangements.

In addition, all states have now enacted laws such as the Uniform Child Custody Jurisdiction Act, which are intended to discourage custody battles and parental kidnapping. Under federal and state laws, parental kidnapping or the abduction of a child across state lines is a crime, with exceptions made for cases in which abuse is involved or the abducting parent has cause to believe that the child is being endangered by the other parent. Other laws prevent international abduction and provide for the return of children illegally transported from one country to another. Stronger laws, along with more agencies to enforce them, have also been established for child support enforcement. These laws are discussed in detail later in this book.

Divorce and Demographics

Throughout history, political, economic, and religious factors have contributed to divorce rates. While the single most important factor in determining whether a particular marriage will end in divorce is the two people involved, certain social and individual characteristics do seem to make divorce more or less likely. Divorce rates tend to go down during times of economic hardship and to rise in times of prosperity. The rates are lower during major wars and escalate when the wars have ended. After September 11, 2001, divorce rates saw a slight drop, while marriage rates rose. Divorce rates usually increase in a socially progressive political atmosphere and decrease in a more conservative environment.

People of Catholic or Jewish faith have a lower divorce rate than do Protestants, although Catholics have seen an increase in their rate of divorce that parallels that of the general population. Religious practices are believed by some to tie in with racial differences in divorce rates. Hispanics, many of whom are traditionally Catholic, have a lower rate of divorce than other ethnic groups, for example.

Cultural factors may affect the entire divorce process. Attorney Judith Finfrock devoted a large part of her San Francisco practice to domestic relations law. Her firm was composed almost entirely of Asian attorneys, and about three-quarters of her divorce clients were members of an Asian ethnic group. "The Asian clients had different concerns than the Caucasians because of their culture," Finfrock explains. "Loss of face in the community was very big, especially for women. There were also cultural clashes to contend with. For example, it has long been acceptable for men to have concubines in the traditional Chinese culture. But wives in America wouldn't put up with it, since such behavior is not tolerated in our society. If a man's mistress became public knowledge, there would be a loss of face for the woman who accepted it. So, in a divorce where there had been adultery, the wife wanted the husband's fault addressed in the court documents, which became public records. California is strictly no-fault, and adultery can't be alleged as grounds, but many insisted it be stated somewhere in the documents."

Social acceptance of cohabitation without marriage has also had an impact on divorce rates in both America and Europe. Since the 1970s, an increasing number of couples have lived together and ended relationships without divorce, and this might have been a factor in the slightly declining divorce rates.

Today, marriage is generally viewed in the law as a civil contract, an emotional bond, and a financial partnership, while the religious or spiritual nature of the marriage vows continues to be important to many people. We expect our marriages to be happy and to offer companionship, sexual satisfaction, and personal fulfillment. In short, both a realistic view of the multifaceted nature of the partnership and high expectations for marriage prevail.

Baby Boomers and Divorce. For the generation that came of age in the sixties and seventies—the baby boomers—two factors seem to play a major part in the frequency with which we divorce. First, we take our happiness seriously. We were perhaps the first generation to believe that we were entitled to fulfillment and satisfaction in our lives and were responsible for creating it. Happiness was more than a goal—it became a duty. We felt an obligation to work toward ending the misery in the world and in our own lives.

Second, the roles and options open to us were changing rapidly. Women were taught that they could and should pursue careers outside the home. Men learned that they could and should be gentle, nurturing, involved fathers. Yet most of us grew up with traditional role models among our parents and other adults. We were uncertain how to make these new roles work, but we were determined to try. We didn't know how to blend and balance what we expected of ourselves; we were torn and confused about what we wanted. Many members of what author Erica Jong has called the "whiplash generation" tried to "have it all" and ended up with exhausting, chaotic lives. We worked so relentlessly in an effort to be successful professionals and committed parents and responsible citizens and loving spouses—all at the same time—that instead of fulfillment, we often wound up with fragmented lives that formed no coherent whole. Stress was no longer an affliction—it had become a way of life. No wonder marriages crumbled under the pressure.

Divorce may be especially challenging for members of the "sandwich generation," baby boomers who are caring for teen-aged children and aging parents at the same time. Yet while the attitudes, legal process, and causes of divorce have changed a great deal over the centuries, the emotional issues have remained largely the same: problems of property division; how debts will be paid; child and spousal support; child custody and visitation; and the inevitable pain, upheaval, blaming, and sense of failure. The good news is that the social stigmas that made divorce more difficult have disappeared or at least lessened, and far more sources of assistance and support are available for those facing divorce today. Also, legal services are now geared toward how to better serve divorced families and improve the lives of all of those who have been touched by divorce, including single individuals, blended families, grandparents, and the children of divorced parents.

Innovations in Today's Divorce

Despite the relentless efforts of some to make it more difficult, accomplishing a divorce today not only is easier in most cases but also offers more choices than ever before. As the legal costs associated with divorce have skyrocketed, more options have become available for couples divorcing, especially for those with no children and relatively simple assets. Self-help books and websites, do-it-yourself divorce kits, law school or court-annexed clinics, mediation, divorce coaches, and other sources of nonlawyer assistance have become increasingly accessible to people seeking to avoid high legal fees.

As the divorce laws have evolved, the role of the legal profession has changed as well. Property disputes now require cerebral wrangling instead of the former battle to the lowest common denominator of marital behavior. Family law is no longer viewed as a poor cousin of more prestigious legal specialties. Divorce lawyers must be familiar not only with matrimonial law itself but also with corollary issues of crucial importance, including business and property valuation, accounting techniques, child custody and support options, and tax law. As a result, respect for family law specialists has risen.

Science, too, has contributed to the change in our beliefs about divorce. Some scientists who have studied human behavior conclude that most people are not biologically designed to be monogamous and stay with the same mate for a lifetime. People are beginning to understand that not every marriage that ends is a failure—some simply are not meant to last forever. Anthropologist Margaret Mead once responded to a question about her "failed marriages" with a statement that although she had been married three times, none of the marriages was a failure. In today's world, other relationships such as jobs, friendships, and community ties are often temporary, and this is considered normal. Divorce and the new beginning that follows can be a healthy transition into a new phase of life, just as a change in career or a move across the country can be.

Sociologist and author Constance Ahrons believes that as life expectancies increase, and as divorce becomes a more accepted fact of modern family life, the rates are likely to either continue to stabilize or increase slightly. She points out that factors such as remarriage and redivorce, which is becoming more common in today's society, must also be considered, as must declining birth rates and the increasing numbers of women who marry later in life or never marry. Longer lives also make serial marriages more likely. Ahrons suggests that longevity may be the single most powerful reason why divorce rates are unlikely to decrease substantially in the future.

The media have also played a part in shaping our attitude toward divorce and the acceptance of family structures beyond the traditional nuclear group. During the 1970s, movies and television began to acknowledge the increasing numbers of divorced families. A few television programs, such as "One Day at a Time"—about a divorced mother and her two daughters—depicted the trials and triumphs of such families, and, most important, showed them as normal, healthy families, not "broken," not desperate, not failures. Films such as *Kramer vs. Kramer* and *The War of the Roses* became more common throughout the eighties, showing the damage that can be done when divorce or child custody turns into war. In the nineties, abundant stories of the positive and negative aspects of divorce and single parenthood abounded on television, in popular series such as "Grace Under Fire," in movies such as *Mrs. Doubtfire,* and in books such as Terry McMillan's *Waiting to Exhale.*

Divorce Magazine was conceived in 1994, when founder Dan Courvette, then an associate publisher of a Canadian wedding magazine, found his own marriage ending. Courvette realized that while there were scores of magazines dedicated to helping couples plan their wedding day, no periodicals existed to assist with the complexities of a divorce, arguably the most stressful and traumatic time in a person's life. So, in 1996, he founded *Divorce Magazine,* billed as "help for generation 'ex.'" The publication achieved rapid success, quickly expanding to produce four regional editions in North America, along with an extensive website. It offers user-friendly resources providing information, advice, and expert guidance in the areas of law, real estate, tax issues, relationships, mental and physical health, children, dating, blended families, and other issues to readers at various stages of the divorce process. Other publishers seem eager to emulate the magazine's success. In early 1998, Japan launched its own divorce magazine, entitled *Liz* in honor of the much-divorced Elizabeth Taylor.

Given our great expectations for marriage, divorce is likely to remain a part of society. Therefore, the various tasks involved in restructuring families will have to remain dynamic. The future is hard to predict, but it seems safe to say that both the legal systems and social attitudes surrounding divorce will continue to evolve as long as human beings and their social institutions exist.

2

Preparing for Divorce

How to Begin and What to Expect

DIVORCE USUALLY TAKES longer than people think it should. As is true in any difficult transition, those embroiled in a divorce are naturally eager to get it over with and move on. Unfortunately, people sometimes make unwise decisions or agree to property settlements or parenting plans that ultimately are not the best or most workable options. Unless the relationship is violent or there appears to be an imminent crisis, it may be better to take your time and make sure everything has been thought through carefully.

When Should I Seek Legal Advice?

As soon as a couple decides to separate, the process of uncoupling begins, by mutual agreement or whatever arrangements fall into place. It is far better to seek legal assistance sooner than later. Speak with an attorney or other competent legal advisor as soon as you are seriously contemplating a divorce. There are three main reasons why this is advisable. First, if you find an attorney with whom you feel comfortable, this will be one less matter to deal with later if things reach a critical state. Second, patterns that you establish on your own after you separate can affect what happens later if certain issues have to be resolved by a judge. These patterns also affect the perception of the parties involved and may impact mediation or settlement negotiations. Your informal arrangements in regard to housing, child custody, and support will often set the stage for the final decree. Third, if your spouse initiates the legal process, you must be prepared to move quickly. Whenever you receive a legal document, you are usually obligated to respond within ten to thirty days. If you have an attorney, all correspondence and legal documents should go to him or her. The attorney should provide you with a copy of every motion, letter, settlement offer, or other significant document he or she receives. Any time you receive a document from your spouse or from his or her attorney, be sure that you speak with a legal adviser as soon as possible. Do not wait, even a few days. There may be work that needs to be done before the responding papers can be prepared, and action is often required within less than two weeks.

When possible, work out temporary arrangements for child support, spousal support, and custody and visitation before you and your spouse move into separate residences. The agreements don't need to be formal, but they should be definite, put in writing, and shared with the attorneys. The date of separation may be significant. In some states, it can affect your financial responsibilities in major ways—another reason why it is best to speak with a lawyer before the actual separation, if possible. This is especially vital if you plan to move away, and absolutely crucial if children are involved.

If you have separated but are not certain about whether you will divorce or reconcile, it is wise to seek a decree of legal separation. Under this scenario, the couple remains legally married, but all the issues that would be addressed in a divorce (including division of property, support, and child custody) are outlined in a legally binding document. If you reconcile, the document becomes moot. If you divorce, it will form the basis for negotiating a final decree. Some couples simply incorporate the terms of the separation agreement into the decree unchanged, whereas others use it as a starting point to negotiate something different when the divorce becomes final.

Educate Yourself

It can be tremendously helpful, from the standpoint of working effectively with lawyers and mediators and for building emotional strength and confidence, to familiarize yourself with the divorce laws in your state. This is usually easier than it sounds. In many locales, lawyers, government agencies, family courts, or professors in the field of family law have put together handbooks, pamphlets, brochures, or websites to help laypeople understand and use the laws of their state. It can be both satisfying and financially smart to use these tools to get the ball rolling. A growing number of websites provide printable work sheets for organizing information and other tools that are helpful in commencing the process. Many of the self-help materials and programs are excellent, especially those that are set up to conform with a state's particular law. However, be wary of any that claim to completely take the place of a lawyer.

Law Libraries

Law libraries are a frequently overlooked resource for a broad range of materials that can be exceedingly helpful to anyone facing a divorce. Public law libraries, usually housed in or near courthouses, are staffed with knowledgeable librarians (who cannot provide legal advice but can steer patrons to sources of legal information) and often provide materials on family court clinics, lawyer referrals, low-cost or free legal assistance, public classes, and similar matters. Most also have computers available for Internet access and free use of legal databases. Law school libraries are another source of legal materials and information, as well as such services as legal aid clinics staffed by law students.

Free Legal Consultation

In many areas, public service lawyers are available to perform free legal services, including divorce representation, for people whose income falls below a certain level. These services are usually provided through legal aid facilities. Many private lawyers occasionally do cases on a pro bono (free) basis to satisfy state licensing requirements, professional rules, or their own sense of ethics. Others sponsor reasonably priced, weekend classes for people involved in relatively simple, no-fault proceedings, in which participants are assisted in completing the required court forms to file their own divorce.

In some areas, volunteer attorneys provide brief telephone consultations free of charge. For example, the lawyer referral service of the Bar Association of Northern San Diego County offers callers a free half-hour consultation with an attorney experienced in the appropriate field to address their question. Other bar associations and similar groups provide such services on either an ongoing or occasional basis—for example, during the week surrounding Law Day (May 1). While these programs are obviously limited, they can be an excellent way to find out whether your case is a simple matter that may be handled on your own or with limited assistance, or if full-fledged representation by an attorney will be required. In the latter situation, most of the services offer referrals to qualified attorneys in the caller's area.

State and local bar associations may also distribute pamphlets or consumer guides, conduct public seminars, sponsor informative websites, offer live or recorded telephone information lines, and provide other services to the public. Contact information for each state's bar association is listed in Appendix B at the back of this book.

Should I Handle My Own Divorce?

The law surrounding divorce (and related matters such as pension rights, taxes, and creditors' rights) gets more complex by the minute. Yet many people, understandably, wish to avoid the cost of hiring an attorney and instead attempt to represent themselves in a divorce. Depending on each situation, this may be perfectly adequate or an unmitigated disaster.

If both parties are honest, emotionally stable, and able to reach an agreement on all issues, a do-it-yourself divorce may be an efficient and economical option. Kits are available online, at bookstores, or through other sources; most contain a set of forms to fill out and file, plus instructions. However, the charge for these kits may run several hundred dollars. Check with your local family court services or law school clinic before plunking down a hefty sum of money for a kit. You may be able to get the same materials, plus handy assistance in completing and filing them, at a much lower cost or even for free. Lawyers or mediators often provide their own checklists and "homework" assignments for organizing property, too.

Generally, even in the simplest divorce, it is wise to seek some level of legal assistance. Completing a legally sound and satisfactory divorce is about more than just filling out the right forms. The documents are only the final step in the process of gathering and negotiating the information that will go into them—information that must be correct, complete, and clearly understood by all. A cheap divorce can be far more expensive in the long run if you bypass getting the expert help you need. For example, the division of property subject to future tax consequences may result in a large and unpleasant financial surprise unless this is addressed in the settlement. If you have any hesitation about doing your own divorce, listen to your instincts and seek competent assistance.

Family law is uniquely fraught with pitfalls. Building a life with another person over a period of years is seldom an easy task, and the same applies to dismantling it. Even if you and your spouse have had a simple life, the complexities of modern society—and, admittedly, the legal system—often conspire to make things more labyrinthine than is readily apparent. For example, consider a childless couple married two years, who rent a cottage and carry joint debt on two credit cards and one car payment. They decide to part ways and agree to a division of their personal property. She gets the cottage and lease obligation, plus one credit card's debt; he gets the car and the debt on it, plus the other credit card's debt.

Sounds simple, doesn't it? But what about her retirement plan at work? And what if he loses his job and can't make the car payment? Although the divorce decree says the debt is his alone, a divorce order is binding only on the couple, not on their creditors. The lender can still come after her for the car payments if he doesn't make them, unless the loan is refinanced in his name alone.

And what about his military benefits? Also, how will next year's tax returns be prepared?

The point is that there is more to getting a clean, final, successful divorce than filing the papers with the right court. Often others need to become involved, such as creditors, pension fund administrators, and government agencies. Even in what appears to be a simple situation, there may be property-value concerns, tax consequences, and future risks to consider. For this reason, the best course of action is to do as much as you can on your own, which may range from nothing, when a couple is acrimonious and can't agree on anything, to getting all your papers in what you believe to be the final form for review by a legal professional.

Don't feel bad if you and your spouse can't agree on everything. Sometimes couples go into a siege and refuse to move forward because they're hung up on one or two points—who gets the coin collection, or where Jimmy spends Thanksgiving. Get as close to an agreement as you can, and then enlist help. Attorneys are negotiators and counselors, too, not just gladiators. They can assist and advise couples in reaching their own settlement, or in mediation. They can also spot inequities or mistakes in a proposed settlement and explain what the law requires (and what the court is likely to decide) in disputed matters. A good lawyer will always try to negotiate a fair settlement first and will consider litigation a last resort.

Alternatives to Traditional Legal Representation

Unless your case is complex or likely to end up in the courtroom, you may not need full-fledged representation by an attorney. A number of alternative sources of legal assistance are becoming increasingly available.

Legal Aid Clinics

Many law schools have family law clinics in which trained law students working under the supervision of an attorney provide services to people involved in a divorce, from basic information to complete assistance through the divorce process. In most areas, government legal aid or court-sponsored clinics provide information and assistance, and divorce education classes are growing in number. These programs provide information, advice on what to expect, and answers to questions. Many also offer guidance in compiling financial information, understanding the legal process, and locating different types of counseling and therapy.

Family Court Service Centers and Other Court-Annexed Services

Most jurisdictions now have a special court to hear family-related matters, including divorce, separation, adoption, and other matters involving children. Many of these courts provide clinics, centers, or classes for people handling their own cases or for those who wish to do as much of the document work as possible in order to reduce their legal fees. Some offer other services as well, such as mediation, counseling, classes in family communication, and similar services to assist families in transition.

The family courts of San Diego County maintain several Self-Help Centers where people can get information on divorce, paternity, child or spousal support, child custody and visitation, and domestic violence restraining orders. Family law facilitators at these centers also hold regularly scheduled workshops to help individuals fill out the court forms and organize other documents that must be filed with the court in a divorce or other family case. Organizing your own papers and information before consulting an attorney can make the attorney's job easier and can save you a substantial amount of both time and money. Packets of forms are available for purchase, and some sessions are offered in Spanish. Both people representing themselves and those who plan to hire (or have hired) an attorney can benefit from such classes, since they give the participants a better understanding of the legal process and its requirements, as well as a forum for organizing essential materials. Be aware that in some densely populated areas, such as Southern California, the wait at such clinics may be as long as eight hours. Call or stop by ahead of time if you plan to seek the help of such services, and see what alternatives may be offered in your area.

Some court-annexed programs offer assistance for families that continues throughout or even beyond the divorce. Hennepin County, Minnesota, which includes the Minneapolis metropolitan area, long a leader in domestic violence intervention, has established a program called Divorce with Dignity. One feature of this program is active case management by the judge, with meetings, regulation of the use of experts, and less litigation. The program's goal is faster, cheaper, and less acrimonious divorces. For example, couples are required to use one neutral appraiser—appointed by the judge—to set the value of a house rather than having two appraisals from opposing parties.

In Twin Falls, Idaho, divorcing parents (and those seeking modification of a custody agreement) are required to attend a short series of classes designed to teach them a businesslike way of communicating with each other, in order to reduce the level of conflict to which the children are exposed. The classes seek to heighten the parents' awareness of the child's point of view and needs, both during and after the family restructuring. They also deal with issues that may arise regarding extended family members or friends—an area that is often neglected when parents divorce but that may be vitally important to the children, as well as fertile ground for continuing controversy if not resolved. This innovative program also provides optional classes for children of divorcing parents, as well as for others such as grandparents, stepparents, or parents who wish to learn the skills offered. The classes are taught by specially trained child custody mediators, and evaluations by those attending the classes have been overwhelmingly positive.

Legal Document Assistants

Traditionally, paralegals and other legal assistants always worked under the supervision of an attorney, in a manner similar to the way nurses and other medical support staff work with doctors. Today, however, just as nurse-practitioners working on their own serve patients in need of limited health care services, paralegals and legal document assistants frequently have their own independent businesses assisting people in various legal matters, especially in the field of family law.

These professionals can provide sound, affordable assistance in reasonably simple cases, as long as everyone involved understands the limitations of what they can and cannot do and proceeds accordingly. People working with legal assistants must generally be willing to do a good part of the work themselves, including gathering the facts and data for use in preparing the required documents, arranging for service of papers on the spouse (or his or her attorney), completing documents and filing them at the courthouse, and making any required court appearances on their own. I have seen divorces prepared by legal assistants proceed efficiently, economically, and with good results in an uncontested divorce.

However, remember that only a licensed attorney can give legal advice or make court appearances on your behalf. If the case takes an unexpected turn, you may still need the services of a lawyer. Some legal assistants have an attorney on call who reviews their work when required and steps in if the case escalates. Others will refer the client to an independent family lawyer if the case becomes too complex or acrimonious. I have seen a few, though, who try to work beyond their capacity, such as when a client is embroiled in a bitterly disputed custody case that has progressed to litigation. Such matters require not just an attorney, but a highly experienced family law specialist. If you choose to use the services of a legal assistant, be sure to ask the necessary questions and get an understanding of what happens if complications arise.

Legal assistants usually offer their services through private offices similar to those staffed by attorneys, but a few have taken innovative approaches. A franchise called We the People offers low-cost legal document preparation centers nationwide, where patrons are assisted in preparing the paperwork required for no-fault divorce or other uncontested legal matters. The service is limited to divorces in which there are no children and no disputes over property. Customers pick up a workbook at the store (some of which offer a drive-up window) and return later with the completed information. The company then prepares the required forms for the person to file independently, or after review by a lawyer.

Limited Attorney Representation

In some locations, lawyers offer "limited scope" representation or "unbundled" legal services. This means that the attorney and client determine what tasks need to be accomplished in the case, so the attorney performs—and the client pays for—only what is essential. This will vary in each case, depending on the individual, lawyer, and issues involved. For example, some people choose to prepare their own legal documents (alone or with the help of a court facilitator, law school clinic, or other nonattorney assistant) and then hire an attorney to file them and make any necessary court appearances. Others want to make their own court appearances but want someone else to do the paperwork and handle any contacts with the spouse and his or her lawyer. Each case may be individually tailored to suit its own requirements and the needs of the people involved.

Information on unbundled legal services is available from state and local bar associations and courts, as well as through the Internet (see Appendix A). If you seek this type of representation, be sure that you and the attorney both have a clear understanding of what tasks each of you will and will not perform, and at what point the lawyer's representation will end. Also discuss what will happen if your case becomes more complicated than you expect.

Legal Service Insurance Plans

Prepaid legal service plans are becoming more and more common. This form of "legal insurance" may be offered through employers or independently. Providers supply attorneys who perform legal tasks for no additional cost or at discounted rates, depending on the plan and the services sought.

As with any form of insurance, these plans can be highly beneficial for some purposes, but they have their limitations. The lawyers provided usually offer initial advice by telephone, which can help you assess the issues and complexity of your case. They may also review documents at no or little additional cost, which can be all that's required in an uncontested, no-fault divorce in which you plan to prepare the documents yourself or with the help of a nonlawyer assistant. Be sure you understand what is and is not covered, as well as the assigned lawyer's background and experience in family law, especially if you use a plan-provided lawyer for full-scale representation. While some, doubtless, are well qualified, people have reported disappointing results in complex cases requiring expertise in family law. Be sure that any lawyer you consider using answers your questions and merits your confidence.

The Internet

During the past decade, the Internet has emerged as a vast and comprehensive source of material on every imaginable topic, including divorce. Cyberspace now contains virtual galaxies of information for those at any stage of the divorce process. A Google search made in March 2006 using the word *divorce* returned 5,600,000 hits. Today, having an online computer is akin to having a desktop library. Websites deal with every topic imaginable and may include interactive discussion groups, online magazines, newsgroups, and contact information for innumerable organizations. They can provide information on local and national laws, sources of professional assistance, publications, self-help materials, and other resources. Most private organizations, public service entities, and law firms today maintain websites filled with a wealth of information. For divorced parents, the Internet provides a vast support system to share ideas, feelings, thoughts, and questions through chat rooms, "blogs," and bulletin boards. Professional counseling and therapy is now being conducted online, and even online mediation—sometimes called "IDR" for "Internet dispute resolution"—is now available.

Various federal, state, and local government offices maintain excellent websites with detailed information about virtually every aspect of family law. Sample parenting and custody plans can be downloaded, and some courts provide a full set of pleading forms that can be downloaded, printed, and then filled out and filed in court. The Office of Child Support Enforcement has a site with links to specific information on the laws and mechanics of child support in each state (see Appendix B).

The number of private Web resources with divorce-related information seems limitless. Many websites are outstanding, brimming with helpful materials on an astounding array of topics. For example, Divorcenet.com, which claims to be the Net's largest divorce resource, provides state-specific materials, along with an impressive collection of articles by professional contributors on a diverse range of subjects such as divorce and military families, taxes, and real estate. It also hosts a support network, including a blog in which people trade views and ideas, and provides forms and other self-help tools. Other recommended websites are listed in the Appendixes.

For people who are not online through a computer at home or at work, most public libraries now have computers that patrons may use to gain access to the Internet, as well as free classes on how to navigate through cyberspace (most people can learn the basics in an hour or two). Be cautious when surfing the Net, however. Some websites advocate actions that run the gamut from unethical to blatantly illegal. I have seen more than a few with appallingly destructive advice to offer. Some engender false hope of reconciliation by promising to reveal magic formulas guaranteed to save any marriage (for only $49.95). Others advocate the use of junk science to "win" a child custody case. Among the worst are those that peddle complete courses on DVD designed to teach one spouse to hide assets from another, how to play dirty to get more than your fair share of the marital property, or how to handle a complex divorce without legal assistance.

Buying into these rip-offs not only will relieve you of a tidy sum of cash but also can result in a legal quagmire that could send you into bankruptcy or even jail. Anyone who advises you to conceal information about your assets and liabilities from your spouse or your attorney, or otherwise counsels deception, is setting you up for trouble—trouble that can range from a collateral attack on a supposedly final property settlement all the way to felony criminal charges. Perjury and fraud are crimes, and judges do not look kindly upon those who lie to the court, even if it's "only" on paper. Also, don't assume that all of the other websites to which you can link from a reputable site are themselves reputable as well. I've seen some excellent sites providing links to some of the vilest. Weigh what you read on the Web, or in print, against your own common sense, and always consider the source.

Choosing a Lawyer

For many people, divorce is one of life's biggest legal, financial, and emotional undertakings. Choosing the right attorney to handle your divorce may be one of the most important decisions you will ever have to make. Remember, not only your money and property but also your security and the future of your children may be affected forever by the quality of the legal help you receive.

Referrals to lawyers can come from many sources. Therapists and counselors who work with people going through a divorce are often able to recommend good lawyers, just as lawyers often recommend therapists. Friends who have been through a divorce and were satisfied with the legal representation they received are one of the best sources. If you hired a lawyer in the past, or are acquainted with lawyers socially, those individuals may be able to provide the names of colleagues who practice family law.

Most state bar associations have lawyer referral services. It's usually not a good idea to choose a lawyer on this basis alone, though, as most of the services are open to any licensed attorney who signs up and pays an administration fee. If an attorney has been awarded state credentials as a specialist in family law, however, this carries more weight, as all states that issue specialty licenses have stringent requirements to qualify for the designation. The American Academy of Matrimonial Lawyers is an elite group of fourteen hundred members with at least ten years of legal practice, at least 75 percent of which has been in matrimonial law. All members must also pass an examination. A list of these attorneys in your state may be obtained free of charge by contacting the organization (see Appendix A).

Whatever you have been told about the stellar talents of a particular attorney, make sure you visit with the person to determine whether this is the right lawyer for you before making a final decision. A lawyer who is wonderful for one client may be disastrous for another. As in any close relationship, you have to be able to develop a comfortable rapport. Sometimes personalities and styles of doing business simply do not click. Remember, you will have to tell this person the most intimate details of your life. Choose someone with whom you feel comfortable sharing this information.

A lawyer who practices in a broad range of general fields may be well qualified to handle a divorce if he or she has taken an interest in family law and kept abreast of current developments through continuing education programs or by regularly handling family law cases. However, when complex assets such as business enterprises, large amounts of money or stocks, or hotly contested custody issues arise, it is generally best to secure an attorney who concentrates most of his or her practice in the area of family law.

Attorney Judith Finfrock also urges clients to be sure the attorney they choose is familiar with the judges in the community: "Unfortunately, there are some judges who make one-sided decisions or enter totally inappropriate rulings. I've seen judges refuse to approve a perfectly fair settlement agreement the couple has reached, because they want to use their power or let their own biases come in. A few are completely crazy and out of control. Lawyers practicing divorce law should be well aware of the reputations of the local judges and be willing to use their right to recuse [disqualify] a judge they don't feel will do right by their client."

The practice of law overall is becoming increasingly specialized. This is especially true in the area of family law as more and more subspecialties develop. There are divorce attorneys who focus specifically on such areas as family-owned businesses, international marriages, military marriages, elder divorces and retirement issues, and parenting issues. If a particular area in your marriage is of paramount importance to you or extremely complex, you may wish to seek referrals to one of these subspecialists through such an organization as the American Academy of Matrimonial Lawyers. Alternatively, ask your lawyer about associating with professionals in the appropriate field, such as a divorce financial analyst, or consider a collaborative divorce (discussed in Chapter 3), in which attorneys work with a team of other professionals throughout the process to reach a settlement of all issues.

Feel free to make appointments with several lawyers and interview each one before deciding (the first consultation is usually free). Go prepared with an idea of the assets to be divided, whether property or custody issues are likely to be contested, and what essentials you want to get out of the divorce. In the book *Divorcing*, renowned trial attorney Melvin Belli lists eight characteristics that should be possessed by a good divorce lawyer:

- The lawyer will be both sensitive and objective. He or she will be willing to listen to and consider your feelings about your particular divorce but also be able to help you channel your feelings into the most positive resolution of your situation in relation to your future happiness.
- The lawyer will be straightforward about billing and charges, so there will be no surprises later.
- The lawyer will not use intimidating legal jargon but rather will explain clearly what the legal terms mean and what the procedures are all about.
- The lawyer will make you feel comfortable asking any question and will never make you feel naive or stupid.
- The lawyer will not promise you the world or give you unrealistic expectations. He or she will try to minimize your costs and avoid unnecessary adversity. Conversely, the lawyer will be willing to work hard to protect your rights and will not sacrifice your best interests.
- The lawyer will communicate with you frequently, so that you don't feel your case is being neglected.
- The lawyer will be familiar with the divorce laws of your state and have experience in how the law is applied in the court in which your divorce will proceed.
- The lawyer will seek to minimize your costs and serve your best interests by encouraging such procedures as mediation, negotiation between you and your spouse, and other efforts to resolve the issues that can be settled outside of court.

Attorney's Fees

What a client may reasonably be expected to pay for a divorce varies tremendously, depending on a variety of factors. Divorce may cost anywhere from nothing to hundreds of thousands of dollars. The range of hourly fees among divorce lawyers of which I am personally aware spans from $50 an hour to $450 an hour. Some lawyers charge a flat fee that will cover all the required work on a case.

A client should thoroughly understand how fees are calculated, what other costs to expect, how payment schedules work, and all other matters relating to fees before any money is paid. Most lawyers will ask the client to sign a written contract, called a fee agreement or retainer agreement, that spells out the details about fees, including hourly rates for the various attorneys, paralegals, and others who may work on the case; whether such rates vary according to the type of work being done; when bills will be sent; and when the client will be expected to pay. Your attorney should be willing to provide you with a written summary of all hourly rates, anticipated costs, and other related information. You should never be charged for the initial interview with the attorney unless you decide during the interview to go ahead and hire that attorney and he or she actually begins to work with you to prepare your case.

Many lawyers charge a retainer, which is a sum of money that must be paid before work on the case will begin. Retainers serve as security deposits, and the lawyer will draw from the retainer to pay the fees as bills accumulate. Some refund any part of the retainer that is not used when the case is over; others keep any remainder as a bonus. Some require acceptance fees in the form of a lump-sum payment up front, with hourly fees additional. Still others charge a bonus, also called a result fee, or kicker, at the end of the case if they win a particularly good result for the client. Many find acceptance fees or kickers distasteful or even unethical, but they are becoming more common, especially for lawyers recognized as leaders in their field. Make sure you understand exactly what the money you are asked to provide will cover. Get a clear, detailed, written agreement, and ask for an explanation of anything you don't understand.

Out-of-pocket expenses in a divorce case can also be considerable. These include court filing fees, mailing, photocopying, expert witness fees, travel costs, investigation fees, and other expenses that can add up to tremendous amounts. Expert witness fees are often particularly high, but these witnesses may be extremely important in a complex divorce case. Appraisers, accountants, psychologists, and vocational experts are often essential. If both parties can agree to have a single, neutral expert perform the required work, this will save money, and the person's opinion will carry more weight if the case goes to court. Using alternative dispute resolution such as mediation or collaboration to eliminate as many contested issues as possible can also save a great deal of money. The level of disagreement between the spouses is the single most influential factor in determining what a divorce will cost.

Many people find themselves in dire financial straits when facing a divorce, and the last thing they want to do is incur more debt. However, borrowing money to pay a qualified attorney and other experts to protect your rights during a divorce may be one of the best investments you can make. Most attorneys today accept major credit cards.

Attorney Judith Finfrock cautions those seeking a divorce lawyer that the size of the fee doesn't guarantee the quality of the results. According to Finfrock, "The best bet is to go to someone recommended by another who has been through the process. Interview more than one attorney. Look for someone who can mirror back what you say, so you are sure the lawyer heard and understood you."

Lawyers should never charge a penalty fee if the couple reconciles and should never put unreasonable pressure on the client to either settle or go forward. Ask the lawyers you interview to give you a reasonable estimate of what the divorce will cost, based on your honest opinion of how many issues are in dispute. Remember that in a hotly contested divorce, an attorney may not be able to predict a realistic total, because much will depend on your spouse, his or her attorney, and other outside factors. Also, in some cases, especially where one spouse is the primary breadwinner while the other earns little or nothing, the one who earns more may be required to pay attorney fees for the other—a point to discuss if this is your situation.

Be aware that if you do not pay your legal fees, the attorney has the right to file a special type of lien at the end of the case or at any time either you or the attorney ends the relationship. You should receive an itemized bill for fees that have accrued at least every sixty days. If you have a question or problem with a bill, talk to your lawyer right away. Most states have some type of arbitration program for disputed attorney fees, generally offered through the state bar association.

A Word of Caution

Watch for red flags when assessing potential attorneys. Be wary of a lawyer who promises to take care of everything you need, guarantees a particular result, or promises to gain a quick resolution of a complex matter for a small fee. Many people understandably would like to turn everything over to a lawyer and avoid the whole process, but this is a prescription for trouble. On the other hand, it is best to let the lawyer handle such matters as direct negotiations with your spouse or his or her lawyer. Discuss the division of tasks and responsibilities with your lawyer, and stick with the plan of action. The attorney should keep you advised of all significant developments as they occur.

Frances Webb, a mediator and a divorced mother, urges people who are still disentangling the legal and financial aspects of their life together to seek sound advice—but to do so cautiously. "Read all the small print when you sign something, and never sign until you know what you are signing," she says. "Don't believe something that sounds wrong or odd, just because a lawyer or banker is telling you it is so. Get independent advice from someone you trust, and make sure everything is put in writing, in a form you understand."

Webb had bad luck with attorneys during her divorce, so she cautions others about automatically placing too much trust in legal professionals. "There are some slimy lawyers out there," she says. "The first one I had not only lied to me but also came up with a bill that was roughly equal to everything I received in a child support matter for which he represented me. My second attorney came highly recommended and seemed to be a good person, but he was in bondage to a big firm that wouldn't let him wrap up the case the way he and I wanted to. Be very careful."

Also beware of the gladiator personality. Lawyers who go into battle looking for a high-profile victory frequently cause far more trauma and expense to their clients than someone whose goal is to reach a fair and reasonable settlement with as little fanfare as possible. It is not uncommon to feel that the best lawyer will be one who takes the position of a warrior and does whatever is necessary to win the case exactly as the client wants it won, fighting to the death if necessary. This type of person may seem appealing in the heat of the moment, when the hurt and anger are fresh. However, barracuda litigation is seldom the best tactic in any type of case, especially a divorce. This type of lawyer inevitably runs up large bills, causes unnecessary delays, and adds to the emotional turmoil inevitable in any divorce. Beware, too, of books, websites, and other self-help materials that encourage this type of behavior. In the 1989 film *The War of the Roses*, Danny DeVito's character, a lawyer who had learned hard lessons, said it best: "There is no winning in this. There are only degrees of losing."

This does not mean it is wrong to take a strong stand on important issues, or to expect your lawyer to do the same if your spouse gets obstinate, but there is often a fine line between fighting for fundamental rights and fighting for the sake of revenge or other inappropriate motives. At the other extreme, clients should also watch out for lawyers who are overly passive. The best lawyer will work hard to achieve a settlement that satisfies the client's most important needs and concerns and will remain ready to make a straightforward, dignified effort in court if necessary.

The Attorney-Client Relationship

By its nature, family law is one of the most emotionally charged fields. While it is important that a relationship between attorney and client be trusting and comfortable, it is equally important to set certain boundaries. Lawyers working in the family law arena are fully aware that they are dealing with people who are undergoing trauma. Most are sympathetic and compassionate and are accustomed to tears and outbursts. However, a lawyer cannot take the place of a confessor, psychologist, or best friend.

Lawyers are often faced with the difficult task of trying to steer a client toward a resolution that is in his or her best interest without offending or appearing to go against the client's wishes. Judith Finfrock emphasizes that the lawyer's first role is truly that of the client's "mouthpiece." She says, "It's up to us to be able to put the client's own words into a concise, structured form that follows the legal requirements, so the judge will hear what the client wants to say."

Yet she also points out that a lawyer must often explain to clients why some of their desires or ideas cannot be legally accomplished. "The position of attorney still carries authority as it should," she says. "We do difficult work, and it gets more complex all the time—in the area of retirement benefits, for example. Most people do respect attorneys and are generally willing to follow what the law requires."

Finfrock has experienced little resistance from clients. She feels that few people want to abuse the system or bring unnecessary hostility into the process. When a client does oppose her suggestions, other factors are usually involved: "With a lot of my male clients, especially, I had the impression they were being egged on by their friends. The guys at the bar after work would be urging them to fight for the kids, take the wife to the mat, put up a real battle. But most clients realize that there is nothing to be gained by fighting. As soon as you tell them they're not going to win anything by putting up a battle, they back down instantly. You have to give them permission to go back to their buddies and say, 'Hey, the lawyer told me I have no choice.' Then they can still hold up their heads on pool night."

David B. Riggert, a family law attorney in Bloomington, Illinois, finds that while nearly half the people who come to him seeking a divorce consultation believe they are ready to proceed with an uncontested divorce, in reality, many have not yet considered essential issues. The realization that more work lies ahead may be frustrating for a client who wishes to proceed quickly and inexpensively, and it may lead them to believe the attorney is churning higher fees. However, an attorney has a responsibility to protect the client's interests, including the duty to uncover issues the client might not have considered—such as whether the parent who will not have primary custody of the children will provide a life insurance policy naming the children as beneficiaries.

Be willing to listen to legal advice with an open mind. A good lawyer-client relationship is one in which concerns can be discussed freely, various options weighed, and a course of action plotted that is both satisfying to the client and legally wise. It is often difficult to see things rationally and set goals during a period of severe emotional upheaval, and part of the lawyer's job is to bring the client back to a logical and rational perspective.

A lawyer should be willing to admit when he or she needs help from outside experts on items such as sophisticated business transactions and tax matters. The lawyer should explain to the client why an outside expert is being hired, how the lawyer came to choose that person, what the expert will do to help in the case, and how much it will cost.

On the matter of fees and costs, the lawyer should be willing, at any time, to tally the costs and fees that have accrued and to explain to the client how and why they were incurred. At the same time, the lawyer should not have to account for every paper clip.

If there is not enough trust between lawyer and client to reach this balance, then perhaps the client should consider looking for another lawyer. It is not uncommon, especially in divorce cases, for more than one lawyer to be involved during the course of the proceedings. If you do not feel comfortable with your lawyer and do not believe that the discord can be worked out after you've made an honest effort to do so, do not hesitate to seek different legal counsel. Lawyers should not take such decisions personally. Also, a lawyer has the right to terminate the attorney-client relationship if the client refuses to meet his or her responsibilities.

In sum, a good lawyer-client relationship is a team effort, but the balance of power always rests with the client. A client should choose a lawyer whose opinion and advice he or she can respect and value. If an impasse occurs, it is the client who will have the final say in all decisions, unless he or she is trying to trick or force the lawyer into unethical or legally improper behavior, which the lawyer must decline.

Should Both Parties Use the Same Lawyer?

From the standpoint of both professional ethics and the client's best interest, most lawyers will not handle a divorce for both parties. There are exceptions, however. When the parties have been able to reach a fair, absolute agreement either on their own or with the help of mediators or other negotiators, one lawyer may simply need to review the documents to be sure that they are in the proper legal form, if this is the only legal task that needs to be accomplished. Yet dual representation in any capacity remains an area of considerable controversy. While some lawyers believe that one attorney should never represent both parties, Judith Finfrock sees no problem with representing both as long as the individuals are aware of their legal rights and have worked out a mutually agreeable settlement that covers all of the necessary issues.

An Overview of the Legal Process of Divorce

Divorce law and most specific aspects of family law are governed almost entirely by the states. This means that the law varies a great deal from state to state, so it is difficult to give general guidelines on what a person can expect. The following information outlines the process followed in most places, but some steps may differ in your jurisdiction.

Furthermore, the steps a couple are required to take will vary depending on whether the parties are able to agree to some or all of the terms of the divorce, the complexity of the property and legal matters involved, and how well the opposing sides cooperate. Naturally, the more disagreement and hostility there is, the more time and money will be spent in the process leading up to the actual divorce, such as pretrial discovery, formal settlement offers, interim hearings, and other legal maneuverings. Fortunately, 90 percent of divorce cases are settled without litigation in court. Many couples work out an amicable agreement and, depending on local requirements, may never appear before a judge. Others go through all the preparations for a full-scale trial and then settle on the courthouse steps. Many others wind up somewhere in between.

Getting Started

Certain basic steps are required to complete any divorce. To start, one party or the other files for divorce. This involves preparing a document that clearly, and usually briefly, sets forth the facts from that person's perspective. It requests the court to take certain legal steps, including dividing property, setting child or spousal support, and resolving custody. This document is usually called a petition for divorce, or petition for dissolution of marriage. In some states, it is called a complaint for divorce. The person who files this document to start the legal process is called the petitioner, or plaintiff. Some states, such as California, have mandatory court forms that must be used for the petition and other documents filed at various stages in the divorce process. Others provide optional forms.

The factual information in the petition usually includes the date and place of marriage, names of the parties, names and ages of any minor children born of the marriage, a description of the property owned by the couple together (marital property), and property the spouse filing the petition claims as separate property. It also lists joint and separate debts. Peripheral issues such as a request to change the wife's name back to her maiden name may also be included. The petition also states the grounds for divorce. It must also contain a statement showing that the court has jurisdiction to grant the divorce. Requirements for jurisdiction vary from state to state, as do residency laws. When the divorce petition is filed, a filing fee must be paid. These fees range from less than $50 to $300 or more. People with income below the poverty line may be able to fill out a form to be filed with the court that will result in a waiver of the filing fee.

Next, the other spouse files an answer, or response, to the petition. This document states whether the other party admits or denies what is stated in each paragraph of the petition. It may also contain that person's version of disputed facts, defenses, counterclaims, or requests to the court for other types of legal action.

Generally, where the parties have worked out a complete agreement (on their own, with the help of their attorneys, or through mediation), they may file all of the required papers, including the petition, response, settlement agreement, and a final order for the judge to review and sign, at one time. This may happen at the beginning of the case or at any stage during the process when all issues are resolved. In some places, if the judge approves the proposed settlement and any related matters, the order may be signed and filed immediately so the divorce can become final the same day it is filed. In others, a waiting period is required (which may be waived by mutual agreement in some jurisdictions). In many cases, this is how the process ends; however, if issues are contested, litigation proceeds.

Discovery

After the complaint and answer are filed, the parties usually begin the discovery process. Discovery is a part of nearly every court case. It allows each side to ask the other questions and request documents about any subject that may be relevant to the case. This involves disclosure of all assets, documents, and information essential to come to a fair resolution. Discovery may proceed formally according to the court's rules, so the judge can intervene if one party does not cooperate, or informally between cooperating spouses. Naturally, the process is easier and faster if people can willingly exchange the essential facts and materials. However, if one person is recalcitrant or less than completely honest, formal discovery is essential.

The discovery process includes "paper" discovery, composed of interrogatories (questions to be answered in writing), requests for production of documents or other tangible items, and requests for admissions, which help sort out the facts that are not contested. Discovery may also include a request for inspection. This is a request to appraise or examine items in possession of the other person that cannot be easily duplicated or provided. Examples include a home or condominium, a business, a boat, and real estate. A subpoena *duces tecum* can also be served on third parties, such as banks, to order that they provide documents at a specific time and place, such as a scheduled deposition or court hearing.

One universal requirement in all divorce cases is full and honest disclosure. Both people must lay their cards on the table and reveal all of their assets, debts, earnings, and property. It is not uncommon for one spouse to try to conceal assets that the person does not want to share. Secrecy is not tolerated by the courts, and a judge will not hesitate to punish a person who tries to hide property or refuses to produce the required documents, by making the person pay the other side's attorneys fees if a court order must be obtained to force cooperation.

If you are trying to exchange informally and your spouse refuses to disclose information about property, earnings, and so forth, a written reminder from you or your attorney that it will all have to come out eventually may be sufficient to gain cooperation. Include a specific list of the information you request (for example, funds held in a savings account; the current value of an IRA; the location of, number of, and amount in any other bank or asset account), along with a reminder that if you have to have your lawyer get a court order, your spouse may be required to pay the fees and costs. Keep a copy; if you do end up in court, this could be essential evidence that you made good-faith efforts to get the information before involving the court and that it was your spouse who refused to follow the rules.

Discovery also involves taking oral depositions, in which one party's lawyer questions the opposing party and his or her witnesses under oath. During a deposition, the attorney for the person being questioned is present to guard against inappropriate actions by the other attorney, such as overstepping the bounds of permissible questioning, deliberate intimidation, or straying too far afield from the matter at hand. If this occurs, the lawyer can raise an objection, which will go on the record for the judge to rule on later if necessary.

The formal discovery process is often difficult, expensive, and seemingly endless, but it's where couples who are unable or unwilling to cooperate informally can finally get down to brass tacks and gain a clear picture of each other's case. Discovery is governed by an elaborate set of court rules. Anyone who refuses to follow the rules may be brought to court in a pretrial hearing, and the party or attorney found at fault can be ordered to pay the fees and costs of the party who had to invoke the judge's assistance to get the discovery process completed. By the same token, if one person tries to use the discovery process inappropriately, such as by requesting voluminous materials that have nothing to do with the case or badgering the other with questions that are outside the accepted scope of the process, he or she can be fined and reprimanded.

This is relatively unusual, though, as most ethical lawyers are well aware of both the boundaries and the importance of discovery. Cooperation is in the best interests of all concerned, though formal discovery may often be time consuming, embarrassingly personal, and downright unpleasant. I once had a client in a fairly complex divorce action who, not entirely tongue-in-cheek, referred to interrogatories as "derogatories" and asked when we were going to "decompose" her husband. As with many cases, once discovery was complete and all the facts were on the table, that case was settled shortly before trial. This is often the most essential function of discovery.

Discovery serves another practical purpose if the case does go to trial. Even though the atmosphere at a deposition is fairly serious, with the presence of the attorneys and with a court reporter taking down every word, it is less intimidating than being in a courtroom. People often speak more freely than they tend to do on the witness stand. Since the deposition (as well as the written discovery) is taken under oath, anything a person says may be used in court, as long as it fits within the requirements of admissible courtroom evidence. Therefore, if a party or witness tries to change his or her story later on the witness stand, an attorney may read the portion of the deposition that is contradictory. This is known as "impeaching" a witness. It virtually destroys the credibility of at least that part of the testimony, so it is a powerful tool.

The rules of discovery are far more liberal than the rules of evidence. Either party in a suit may request anything that is "reasonably calculated to lead to the discovery of relevant evidence," not just items guaranteed to be admissible in court. Thus, most questions about property, business holdings, and other assets are generally permitted. Judges are not amused when one person tries to hide information. It creates more work for the judge and damages the person's credibility. Therefore, in a divorce case, virtually everything involving property, salary, pensions, and all related matters must be disclosed. Again—this cannot be emphasized enough—beware of anyone who advises you to conceal property or information about your assets. Such a strategy not only is dishonest and illegal but also almost inevitably backfires.

Conversely, judges also get impatient when people try to use the courts as a forum to vindicate their hurt or anger by bringing in matters that don't pertain to the business of ending the marriage. Discovery motions and other pretrial motions are sometimes overused and abused to hinder the process or annoy an opponent. The relevant issues in a no-fault divorce are the division of property and debt, child and/or spousal support, and child custody. The court does not want to hear about his affair, her drinking problem, or the details of fights unless it directly impacts on the central issues—for example, if he spent all their savings on his girlfriend, if he beat his wife and she has a separate claim for her injuries, or if her alcoholism has made her unable to care for the children.

Interim Orders and Related Issues

Certain overriding matters must be addressed while the divorce is pending, including child and spousal support, living arrangements, access to property, payment of debts, and child custody. Therefore, when a divorce does not settle quickly, the court may require the filing of interim or temporary orders, which state how these matters will be handled until a final agreement or order is filed. In some areas, they are required. In others, they may be waived if both parties agree in writing and if there are no children involved. As with the final decree, the couple can either work out their own temporary agreement or let the judge decide.

Remember, any temporary agreements you reach informally with your spouse, especially those involving property division or financial decisions, are best turned into a formal written interim order to be filed with, and reviewed by, the court. Such agreements are often called stipulations. These are highly favored by courts because they demonstrate that the parties have agreed on certain things and the court won't be required to intervene. Generally, there is no court appearance required. You can summarize the matters you have agreed to in your own words and then ask your lawyer to put the document into the correct legal form, which is then signed by both parties and/or attorneys and filed with the court.

Temporary orders are supposed to be just that—temporary—but be on guard. They may set the stage for what is to come, especially if the divorce is protracted. This is especially true in matters of child custody and visitation. Courts are reluctant to create upheaval in the lives of children who have settled into a new routine, unless given a good reason to do so. Thus, if you find yourself in a situation that makes you unhappy—for example, your spouse took the children, moved out of state, and now dictates when you may see them—act quickly to get a temporary order in place that sets legal rights and parameters with which you can live.

While the divorce is pending, it is advisable to avoid certain actions that can cause unnecessary risk or complication. Establish your own credit as soon as possible rather than continuing to use credit accounts held by both you and your spouse. Don't continue to mingle your assets with your spouse's in bank accounts. Be cautious about starting a new business or buying shares in a new venture until the divorce is final. This does not mean that you cannot get on with your life and take such steps as changing jobs or moving, but it is best to discuss major changes with your attorney, because even things that don't seem relevant can have an impact on the outcome of your case. If you do make such transitions, consider whether a new interim agreement should be filed. Informal hearings before the judge may be held on interim matters at any stage of the proceedings.

During the divorce, spouses have often been known to lock each other out of the house or dump the other person's belongings on the lawn. In Terry McMillan's novel *Waiting to Exhale*, a character involved in a bitter divorce has a garage sale in which she sells all of her husband's belongings for $1 each, including his antique automobile. A woman I know loaded all of her husband's clothing into garbage bags and set them on the curb, and then called him to say that either he or the trash collectors could pick them up before garbage day. Such maneuvers are no doubt tempting if your spouse has behaved badly. However, you don't have the legal right to prohibit your spouse from entering the house or to dispose of his or her belongings unless a court has said so.

If your spouse has abused you, you can obtain a protection order (also called a restraining order) that legally requires him or her to stay away. This process is usually quick and easy. Check with your attorney, a local domestic-abuse shelter or hotline, or the police to learn your options. If you get a restraining order, be sure that your local law enforcement precinct or station has a copy and knows that you are worried about your safety. Many law enforcement officers will help you by providing safety tips, patrolling your neighborhood more often, or checking with you regularly. Call or visit the websites of appropriate sources to find out what is available.

Settlement or Trial?

As previously discussed, most divorces settle before trial. At any stage of the process, the parties may create a full or partial settlement agreement. If they can agree on all the issues in the divorce, both lawyers (or a mediator or other professional advisor) will work with one or both to draft a settlement agreement. This will be incorporated into a final decree or order that will be approved and signed by the judge. If there are still issues that are disputed, a partial or "bifurcated" decree may be entered, with the court reserving the right to decide on the issues still in dispute. Most lawyers believe it is better to hold off on the final decree until all issues are resolved.

If necessary, a full trial or hearing will be held. The parties present evidence, including the testimony of witnesses and experts, and then they await the decision of the court. In most disputed cases, a judge will decide the outcome of a divorce action, but jury trials are still available in some states. Again, only about 10 percent of divorce cases go to court on any of the issues involved, with child custody the most common bone of contention.

Nearly everyone who has been involved in litigation, whether as a party, a witness, or a legal professional, agrees that settlement is almost always preferable to going to trial. When the people involved are able to work out their own agreement, they are much more likely to abide by its terms and to resolve any difficulties that come up later. A trial is always an expensive vexation and can severely increase the discord between the people involved.

Sometimes people believe that if a settlement is not reached early in the negotiations, the situation is hopeless and a trial is inevitable. This is actually the opposite of how things work. Often cases settle the day before a trial is scheduled to begin or, literally, on the courthouse steps the morning of trial. As one prominent family attorney has stated, an imminent trial brings people as close to reasonableness as they ever get. The only way to reach this point, however, is to keep preparing diligently for trial, with the assumption that the case is absolutely, without doubt going to court. As I recently heard one attorney-mediator put it, "Pray for peace, but prepare for war." Last-minute glitches in settlement agreements seem almost as common as eleventh-hour resolutions.

Divorce by Default

If one party has disappeared, does not want the divorce, or, as in one case I handled, simply refuses to be involved in the process, the divorce can still be accomplished. All states have provisions in their laws for "default" judgments against a party in a lawsuit who cannot be located or will not cooperate in the legal process. This usually requires proving that the person was properly served with process according to state requirements; showing that all the required attempts were made to contact the person; filing affidavits or other papers to show that the court record has been properly maintained and the person is not unreachable due to military service; and allowing a reasonable passage of time to show that the person had a fair opportunity under the law to enter an appearance had he or she wanted to do so. Any default judgment can be overturned later if the person comes to court within a specified period and proves that the case was not handled according to the rules. Once the time to challenge has passed, however, a carefully crafted default decree is every bit as binding as a decree in which both parties appeared in court.

Letting the Judge Decide

Often, if a couple cannot reach an agreement with respect to one or more issues, the parties will declare an impasse and leave it to the judge to decide how to resolve the dilemma. As a general rule, those who take this route should remember two points: first, judges do not like to be given this responsibility, and second, the decision of the judge may not make anyone happy.

Furthermore, even in a fault-based divorce, the courtroom is no longer considered a forum for vindication of wrongdoing. Judges have neither the desire nor the duty to take half a day of court time to hear about how Jane wants the condo in Aspen because little Joey was conceived there, or that John shouldn't have it because that was where he started his affair with Tiffany, which led to this mess in the first place. This doesn't mean the judge does not care or is unsympathetic to the human feelings involved, but a judge is not a counselor, and his or her job is limited to making sure the property is divided fairly and legally and that support and custody issues are appropriately resolved. In such a case, neither Jane nor John will likely get the condo—it will be ordered sold, and the proceeds will be divided. So, it's far better to try, if at all possible, to work out an arrangement with which everyone can live, whether on your own, through attorney negotiations, or with the help of a mediator.

If you do go to trial, the process is reasonably standard in most courts, although some procedures and the degree of formality may vary. Generally, the attorneys will give opening statements, and the petitioner will put on witnesses, introduce evidence, and present his or her case, followed by the respondent. The petitioner may then present a rebuttal. The respondent may also present what is called a surrebuttal. Finally, the parties present their closing arguments. The judge may request memoranda or briefs to be filed before or after the trial on legal issues. It may take the judge some time, generally not more than a couple of months, to decide the outcome and enter an order that divides property, sets custody and support, and states any other rights and responsibilities of each party.

If your case ends up in the courtroom, remember that you are there to make a favorable impression on the judge and to sell both your case and yourself. Dress in a neat and reasonably businesslike manner. Avoid extremes in appearance or behavior. As I was told as a fledgling attorney, the first rule of litigation is always "Don't piss off the judge." Force yourself to remain calm, speak clearly, and if you don't understand a question, say so rather than try to answer it. Testify truthfully and accurately, and don't offer information beyond the question asked. If you believe that something needs to be explained and you weren't given the opportunity to confer with your attorney, ask to do so.

Prepare and rehearse with your attorney before you take the witness stand. Get some idea of what to expect. Be sure to share all relevant information with your attorney, including details that could be embarrassing or damaging. Remember, your attorney has a duty to keep this information confidential. It can be devastating if the other side somehow learns of something detrimental and your attorney is not prepared to handle it. The court is not the place to seek vengeance against the ex. Keep your emotions in check, and don't refer to "that bastard" or "that slut." Strive to project an image of dignity, and stay on the high road if the opposing attorney tries to shake you during cross-examination. Sometimes unethical attorneys will try to make a witness appear hysterical. Don't give them the satisfaction, and keep your cool at all times.

Divorce trials are never pleasant, but they need not be overly traumatic. Thorough preparation and practice with your attorney will give you the confidence and skills you need to present your case in the best manner possible.

Appeals

A person who believes the court decided a case in a way that was legally impermissible may appeal that case for review by a higher court. In cases based on state law, this generally means the state court of appeals or the state supreme court. It is the job of the appellate court to review the decision of the lower court and determine whether the decision was made on the basis of a legal error, whether the decision was not supported by adequate evidence, or whether the judge went outside the boundaries of his or her discretion. Different standards are applied depending on the type of case and the nature of the challenge.

In matrimonial cases, an appeal is often brought not so much because a party genuinely believes that the wrong decision was made, but to try to leverage a settlement with better terms than those set out by the lower court. Appeals are costly and time consuming, so a person who received a generous award by the lower court may be willing to give some of it up in order to bring the matter to an end and avoid what may be greater expense and frustration in the long run. If an appeal is truly frivolous and obviously brought for improper reasons, sanctions can be imposed.

A legitimate appeal may be well worth the effort when the lower court made a mistake or a bad decision. In addition to righting a wrong in an individual case, an appeal may result in a reported decision from the higher court, which sets a precedent—a binding legal rule that must be followed by lower courts in the jurisdiction. This is how a significant part of the development, clarification, and evolution in the law takes place.

Nevertheless, the decision to appeal should be thought through carefully. Appeals in spousal support and child custody cases have increased dramatically in recent years, with the number of appeals in family law cases overall quadrupling since 1992. Hotly contested cases have been known to drag on for four or five years while a family remains in a constant state of stress and uncertainty. There may be circumstances in which such protracted litigation is justified, but they are few and far between. Throughout the litigation process, those involved should consistently be considering whether the benefits of slogging through to the next step truly outweigh the burdens and should keep a vigilant eye trained on ways to put an end to the battle—especially where children are suffering as a result.

General Cautions Regarding the Legal System

The legal process can be treacherous. While it is safe to say that most judges, social workers, psychologists, and others involved in family law are honest, dedicated professionals, far too many abuses still happen. Stories of inequity, incompetence, and sexism abound. In short, the quality of justice varies greatly depending on the location and the people involved. Even judges who are trying to do their best by those who appear before them often issue orders that turn out to be detrimental to one or all of the parties involved, simply because they don't see any other option or are too weary to take the time to find a better way.

Also, especially among new lawyers, divorce cases tend to have an inappropriate reputation as being "easy." Even a divorce that seems to be perfectly simple, with no major disputes over property or custody at the outset, can escalate into a battle that may drag on for years and require substantial legal expertise before it can be resolved. I once took a case that was supposedly uncontested. Only one piece of property, an antique buffet, remained in dispute. Not only did the couple fail to reach any agreement as to who would get the buffet; they also began questioning property they had already divided. Then one person decided the child custody arrangement wasn't satisfactory after all. In the end, the whole thing spiraled out of control. The case dragged on for months and took several mediators, appraisers, lawyers, and judges to bring it to a final resolution.

Also by its nature, the legal system is subject to manipulation and misuse by those who wish to wield it as a weapon against a spouse. And unfortunately, some unscrupulous lawyers deliberately prolong the process to run up fees. I have met some of the finest human beings I have ever known in this profession as well as some of the most loathsome and contemptible. While I am happy to say that the vast, vast majority of the lawyers I know are good, decent people, there are a few sleazeballs out there waiting to exploit any available target.

A client facing divorce is emotionally vulnerable and must necessarily lay bare to the lawyer the details of his or her private life and finances. For this reason, people facing divorce make easy prey for crooked lawyers. This does not mean that a client seeking a lawyer to handle a divorce should be paranoid. As in any profession, there are a few bad apples, but just how many may be exaggerated. The tabloids, as well as the more mainstream media, tend to jump on any story full of lurid details of cheating, conniving, and love gone wrong. Stories of abuses by divorce lawyers make juicy copy and hit the headlines far more often than any mention of the great majority of good lawyers who are working hard to get their clients a fair shake.

Of course, penalties exist for unethical behaviors if they can be proved, but this is relatively rare. Judges are often reluctant to draw the line between "zealous advocacy" and violations of court and professional rules. Furthermore, judges often express frustration when the classic "swearing match" goes on in the courtroom. It is often difficult to tell, in an emotionally charged arena, which person is lying and which is telling the truth. And there still are a few judges out there who simply don't give a damn.

Does this mean that nothing can be done, that everyone involved in a divorce is simply at the mercy of the legal system and the courts? Absolutely not. Every state has a lawyer disciplinary board and a judicial review board, which can hear complaints against unscrupulous lawyers and judges. More and more states are amending their codes of conduct for lawyers and judges to prohibit sexist or other unethical behavior and to provide more effective penalties for those who violate the codes of conduct. Some courts, overburdened by frivolous and unnecessary litigation, are starting to crack down on those who abuse the process for purposes of harassment or delay.

A growing number of private organizations are sprouting up to assist those who are victimized by the legal process. People who band together with others who were treated unfairly can and do get results. Do not hesitate to contact your state's bar association or another relevant group if you have been treated inappropriately by someone involved in the justice system.

3

Mediation, Litigation, and Other Alternatives

A DIVORCE TODAY often involves several professional advisers working in various capacities to help the couple either reach a settlement or prepare for trial. Two of the most familiar are attorneys and mediators. While attorneys are generally viewed as advocates representing clients on contested issues, with mediators seen as peacemakers guiding the parties to an out-of-court resolution, these roles frequently overlap. Some professionals serve as both attorney and mediator, acting as an impartial legal adviser to both parties and assisting them in covering all of the legal bases in reaching a settlement, including preparation and filing of the court documents.

Additionally, it has become increasingly common for both attorneys and mediators—as well as other professionals—to be involved in a divorce case from the outset. This process, sometimes called "collaborative divorce," combines legal advocacy and alternative dispute resolution, with the goal of reaching a fair settlement without litigation, even in hotly contested cases.

However, it also remains common for couples to try to resolve all or part of the case through mediation alone and then hire lawyers to litigate any remaining issues. If the couple sincerely wishes to resolve their differences on an egalitarian basis, and the balance of power between the parties is reasonably equal so that neither requires a personal advocate, a final settlement can be achieved through mediation alone. Couples may then hire one lawyer, or retain a lawyer for each person, to review the paperwork and prepare it for filing if the mediator does not provide this service.

Conversely, each party may hire a lawyer at the start of the divorce process; the attorneys negotiate an agreement to the extent possible and then send the parties to mediation to work out the remaining bones of contention (standing by to advise on legal questions, if necessary).

Any of these methods can work well, but the relationships between these professionals may be complex. If you choose an approach in which different professionals are involved at the same time, be sure you understand how they feel about each other and about the process. In the vast majority of cases with which I'm familiar, the attorneys and mediators worked together harmoniously, with all comfortable in their respective roles. Most lawyers favor mediation in appropriate cases. Attorney Judith Finfrock, a strong supporter of mediation, notes: "Sometimes the party who is at fault, especially when it is the man, feels that no one is listening to his (or her) side. In mediation, everyone gets to be heard, and this is what these people need. Once they've had their say, they can get down to the business of settling things."

However, I have heard reports of attorneys who discourage mediation or refuse to cooperate with mediators. I would recommend caution regarding any attorney who disfavors all mediation (as opposed to preferring one form of mediation or mediator over another, or suggesting that it may not be appropriate in a particular instance). This may be a sign that the lawyer has the type of "gladiator" mentality that can only increase the cost and trauma to all involved.

Mediation

Mediation has become a popular alternative for divorcing couples who can't reach a complete agreement on their own and yet want to avoid the rancor and cost of litigation. In mediation, the parties to the divorce meet with one or two mediators in an informal setting. The mediator(s) will serve as a neutral third party (or part of a team) to guide and assist settlement negotiations. Mediators point out available alternatives and work with a couple to forge an amicable solution to disputed issues. Many people believe the team approach, which usually combines an attorney and a counselor or therapist, provides the most balanced method.

One main goal of mediation is to turn two people who are at odds with each other into a partnership capable of working together to solve a mutual problem. In addition to helping couples resolve the immediate problems of the divorce, mediation teaches cooperative skills that can remain useful in subsequent years if new issues arise. If the parents cannot reach their own agreement on child custody or visitation issues, mediation will often be mandated by the court, whether the dispute arises during the divorce or later—for example, when one parent seeks to modify an existing order.

The primary goal of either a private or court-appointed mediator is to guide the parties to reaching their own resolution of each contested issue, but a court-appointed mediator will make recommendations if the parties cannot reach an agreement during mediation. The suggested resolution is presented to both the couple and the court. Often the couple will voluntarily adopt the recommendations unless one person feels strongly that they are incorrect or unfair.

When mandatory mediation is ordered by the court, the order must be taken just as seriously as any other. A missed mediation appointment not only creates a bad impression in the eyes of the mediator and the judge—people you do not want to annoy—but also may lead to fines or other penalties. In California, for example, sanctions of up to $1,500 may be imposed for failure to appear at a mediation appointment—and the family law judicial officers regularly levy such fines when parties fail to show or call to reschedule.

Mediation is not limited to divorcing couples. It may also be used to help both straight and gay couples who have lived together in a long-term cohabitation come to an agreeable settlement at the end of the relationship. Mediation is also helpful during the years after a divorce, especially when disputes over children occur or the necessity to change custody or a support order arises. Sometimes mediators work with whole families to help resolve discord in such areas as step-parenting and teenagers' behavior.

Choosing a Mediator

Choosing a good mediator can be tricky. As with lawyers, some mediators specialize in family issues, while others handle a wide range of disputes. Even within the area of family mediation, there are subspecialties: some mediators focus on custody issues, some deal with property and support, and others specialize in long-term financial planning.

Parents ordered to mediate custody or visitation disputes by the court generally have the option of choosing to use a private mediator or mediation team instead of the court-appointed mediator, and this may be the better route to take. While the latter have the advantage of providing free or low-cost services, they are inevitably very busy, with some assigned to mediate two cases per day. Also, there may be a delay of several weeks or even months between the times the order to mediate is issued and a mediator becomes available.

Also, court-appointed mediators are limited to dealing with custody and visitation issues. They cannot address other contested matters such as property division or alimony. And, while most couples who have experienced court-based mediation feel that these mediators do a phenomenal job under difficult circumstances, some have reported feeling that the process was a waste because the mediators simply didn't have time to study and understand the parties' circumstances or grasp the reality of the situation. Therefore, give careful consideration to what is truly at issue—or may become a contested issue—before deciding whether to use a private or court-appointed mediator. Private mediators generally charge fees by the hour or the session, although in some areas, free or low-cost mediation services are available through public or private sources.

Mediator, author, and attorney Roberta Beyer recommends finding a mediator through referrals from attorneys, counselors, clergy, and friends. She advises people who are considering one nonattorney mediator, rather than a team, to ask how the legal issues will be reviewed: Does the mediator have special training, require that each party be represented by legal counsel, or refer legal issues to a lawyer? Also, ask the mediator to tell you about membership in any professional organization, the length of experience or number of cases mediated, and whether the practice is primarily devoted to mediation or is an adjunct to another profession. Finally, be sure to ask about cost, payment arrangements, scheduling, and other nuts-and-bolts information.

The Benefits of Mediation

One essential component of a successful mediation, or any other successful negotiation, is willingness by both parties to compromise. Settlement of all issues seldom happens overnight. It may take extensive and continued negotiation, whether the process is handled by the spouses themselves, lawyers, mediators, or some combination.

Roberta Beyer practiced family law for more than ten years before devoting her efforts to mediation. "Early on, I realized that the adversarial way of trying to resolve family disputes was also the worst way," she says. "It was centered on blame and fault. Plus, it was oriented toward the past. Even after the no-fault grounds became the most common basis for divorce, there was still an emphasis on fault—for example, in custody disputes. People focused on the worst in the other partner to their own advantage. Fault always managed to creep back in." Beyer says she loved her work as a mediator from the start: "I felt that I was finally using my law degree in a productive way. It is so gratifying to me to help people work things out rather than take sides in a battle. There are tremendous differences in what the two systems involve."

People who have been through different processes and compared the merits of each agree that mediation is preferable to battle. "It's much more constructive to mediate," says Becky Ralston, who has been through two divorces, "to negotiate a settlement in a nonadversarial setting. You have x amount of assets to split up, and if you continue fighting over it through your lawyers, if you're not careful, you won't have anything left to fight over."

Ralston, who worked with both a mediator and a lawyer in her second divorce, hastens to add that she also valued the services of her attorney. "I had a lawyer who was worth her weight in gold, who had clout in the local family law community," she says. "Therefore, the lawyers were able to narrow the issues to what we could mediate and get to the point where we could have a fair settlement without too much fuss. She was a very ethical attorney. She had me do a lot of the legwork to save money, and when she had brought us close to amicable terms, she encouraged us to mediate our remaining differences."

Ralston and her husband chose a psychologist to mediate when they reached an impasse on certain property settlement issues. "The guy was a saint," Ralston remarks. "Because of the professionals who helped us come to terms, we still have a relationship on some level—we can deal with certain business we still have to handle together and remain friendly."

When Beyer began mediating, she worked alone. Now she teams with a psychologist. "As a team, we can address all of the issues that need immediate attention," she explains. "When counselors or psychologists mediate alone, they usually are good with the parenting issues but have trouble with the legal aspects of the property, tax, and debt issues. And when attorneys mediate by themselves, we aren't able to deal with all of the underlying issues besides the legal problems. I've been working with a great psychologist in a team approach for four or five years now. I help the couple with the legal matters, while my partner helps them deal with communication and the emotional issues."

Psychologist and mediator Stephen Feher, Ph.D., has worked both with a lawyer partner and alone. When mediating solo, he refers clients to family attorneys if they are not yet legally represented. He has also worked in court-annexed programs as a settlement facilitator, in partnership with a lawyer or judge. Feher prefers to team with a female attorney in mediation. "A gender-balanced team has certain advantages. Sometimes with two men or two women, the partner of the opposite sex feels that three men—or three women—are ganging up on the individual," he explains.

Beyer is a believer in full-service mediation. She has found that the inability to address all the issues to be resolved is a problem in many of the court-annexed mediation programs. "In our community, the court clinic deals with child custody and visitation issues only. Yet everything spills over so much; property, custody, and support are tied together," she remarks. "The mediators should be able to help the partners resolve all of their conflicts, because this is so important for the children. Studies on children in families going through a divorce show that one of the chief concerns for the children is that the parents not remain in conflict. That's a main reason it was important to me to be able to offer a full-service, therapeutic style of mediation. When people divorce, they remain parents, and they have to be able to parent together. We help them work on restructuring their relationship so communication between them will be positive after the divorce, as well as prepare them for better communication in subsequent relationships with others."

Communication likewise is fundamental to forging a sound legal agreement. As Beyer emphasizes, "If we don't help the couple deal with the underlying issues, the agreement is likely to fall apart later on. If they can't communicate, problems are inevitable, especially when child custody is involved. The mediation process itself tends to make for stronger agreements that are more likely to stand the test of time than court-ordered settlements. People are happier when they make their own agreements. Compliance rates in mediation agreements are much higher statistically. When you get the emotional issues aired, it keeps the settlement in perspective."

Although she finds the team approach preferable in her own practice, Beyer notes that there are some very good mediators who do it alone. "Many mediators do a great job on their own, as long as they are able to deal with all of the issues. Therapeutic mediation is good in any case. We have to realize that when a couple is stuck over Grandma's piano, the piano is not what's at stake. Property often becomes a symbol of emotional issues." Beyer believes this attention to emotional matters is crucial to the overall mediation endeavor: "The process of divorcing is tough and scary for the people involved. Our goal is to move them into a good, civil, positive business relationship."

Mediation is generally far less expensive than trying to reach a settlement through litigation. "Mediation usually costs about one-third of what it costs to go to two attorneys, even if the relationship is not adversarial and no court action will be required. If the case does go to trial, the figure would be closer to one-tenth," Beyer explains. "A divorce can be a financial nightmare, and nobody plans for that cost in the normal budget."

As do most other mediators, Beyer believes that attorneys should retain some involvement in a mediated divorce. "Divorce law has become so complex; in many ways it's like medicine," she states. "When there are complicated assets, we advise a couple to see an attorney specialist to review the agreement and make sure everything is sound, such as when there are complex pension issues." She adds, "As a family law attorney, I'm capable of dealing with most of the matters that come up. But I wear a different hat as a mediator. In a typical case, 90 percent of the work to complete the divorce documents will be done here, and the rest will be executed by another attorney for a relatively small amount of money, depending on the complexity of the case."

The mediation process varies according to the people involved and the nature of the matters to be settled, but a fairly standard process is followed in most cases. "The appointments are scheduled for two hours, which is generally just about right," Beyer explains. "We try to meet every week to keep the momentum going, but we may have to wait longer between meetings if the couple needs appraisals of property or must deal with other matters. Most couples come to as many sessions as it takes to agree. Some come to one session and then work out an agreement on their own." Beyer and her partner use a variety of techniques to address special problems, including meeting with each person alone, or even threatening to end the mediation and send the parties back to their attorneys if both refuse to budge. The bottom line, she states, is finding a process that culminates in an agreement that is fair to both people and likely to stand the test of time. "We are always happy to work ourselves out of a job. We're successful in getting an agreement on all or most issues in 80 to 90 percent of our cases."

When Mediation Might Not Be Appropriate

While most professionals in the field of family law favor mediation, some have misgivings about its use when the relationship is acrimonious or the balance of power is significantly one-sided. As family law attorney Kathleen Robertson explains, "Mediation without attorneys works only when there is an equal playing field, and in practice this doesn't happen very often. One client brought me an agreement for my review that had been drafted after mediation. It took me a five-page letter to point out everything in the agreement that was unfair. It was obvious that she was completely under the control of her husband. I learned that every asset he controlled had been grossly misrepresented in the mediation. She refused to sign the agreement and ultimately received a better settlement."

However, a skilled mediator may be able to offset such inequities in appropriate cases. According to Beyer, "The people in high conflict are the ones who really need our help. True, if there is a power imbalance along with an unskilled mediator, bad results can occur. A good mediation team's job is to balance the power. Mediation itself is empowering. If a person with no power in a relationship goes to an attorney and simply hands over her problem, this doesn't help her at all. With good mediation, there is learning, and the person becomes a part of the decision-making process. We work very carefully when the balance of power is unequal. If we see one person being rolled over, we try to urge the other to be more fair. However, if they can't reach a fair agreement, and we see that one partner is trying to bully the other, we have the right to terminate the mediation and send them to attorneys. We have a moral and ethical obligation to see that any agreement we help a couple reach is fair to both partners and fair to the children."

There is a raging controversy as to whether mediation can ever work when a relationship has been violent. Beyer remarks, "It can work with highly skilled mediators if there is no current physical abuse, if clear boundaries can be set, and if both partners are in counseling. First and foremost, the process must be safe. Unless both people are seeing therapists and willing to set trustworthy limits, such as having no contact with each other outside the mediation, then mediation is not appropriate.

She adds that there are other instances in which mediation should not be recommended. "Successful mediation requires honesty," she states. "If one person is hiding assets or lying, it won't work. Then the couple needs to go into court and use the formal discovery process." Likewise, mediation is inappropriate if one spouse has been involved in any criminal financial transactions. "That makes it too complicated—the attorneys need to handle all the issues involved," she says. Beyer and her partner can generally tell if one of the partners is not being honest. "We can usually ferret out what is being hidden or explain why it will come back to haunt them later if they are dishonest. This is seldom a problem. Most of the people who come here want an amicable, civilized divorce. We really have few cases in which the people are violent or dishonest."

Mediation may also be inappropriate, according to Beyer, when the mediator has had a prior professional relationship with either spouse. "If an attorney has represented one, or a therapist has counseled one, there may be a lack of impartiality. Also, a mediator wears a different hat from a lawyer or counselor, even though many professionals do both types of work. The client may want to see the person again in the other capacity, and it can get very confusing." She also emphasizes that people often look at things from a different viewpoint after the divorce. "If there is any possibility of partiality by the mediator, a client may not view it as a problem during the process but could look back six months later and feel troubled."

Collaborative Divorce

"Collaborative divorce" is one of the most exciting, and most practical, concepts to emerge from the changing landscape of divorce law and practice in recent years. It is an interdisciplinary team approach, in which a group of professionals work with a divorcing couple to help them reach a fair resolution of all issues without litigation. In addition to the attorneys representing each party (who advise them on the law and draft the settlement), financial analysts, mental health therapists, vocational experts, divorce coaches, and various other professionals may participate. The process stresses honesty, integrity, cooperation, and compromise, with an orientation toward the future. The parties and their counsel commit to making every effort to resolve their differences justly and equitably, without litigation, in a nonadversarial setting. If the negotiations do break down in a collaborative divorce, both parties will be required to get new lawyers to represent them in court.

Collaborative divorce, like mediation, is usually far less expensive than litigation and proceeds more efficiently. One set of professionals works as a unit to orchestrate a settlement addressing all of the complexities involved, rather than two highly paid teams meeting as dueling expert witnesses in the courtroom. The collaborative process also tends to foster a higher degree of respect and dignity among the parties, which in turn is much less traumatic for any children who are involved than a courtroom battle. State bar associations may provide referrals to collaborative divorce attorneys, as do numerous Internet sites. See the Appendixes for listings.

Litigation

Many argue—and I tend to agree—that adversarial litigation should rarely, if ever, be used to resolve disputes within families. As stated by the Twin Falls, Idaho, magistrate court on its website, "Families cannot be divided by declaring winners and losers. When we go through the adversary process, children always lose. The goal of mediation is to make children winners."

Even in childless divorces, litigation is inevitably agonizing and damaging to everyone involved. Jane and Ron Foster decided to divorce shortly after Jane left the government firm where they both had worked to start her own design business. "We thought we had everything worked out," she recalls. "We didn't have children, and we made a written agreement dividing most of our property, but as things progressed, we began to disagree about how to divide the equity in the house, some loans, and my new design firm," she says. Their case eventually went to litigation. "The courtroom was the last place I thought we would end up," she remarks. "We had nothing of extreme value, but we just couldn't reach a final agreement on these issues."

She remembers the pain of appearing in the courtroom as a litigant against her husband: "How sad that it had come to this, with the man I had married, loved, slept with, traveled with. He seemed so desperate—and so was I. It was even sadder when Ron resorted to lying on the witness stand. My attorney proved he was not being honest, and the judge was not kind to him at the end of the trial. It was a nightmare, and I sometimes wonder if it was worth it. Looking back, I'm glad I stood up for what I knew was right, but I wish there had been a better way to get through it, for both of us."

Unfortunately, in some cases, no matter how hard one or both people may try to find a better way, litigation will be inevitable. If you find yourself in a divorce that seems bound for trial, it will be important to have an attorney who is prepared to take you through a full-scale litigated case while at the same time doing everything possible to try to resolve some, if not all, of the issues involved before you hit the courtroom.

Tony Kaye, a divorced father of two who went through a wrenching child custody battle, advises those in similar circumstances to try to view the litigation process in a businesslike manner. "Hire the best attorney you can afford, tell him or her what you want to achieve, and then get out of the way and let the lawyer work," he says. "Handle all communication with your spouse through the lawyers. Otherwise, you'll let your emotions get involved. You can end up getting your buttons pushed until you just give up." Kaye let himself be railroaded into a custody agreement he did not feel was best for his children. A short time later, his instincts were proved correct when his wife, who had insisted on primary physical custody, began neglecting the children and ignoring his visitation schedule while she pursued a new relationship. That was when Kaye ended up in litigation, spending several thousand dollars to achieve the arrangement he had favored all along. "If I had just hired a strong attorney and then stayed out of it the first time around, I would have avoided a lot of expense and a lot of grief," he says.

Choosing and Working with an Attorney

Kathleen Robertson has practiced exclusively in the area of domestic relations law, first at a large law firm and more recently as a sole practitioner. She urges those facing a divorce to work with an attorney who is a specialist in the family law field. "There are a lot of lawyers who just dabble in domestic relations work, and they are at a disadvantage," she explains. "Historically, the area of family law has been looked down upon. Male attorneys especially didn't like to practice in that area because you don't get a lot of glory or big money, and it's a very emotional environment. But family law has become extremely complicated. Today, people are beginning to recognize it as a more highly specialized and respected field of practice."

In line with many other professionals, Robertson advises anyone seeking a divorce attorney to ask friends for recommendations. She also suggests using bar association referral services and checking to learn which attorneys are registered specialists in the field—although she quickly adds that many good family attorneys are not registered as specialists. She also urges people contemplating a divorce to educate themselves on the process through local classes, seminars, or clinics.

Regarding working with an attorney, Robertson advises clients to ask a lot of questions. "Be sure you get a representation letter that is detailed and that outlines what you can expect in the way of fees and other matters. Contingency fees are not allowed in divorce actions; in New Mexico, where I practice, there is a statute prohibiting them. I always talk to the client about the fees and other information as soon as we have agreed that I will take the case. I also give an information questionnaire to every client; then I set up a consultation in which we discuss all of the issues involved in the case in detail. I give the client an overview of what issues are black and white, what issues fall into gray areas that don't have a predictable outcome, and the steps we will go through in the divorce process. It's important that the client and attorney work with each other and that both have realistic expectations. Some clients are looking for a 'mad dog' attorney to punish the spouse. I have to explain to them that this approach is bad for them, their kids, and the system."

Robertson counsels her clients on what to expect on a practical basis. "People often envision that they can maintain the same lifestyle after the divorce," she says. "I have to explain to them that this is not likely to happen. I don't have a magic wand to make it happen. All I can do is try to get them the best possible result under the law. I also recommend therapy for almost all of my clients, if they're not already seeing someone." She notes, "Nearly everyone divorcing has what I call 'situational schizophrenia.' There are some therapists whom I know and respect, and I will personally recommend them."

She adds that it is often hard to draw the line between being supportive and meeting her professional obligations: "As a domestic relations attorney, I have to maintain a certain amount of objectivity and distance and not become too buddy-buddy with my clients. I can't let them start seeing me as Glinda, the Good Witch. If the attorney becomes too enmeshed in the client's personal life, he or she can't do a good job. We're not rescuers; we're advocates. Therefore, a client seeing a therapist is often better able to work with the attorney on legal issues, because the client doesn't expect the attorney to fill the role of therapist as well. Family lawyers still inevitably become more involved in their clients' emotional lives than attorneys representing clients in other legal matters. Of course, you have to be empathetic with a client, because everyone is out of control during a divorce. Many clients seem to prefer female attorneys because women are seen as being more comfortable with emotional extremes."

Robertson believes that while boundaries must be drawn, the role of legal counselor remains a central part of the lawyer's job. "Especially in today's legal climate, it's important to have an attorney who will listen to the emotional reasons for the decisions being made by the client. For example, a person often has strong emotional ties to the home. An attorney must realize that while keeping the home may not be the most advisable financial decision for the person, it is his or her choice. I tell clients, 'This is your divorce!' I make sure they understand that they have to be the one to make the decisions."

When clients insist on making a decision that Robertson doesn't feel is in their best interest, she sends them a long letter documenting all the problems that are likely to occur as a result, with a reminder that they can't go back and change the decision later. "I tell them both directly and in a letter that the course of action is inadvisable, but they are entitled to make what I feel is a bad decision," she says.

Successful Litigation

Robertson is among the majority of family attorneys who believe a settlement reached by the parties is always preferable to going to court. She asserts, "It's best to limit the controversy, in terms of both dollars and emotions. Divorce is expensive, but there is a plus side to that, because the financial ceiling allows the battle to end at some point. The more economically sound decisions are usually the wiser ones anyway. For example, when people agree to split the cost of one expert witness, not only do they save money, but also the opinion of this person will have much more weight with the court than two hired guns doing battle. A settlement may be reached after the neutral expert has made a report to both parties."

As Robertson recounts, the practical process of getting the divorce accomplished is the same in most cases: "First, I give clients the information questionnaire, which requires them to do some homework and get the necessary information and documents together. Then I have them bring in the information I need to draft the petition to get the divorce going. I then prepare a temporary domestic order, which is a document that must be filed, under our local rules. It is a standard form that lists property and debts and requires that documents be exchanged between parties. Each party must file an affidavit, including proof of income, rent or mortgage, fixed expenses, and full disclosure of assets so the court knows that nothing is being hidden. Next, I take care of any other interim relief that needs to be established, such as interim spousal or child support. Many clients don't realize that this interim relief is available. The interim order from the court outlines how fixed debts will be paid and who will pay what, so that the community's credit won't be hurt. Voluntary contributions, such as payments made into a 401(k) plan, usually stop during the interim period until the divorce is final."

The information questionnaire she provides the client covers issues not specifically dealt with in the interim order. "It also covers the client's personal history, work, education, and so on—everything I will need to put the case together. We look at the children's special needs and the emotional issues—who wants the divorce, why the client thinks it's happening, what he or she believes are likely to be sticky areas in reaching a settlement. If there are domestic violence issues, we must make these the first priority and deal with them right away. I obtain a broad restraining order if there is any danger to the client or the children. I also ask for a court-appointed psychological expert to assess the family immediately, and I request that the abuser have only supervised visitation with the children until the expert has made an evaluation. In short, the first step is to get things stabilized," Robertson explains. "Violence and money are two big issues that have to be dealt with in interim matters. Then I can get to the nuts and bolts of the case. Whenever possible, I try to complete discovery informally. There are pros and cons to this, since informal discovery is not conducted under oath, but it costs a lot less, and the client usually knows whether the other party will be honest or not. It's a cost-benefit analysis."

Robertson favors a settlement in which assets can be traded off rather than liquidated, as long as the value can be accurately assessed and an equitable settlement reached. She states: "It's usually better to trade assets. For most couples, the two biggest assets are their house and their retirement plans. We have to look at the present-day value of each and also be sure we are trading apples for apples. I always try to retain one actuary to perform valuations on all retirement benefits requiring valuation, so that the same set of assumptions is used in appraising each asset. Again, it's best if one expert can be agreed upon by both sides."

An experienced family law attorney will also be familiar with ways to cut corners in cost without compromising a client's rights. "For real estate," she says, "I start with a market-value analysis, which a real estate agent will perform for free. If the couple can agree that the value is accurate, there may be no need to pay for a formal appraisal. Equity in the house can be determined by subtracting the mortgage balance from the agreed-upon value. Cost-of-sale and tax issues can be a problem if a house must be sold, and this must be analyzed on a case-by-case basis. I make sure the client knows what he or she will be facing in the way of direct costs, as well as indirect costs such as capital gains tax in the future. I work with CPAs in almost all cases."

When Children Are Involved. It is much better for both the couple and their children if a couple can agree to a settlement on custody and support issues. As Robertson points out, "People must realize that what is in the best interest of the child is not necessarily what seems to be in the best interest of one of the parents. In this jurisdiction, we have a court clinic that mediates contested custody issues. Some clients who wish to mediate other areas of disagreement find that private mediation is the route to take so that the entire case can be settled and an attorney can then prepare the final document."

Robertson, herself a divorced mother, stresses that big changes are happening rapidly in many areas of family law, including child support, another reason clients need a qualified family lawyer. "Many states are changing their laws to be more in line with the federal child support guidelines, calling for one schedule that recognizes that each parent has a duty to support the child. Also, many states now have laws specifically dealing with college tuition." She also warns that the statutory child support guidelines do not take into account expenses for extracurricular activities or medical costs not covered by insurance. "I raise all of these issues and deal with them in separate paragraphs of the final order," she says.

Robertson is often frustrated by divorcing parents whose views of the future are not realistic. "This is a big problem," she maintains. "Clients sometimes fail to accept that they still have to be parents with the divorced spouse. They will have to communicate with each other. They get into this mind-set of 'my way or no way,' and emotions run rampant. It's sad, and it's way off the mark. Children need predictability and stability, as well as protection from the bad feelings between parents. Parents need to at least be neutral with one another when the children are present. When I draw up a parenting plan as part of the settlement agreement, I urge people to include a mediation clause. It generally states that if there is a dispute involving the children, one parent will make a request to the other in writing. Then the other responds. If they can't reach an agreement, they will go to mediation. Going to court again should be the last resort."

Spousal Support and Other Issues

Robertson notes that while spousal support may not be available in many cases, she always discusses it with her clients. "It's important to remind anxious clients that they may have long-term needs that they don't know about yet. For example, someone who has been married forty years and divorces may be incapable of self-support. Social Security benefits, spousal support, and retirement benefits must be reviewed and considered as sources of income. I look at every case as a potential spousal support case until I see that there is either no need or no ability by the other party to pay."

A domestic relations attorney must also remain familiar with other areas of the law in order to do a thorough job. "Other litigation areas often overlap," she explains. "Intentional infliction of emotional distress or other spousal tort claims may need to be pursued. Bankruptcy issues may arise. A good, creative attorney has to recognize and raise these issues. It's really complicated; you have to have so many areas of expertise to do this right."

Robertson urges clients to be candid with the attorney about any mistreatment of themselves or their children during the marriage. "Sometimes clients who are familiar with the no-fault system won't even bring up these issues, but they should. For example, if there has been abuse, the attorney needs to know so that the client won't be sent to the court clinic for mediation with the abuser. Shuttle mediation, in which the parties do not see each other and the mediator goes back and forth, is an alternative sometimes used in place of traditional mediation. Clients should be absolutely honest with the attorney about any emotional or physical abuse, intimidation, or threats. The cycle of violence often escalates during the divorce process," she says.

Legal Fees

Attorney's fees can be awarded differently in a family law case from the way it's done in most other cases. The party with higher earnings may be ordered by the court to pay attorneys' fees for both parties, but each client may be required to pay his or her own attorney first and then receive reimbursement from the other party, as ordered.

Robertson also points out that a client who engages in obstructive or inappropriate behavior that results in escalated legal fees can be ordered to pay the other party's fees. She generally requires her clients to pay an advance to begin representation. Robertson cautions that it is often impossible to tell how much a divorce will cost. "It all depends on the other attorney and whether the parties are going to be reasonable or unreasonable."

4

Special Complications

Owing to one reason or another, many divorces cannot be concluded quickly and simply. When one or more complicating issues are involved, people need to be aware of the options and challenges they face, as well as potential pitfalls and sources of help.

The Violent Marriage

It is estimated that as many as 25 percent of all American women who initiate a divorce action are victims of domestic violence. Recent studies indicate that many men are also escaping violent marriages, although the numbers are harder to document due to lower reporting rates. It is also estimated that more than 90 percent of the victims of domestic violence are women, but again, an increasing number of men are beginning to report such abuse as well. In all circumstances, ending an abusive marriage requires special handling and caution.

Here, I am referring to a marriage in which one person routinely abuses the other physically, emotionally, sexually, or in a combination of ways. These relationships are almost always one-sided: one partner attempts to establish complete control over the other. The dynamics are totally different from a mutually combative situation, in which the partners often "fight." Such marriages are characterized by constant arguments, but the arguments rarely deteriorate into physical brawls. If they do, the relationship usually ends quickly or improves rather than continue on a violent path. Relationships marked by ongoing domestic violence are different, and ending them, while always desirable, must be handled with care.

When one spouse has abused the other, the rules of the game are inherently changed, because the people involved do not have equal bargaining power. The longer the marriage has lasted, the worse the problem will be. People who have suffered abuse over a period of years may have a severely distorted perspective of reality and of their choices. Many suffer from post-traumatic stress disorder and require professional help to rebuild a healthy, stable life. It is essential that they—and everyone else involved—understand that it is the abuser who is responsible for this vicious, criminal behavior. The abuser is always to blame—never the victim of the abuse.

When one partner in a marriage abuses the other, the person's primary goal is control, including control of the victim's ability to leave. Ironically, when a marriage has been abusive, the most dangerous point in the relationship is often the point at which it ends. More women are murdered by a husband or boyfriend when they try to leave the relationship than at any other time. For this reason, anyone divorcing an abusive partner should take special precautions, from the day the decision to leave is made until the divorce is final, and even afterward. Many abusers keep trying to terrorize, cajole, or manipulate the other person into returning, even long after the divorce. Some studies estimate that 50 to 75 percent of the women who leave men who have abused them are stalked afterward. Children may also be in great danger at this time.

To help guarantee safety, anyone divorcing an abuser should be certain that those who know the victim's whereabouts or other confidential information will not reveal it to the abuser. Fortunately, many court systems, shelters, and other agencies now employ specially trained advocates. These people, or other professionals, can provide special help to victims of violence in using the legal remedies and social services available. A call to the local shelter, court, or state domestic violence coalition (all states now have one) can provide information on services in the area (see the Appendixes). These organizations can also help victims formulate a safety plan to help ensure security before, during, and after the separation from an abusive spouse. Family law attorneys will also be aware of the special services for victims of family violence.

A person who has suffered injuries because of abuse may have a tort claim for personal injury that can be brought in conjunction with the divorce action. Any attorney representing a victim of domestic violence should be familiar with this option and how to use it. In addition, a restraining order should be filed while the divorce is pending, and a permanent injunction or other specifically tailored order should be made a part of the final decree. The orders should either prohibit the abusive spouse from contacting the victim in any manner or set strict limits if child visitation is involved.

As discussed in Chapter 3, mediation is generally inappropriate in cases in which the marriage has been abusive, especially if the threat of violence remains. Successful mediation depends on two people with equal bargaining power who can reasonably consider their alternatives and reach a fair agreement. Where one partner has been consistently bullied and controlled by the other, this is usually not possible. The victim often agrees to unsatisfactory terms out of fear, intimidation, or a desire to get away from the abuser. Also, it is unfair to force the victim to spend the hours it takes to mediate an agreement in the presence of the batterer. In an abusive situation, it is usually far better—and often essential for the victim's safety—to restrict all negotiations to communications between attorneys or other advocates. Most courts that have mandatory mediation programs will make exceptions if the marriage was abusive. For those that don't automatically exclude violent marriages from the mediation process, an attorney, a court advocate, or a social service worker can intervene and convince the court that mediation is not appropriate.

Child Custody and Visitation

Child custody and visitation must also be given special attention when a violent marriage ends. Most courts today place substantial weight on evidence of any abuse in the home in determining custody, although some are still stuck in the Dark Ages and blame the victim for "allowing" the children to remain in a home where one parent beat the other. Incredibly, courts have been known to rule that even fathers who had murdered the mothers of their children were not necessarily unfit parents! Thus, it is essential that the abused parent have sensitive, competent legal representation.

Most experts who work with children agree that growing up in a violent home is one of the worst things that can happen to a child, whether or not the child is directly abused. Those who have studied violent homes believe that almost all children in homes where one parent batters the other are aware, at least on some level, of what is going on, and they suffer terribly for it. As stated by top divorce attorney Raoul Felder in Emily Couric's *The Divorce Lawyers*, "When you hit a kid's mother, you are hitting a kid, you are doing damage to that kid. You can't really separate the two . . . the household is crazy by definition at that point. The law is not adequate to deal with crazy situations." Felder maintains, and many colleagues agree, that spousal abuse alone should affect that parent's rights as a custodian of children. Many advocacy groups argue that joint custody should never be awarded in cases in which one parent was violent toward the other, and courts are starting to change their laws and rules accordingly. This makes sense, because someone who abuses a child's parent has already demonstrated a lack of regard for the welfare of the child.

In 1990, the U.S. Congress passed a resolution recommending that custody not be given to a parent who has abused his or her spouse, because doing so would be detrimental to the child. The resolution is persuasive, but it does not have the force of law. Judges still have broad discretion to make their own determinations about what is in the best interest of the children in states that have not enacted their own laws governing this situation. Therefore, victims of domestic violence should be certain to inform their attorneys about the full history of abuse in the marriage and should request that a court-appointed or privately hired mental health professional be involved in custody decisions.

If the abusive spouse does get custodial or visitation rights, the option of supervised visitation and/or special provisions for the exchange of the child should be considered carefully. Many communities have found innovative solutions to these problems, such as establishing centers where the parents can exchange the child safely, without any contact, or designating locations such as the YMCA or YWCA that provide facilities for comfortable, subtly supervised visitation and recreation. Also, custody orders may be modified for good cause and can be changed later if the abuser convinces the court that he or she has stopped the criminal behavior, has sought treatment, and is committed to building a healthy relationship with the child.

Safety Concerns

An attorney handling the end of a violent marriage must be prepared to perform all the tasks essential for the client's safety. Attorney Judith Finfrock estimates that about 30 percent of the divorces she has handled involved domestic violence between the couple at some point. "In these cases, I also had to see that restraining orders were in place and arrange for a mutual exchange of the children for visitation at a safe place so that the parents would not have to see each other. I will not hesitate to advise a mother to withhold visitation if she or her children are in danger," she says. "By doing so, I know I take a risk, because while most judges will agree that this is the right course of action if past violence can be proved, others hold visitation rights sacrosanct, and a lawyer can get in trouble for advising a client to go against them. But consider what's at stake."

Unfortunately, the quality of justice that a battered spouse receives often depends on geography. Some communities have excellent programs in which anyone beaten by a spouse will be provided with assistance in obtaining a protection order; the abuser will be immediately arrested (and often given the alternative of staying away from the victim and attending a treatment program or going to jail) and prosecuted. Sad to say, in other areas, services range from piecemeal to nonexistent. Still, more and more communities are waking up to the horrible toll taken by domestic violence and are starting to treat it as the potentially deadly crime it is.

Ideally, domestic violence victims who are planning to make the break from their marriage should first find out what services are available and how such cases are treated in their community. Every state now has a coalition against domestic violence. Check the government pages of your local telephone directory or the Internet. Many have toll-free numbers as well as websites and emergency hotlines. Some cities now have local groups as well, and special help is available in nearly all areas of the country. Hotlines can refer you to shelters, support groups, and social service agencies. The National Domestic Violence Hotline is staffed twenty-four hours a day by trained counselors who provide crisis assistance and information about shelters, legal assistance, health care, and counseling. Its number is (800) 799-7233 (SAFE) or for TDD, (800) 787-3224. Local police, prosecutors offices, emergency medical personnel, the United Way, the YWCA, and similar organizations can provide help or referrals. There are also numerous websites and books geared to domestic violence victims, including my *Domestic Violence Sourcebook* (see the "Resources and Suggested Readings" section at the back of this book).

For women or men who have been abused, taking that first step toward a divorce can be empowering. Remember, however, that it is essential to have a personal safety plan in place that covers in detail the periods before, during, and after departure; as well as the duration of the divorce process.

Child Abuse

Direct child abuse, while sometimes related to spousal abuse, also occurs in homes in which only the children are victims. Staggering numbers of children are physically and/or sexually abused. Today, not only do the laws make child abuse a crime and provide for state intervention in situations in which child abuse is present or suspected, but there are also laws requiring people who have close contact with children, such as doctors and teachers, to report suspected abuse. Notwithstanding, this crime often goes undetected, despite the ongoing public pressure to stop it and the presence of child protective agencies in every state.

In a divorce action, a parent seeking sole custody of a child who has been abused by the other parent should be able to take advantage of the many sources available to help protect the child's interest, often free of charge. Such resources include publicly employed psychologists, social workers, and child welfare advocates. A call to your local family services or child welfare agency can put you in touch with help. There are also special hotlines that provide information and referrals, along with organizations working to prevent and stop child abuse (see Appendix A).

The first action that a victim of violence or the parent of an abused child should take when seeking a divorce is to locate an attorney familiar with the dynamics and dangers of family violence and make it clear to him or her that immediate assistance is needed. Provide your lawyer with detailed information about the abuse, and ask for help in familiarizing yourself with the available services in the community. Documentation is important, and records of medical treatment, social service intervention, reports of suspected abuse, and police involvement all may be crucial to the case. Be sure to share both formal records and informal recollections with your attorney.

If you can't locate an appropriate lawyer on your own, ask for assistance through a local shelter, state or local coalition against domestic violence or child abuse, or domestic violence or child abuse hotline. If you have problems coping with the stress of dealing with children during your divorce, or believe you might have treated your children abusively in the past, you must get professional assistance immediately—both for the sake of your children and to protect your rights to custody and/or visitation. Appendix A lists organizations such as Parents Anonymous that can provide advice, information, and referrals to professionals in your area who can help.

The Displaced Homemaker

No-fault divorce has simplified the legal process and doubtless has made divorce an easier and more straightforward procedure for the couple composed of two mature, reasonable people who have amicably decided to end their marriage. At the same time, the no-fault system has created great difficulty for some individuals, particularly for women who have been abused by their husbands or have spent many years out of the workforce as homemakers and mothers.

In her book *The Divorce Revolution*, Lenore Weitzman, Ph.D., contends that the advent of no-fault divorce has transformed the entire landscape of American family law. She echoes what is perhaps the most common criticism of no-fault divorce: namely, that for women and their minor children, it often leads to a sharp decline in the standard of living after a divorce. Other experts share Weitzman's concern. "The implementation of no-fault divorce by most states in the 1970s and 1980s is arguably one of the most important changes in women's work lives in the past hundred years," says Patricia Murphy, Ph.D., a vocational rehabilitation counselor and author who frequently testifies as an expert witness in divorce cases. The involvement of a vocational expert—who may be appointed by the court—can be fundamental in determining the amount, type, and duration of support that is necessary.

Murphy generally favors the concept of rehabilitative alimony, as it gives recognition to the vocational impairment that inevitably occurs when a person spends a period of years out of the paying work world. "The status of a displaced homemaker is roughly equivalent to that of displaced male workers who lose their jobs when a factory closes," Murphy explains. "Both are in need of rehabilitation, such as career counseling, vocational evaluation, training/retraining, résumé development, and assistance finding job leads." The problem arises when the courts fail to recognize the reality faced by a woman entering the world of paying work outside the home after being absent from it for a number of years or, for some, never having been in that world at all.

The importance of recognizing the value of homemaking and child care activities also needs to be addressed. As Murphy says, "The inclusion of an actual dollar valuation of these activities in the divorce process will go a long way in identifying the homemaker as a worker and, perhaps, in establishing a better set of facts for decisions about spousal support and rehabilitation needs."

Murphy provides an example from a case in which she was involved. Her first task is always to identify a client as a worker. In this case, Liz, a Utah woman, had worked primarily as an unpaid homemaker and mother. Although she had a degree in nursing, she had only a few months' work experience and had been a homemaker for twenty-five years. Her nursing license had expired, and she would have needed at least one year of college to bring these skills up to date, along with meeting other licensing and registration requirements. Moreover, she no longer had the desire or the ability to be in the nursing profession. Liz had been severely abused by her husband and had lost the vision in her left eye as a result, which precluded her from performing certain jobs, including nursing work.

After Liz and her husband separated, she held several low-paying jobs without benefits. The divorce left her confused and frightened about her vocational goals and her employment potential. Liz also suffered from post-traumatic stress disorder (PTSD). Though often not recognized as a disabling condition, the disorder gave rise to personality traits such as fear, depression, guilt, passivity and low self-esteem, which further impeded her ability to function in the workplace. Battered women often suffer from a particular form of PTSD known as battered woman syndrome (BWS). The diagnosis of BWS allowed Murphy to understand why Liz had been unable to move up vocationally. She had been employed at a battered women's shelter and was strongly motivated to continue to provide a service to formerly battered women. However, she could not make more than $8 per hour at this position.

Murphy worked with Liz to analyze the various jobs that could help her fulfill her goals, raise her income, and develop new skills that would be transferable to other settings in the future. Together they settled on a plan through which Liz could establish a carpet cleaning business and hire formerly battered women as employees. The flexibility of the business would allow her to take college courses to develop more skills in small business management and related areas. She could also enroll in courses to assist her in overcoming her low self-esteem and other impairments related to BWS.

Murphy came up with several alternative approaches for calculating the support and compensation Liz should receive, including examples that could not be developed as vocational rehabilitation plans, such as a return to nursing, and what she had lost as a consequence. Other approaches took into consideration the value of her services to the family, her current projected earning abilities (based on U.S. Department of Labor statistics), the cost of rehabilitation and psychotherapy services, and the cost to purchase the franchised carpet cleaning business and set it up, plus the cost of the recommended two-year community college program.

In the final analysis, Murphy was able to demonstrate that an award encompassing the total cost of the vocational rehabilitation plan to get Liz started in her chosen business made the most sense both economically and in terms of quality-of-life concerns for Liz. The damages she could reasonably have claimed through a domestic tort action were far greater than the cost of the rehabilitation plan. "These analyses offered Liz's attorney a powerful tool in both the no-fault divorce process and the domestic tort process," Murphy explains.

Testimony by vocational experts is now allowed by most courts, although the context in which it must be introduced into evidence varies. "What is disallowed in the no-fault divorce process may be allowed in the domestic tort process," Murphy says. However, she cautions, it remains unclear whether psychological and/or physical injuries of abused women can be used in straight no-fault divorce cases. Therefore, she advises vocational experts to prepare no-fault divorce cases as if a domestic tort case will be filed, even if it may not be practical due to difficulty, time constraints, or remaining barriers in state law.

The Equality in Marriage Institute was founded by Lorena J. Wendt, who went through a very public divorce in the late 1990s that became a test case for valuation of the services of homemaker spouses. The Institute provides information and assistance for others in similar circumstances and maintains an extensive website. See Appendix A for contact information.

Annulment

When a marriage is legally annulled, it effectively never existed, in the eyes of the law. Grounds for annulment vary from state to state but generally require proof of something that would render the marriage "voidable" or that would prevent a valid marriage from having occurred in the first place. For example, fraud, minority, bigamy, or one person's physical inability to consummate the marriage may be among grounds for annulment. The procedures for obtaining an annulment (or, as it is called in some places, "nullity of marriage") are generally similar to those required for obtaining a divorce.

Annulment is fairly rare today, but it still occurs. Before pursuing this course, both spouses should weigh all possible repercussions carefully. For one thing, annulment may have serious consequences for the immigration status of a person who is not a U.S. citizen. It may also affect entitlement to employment benefits or other property rights. Remember, though, that annulment will be granted only in very limited circumstances. If a couple was validly married and then lived as husband and wife for even a brief period, annulment is generally not an option.

Divorcing Catholics may also wish to consider annulment of their marriage according to the church's canon law. Church annulment involves a declaration by an ecclesiastical tribunal. In contrast to civil annulment, it does not have any legal bearing on a divorce that has taken place or is pending; it is purely a matter of religious doctrine, required before a Catholic wedding may be performed for someone who has been previously married. According to information provided by the Archdiocese of New York, annulment does not deny that the relationship existed, nor does it imply that the marriage was a product of ill will or moral fault. Rather, one of the partners to a marriage can petition a church court to investigate the canonical validity of a past marriage (whether a Catholic marriage or not), a process that is normally initiated after a civil divorce has been obtained. A representative of the appropriate tribunal of the archdiocese then advises the person about what will be required, explains the grounds for annulment, and outlines the procedure. If there is found to be a basis for a formal hearing, a petition is drawn up, and the matter proceeds in a manner somewhat similar to that of a civil hearing, including a right to appeal a negative decision. Catholic annulment may be a lengthy process. Those seeking an annulment in New York are cautioned that the process may take more than two years to complete and are advised not to plan a church wedding until the final decision is rendered.

Special Concerns for Military Families

Divorcing couples with one or both partners in the military service face certain concerns not shared by civilian couples. Special military laws, rules, and regulations can affect how a divorce proceeds. Federal laws, such as the Servicemembers Civil Relief Act, as well as the laws of some states, can also impact the divorce—for example, in some states, residency requirements are relaxed for military personnel. In addition, spousal and child support are subject to special rules that affect both calculation and collection of support. Issues of jurisdiction, taxation, residency, default, service or papers, and venue may also be tricky.

Both active and retired service personnel may be affected by these laws. Military pensions and survivor benefit plans require particular attention, with laws such as the Uniformed Services Former Spouse Protection Act governing division of these assets. Military retirement pay and related benefits acquired during the marriage are generally considered marital property, subject to division between divorcing spouses depending on state law and individual circumstances. These matters need to be handled carefully by a qualified attorney, who must be certain the appropriate government offices are notified if benefits are to be divided.

Fortunately, numerous programs and agencies are available to assist military personnel and their families who are coping with divorce and other family law issues (as well as a variety of programs designed to strengthen and support military families to prevent their disintegration). One of the broadest is Military OneSource, which was established by the U.S. Department of Defense to act as a clearinghouse to steer soldiers and their families to sources of support. This program provides assistance to military families with nearly any problem—from a midnight plumbing disaster to a child custody clash—and complements similar programs offered by each branch of the service. Military OneSource is staffed by nonjudgmental social workers or counselors with special training in military life, who are available around the clock by telephone or online. See Appendix A for contact information.

Also, the American Bar Association has established a program called Operation Stand-By to assist judge advocate general (JAG) attorneys representing service personnel with family law issues.

Operation Stand-By provides volunteer family lawyers from each state who can help JAG lawyers navigate the law of a client's home state and deal with any thorny issues that may arise. For more information, contact the ABA (see Appendix A).

Child custody and visitation can be especially tricky for military families, since people in the service do not have the same choices and degree of control as the civilian population regarding where they will live and for how long. Furthermore, some military bases do not provide housing for family members. Therefore, anytime a military parent has full or joint custody of a child, these contingencies should be addressed in the decree.

Premarital Agreements

Contrary to what many people believe, premarital agreements are not new, though they have become more common in the last thirty years or so. They have existed since the turn of the century and came into regular use during the 1920s, when wealthy men wishing to marry younger "trophy wives" feared that their wives might claim their fortunes upon the man's death or if the couple divorced. For the next fifty or sixty years, courts frequently refused to enforce such agreements as being against public policy. Times have now changed, and most judges today are prone to abide by the agreements, if they meet certain requirements, which tend to vary by state. Approximately half of the states have now adopted some version of the Uniform Premarital Agreement Act, which sets out specific standards. Other states continue to either rely on their own common law or draft their own statutes governing these contracts.

Pros and Cons

Premarital agreements (also called prenuptial agreements, or "prenups" for short) are becoming more and more common as people marry later, as well as marry for a second or third time, and as women more often enter marriage with substantial property or lucrative careers of their own. Many people favor premarital agreements as a sensible and practical way to deal with a fifty-fifty risk factor as divorce rates hold steady around this mark. Some compare them to a property settlement that's created when a couple is still in love. Nevertheless, these contracts are controversial. Whereas some of the country's leading matrimonial lawyers will tell you no marriage should begin without one, others condemn them as nothing but trouble to be avoided at all costs. My own opinion lies in between these two extremes. I feel that these tools can be valid, but they need to be approached with caution, for several reasons.

First, many premarital agreements carry the subtle suggestion that the couple does not expect the marriage to last. Consequently, one or both partners may go through the marriage under the shadow of a little dark cloud indicating a lack of trust, an absence of faith in the union. One lawyer who practiced family law for many years told me he has never seen a marriage subject to a prenuptial agreement that did not eventually end in divorce. It seems, too, that the agreement is almost always pushed on one spouse by the other. As a client of mine once remarked, "I couldn't believe it when he brought me this thing to sign two days before our wedding. It made me feel less of a woman." Unless the marriage is truly a union of equals, with similar levels of sophistication, financial savvy, and confidence, a prenup will almost certainly smack of one spouse's "protecting" assets from the other, which logically implies an expectation of divorce.

Second, nearly any legitimate aim of a premarital agreement can be accomplished by more traditional legal tools, such as wills, deeds, trusts, and various types of contracts. These tools, in addition to being free of the stigma of mistrust, tend to be stabler and more efficient in accomplishing their goals. Some judges find premarital agreements distasteful and will look for any way (and there are many) to avoid enforcing their terms. Most of the same judges, however, are perfectly comfortable enforcing a will, trust, or deed. Another advantage to using more traditional devices to manage assets is that they may provide tax benefits not available under prenuptial agreements.

Third, couples often face unexpected events over the course of a marriage, and changed circumstances can bear on the meaning and effect of the prenup. For example, I once worked on a divorce case in which a wealthy oil baron had insisted his wife sign a premarital agreement. It essentially stated that each would own his or her currently held property and all proceeds from it as separate property, and any gifts from one to the other would become the recipient's separate property. During the ten years that the marriage endured, circumstances changed drastically as oil prices dropped, and the man at one point feared his company might go bankrupt. At that juncture, he transferred a large amount of money to his wife by giving her several certificates of deposit as gifts. When he decided to leave her, the instruments were still in her name. Under the terms of the premarital agreement, they had changed, or "transmuted," into her separate property, according to the couple's intentions at the time of the transfers—so she kept the funds in these accounts when they divorced. Certainly this was a result he did not foresee or intend at the time he persuaded her to sign the agreement.

All the same, I do believe that premarital agreements have their place. Between two mature and emotionally strong partners, a jointly created prenup can establish how each person's assets and debts will be managed, both during the marriage and in the event it ends through death or divorce. This can help clarify the couple's financial arrangements and avoid potential confusion or disagreement—not only between the couple but also on the part of others, such as adult children.

Enforceability

The main concern of courts in deciding whether a premarital agreement should be enforced when a couple divorces is whether it is fair in its terms and was openly entered into between people operating on equal footing. Courts commonly look at such criteria as whether each person had separate, independent legal advice; whether the person who prepared the agreement used "duress," or pressure, to compel the other person to sign; and, above all, whether there was full disclosure by each party of all assets and debts. A prenuptial agreement may be held invalid and unenforceable by the court if it appears to be the product of "undue influence"—that is, if either the husband or wife dominated the other, who was weaker, had greater needs, or was in distress at the time the agreement was signed. Agreements that are very one-sided are inherently suspect—for example, situations in which one person is wealthy and the other would receive nothing upon divorce. Those that are signed a very short time before the wedding are likewise disfavored. Vast differences in age, education, or experience between the couple will also raise questions. Ironically, people often sign premarital agreements—documents that may inherently suggest a lack of trust—without reading them closely or obtaining independent legal advice, because they love, trust, and believe in the person they are about to marry.

Since the character of property as separate versus marital property may change depending on how the parties treat it (as discussed later in the book), lax record keeping may also provide a basis for challenging a prenuptial agreement. Generally, property acquired during the marriage is presumed to be marital property. This means that the court will start with this assumption, and it will be up to the person stating that a particular item of property is separate to produce the evidence to prove that this is so. More than a premarital agreement stating general intentions may be necessary, especially if property has been mixed (such as money in a joint account), bought and sold, or otherwise transformed from its original character.

No one factor alone will usually be sufficient to convince a court that a premarital agreement should be disregarded, unless it is something extreme (such as lying about assets). Sometimes part of an agreement will be unenforceable, but the rest will be allowed to stand. For example, premarital agreements cannot legally set limits on the amount of child support to be paid in the event of divorce, because public policy requires current law and family circumstances to be considered in this regard. When confronted with such an item, a court might delete the section of the agreement purporting to set child support and enforce the rest of it, rather than toss out the whole thing. This is a common practice with any type of contract.

If you are leaving a marriage that was governed by such an agreement, discuss these matters thoroughly with your attorney, whether you favor the terms of the agreement or not. If there is the slightest hint that there was coercion when the agreement was signed or unfairness in its terms, many judges will simply invalidate the agreement and make their own decisions on property division.

Divorce in Later Years

According to the American Association of Retired Persons (AARP), the number of people over the age of fifty ending long-term marriages is increasing. In a 2004 *New York Times* article entitled "The Thirty-Seven-Year Itch," it was reported that both government statistics and anecdotal evidence indicate that increasing numbers of Americans aged sixty-five and older are divorcing since the turn of the twenty-first century.

Opinions as to why more older people are divorcing vary, but a widely held belief is that shifts in both life expectancy and social attitudes play a part. Compared with previous generations, people in unhappy marriages nowadays are less likely to stay out of a sense of duty or lack of options, especially if the discontent has been building for years. Moreover, healthy people of sixty-five or even seventy may realistically expect to have another ten or fifteen years in which to pursue their dreams and desires—enough time to bring a dream to fruition, but not enough to fritter away in indecision or dissatisfaction.

That said, even among the most vibrantly healthy segment, older people have special concerns that must be given attention when they end a marriage, such as Social Security benefits, long-term health care, housing options, and estate planning. Just as with divorcing people of any other age-group, seniors should reassess estate planning and health care documents such as life insurance policies, burial plans, trusts, living wills, durable powers of attorney, and any account or asset that names a beneficiary. Retirement plans and benefits must also be handled with care both in terms of dividing the marital property held in such assets and in the context of future planning. The retirement of a spouse who is paying alimony or support can result in changed circumstances that legally or practically reduce the amount he or she will be able to pay—a special concern when long-term spousal support is ordered. Generally speaking, people divorcing later in life should be represented by a lawyer who is familiar with the special needs of older clients, or who will associate with a specialist in elder law.

From an emotional standpoint, divorce is difficult at any time in life, but it creates unique burdens for senior citizens. Older women who divorce often encounter serious financial hardship, especially if they spent the bulk of their married lives as homemakers. In addition to the challenge of adjusting to a vastly different and unfamiliar way of living, older women seeking employment after divorce often struggle to secure an appropriate job. On a positive note, this appears to be changing, as more women over fifty-five now have, or have had, careers of their own and are therefore better prepared to be self-supporting. A recent AARP survey found that slightly more women than men in its responding group (encompassing divorcing people aged forty through eighty) initiated the divorce.

Older men who divorce grapple with a different set of problems. Those who were in traditional relationships in which the wife handled all the domestic chores must learn to perform these tasks for themselves. Also, some psychologists believe that men suffer more from lack of companionship and family contact after a divorce, especially in later years. Here again, though, the picture is improving. Men who divorce today appear to be faring better than their predecessors: 81 percent of those responding in the AARP study eventually remarried or entered into another form of exclusive, long-term relationship (as did about 75 percent of the women, with many of those who remained single reporting they did so by choice). In the study, people divorcing after age fifty generally reported being happier and emotionally healthier after a miserable marriage dissolved.

The support of new partners, friends, and family members, particularly the children and grandchildren, can be a lifeline for divorcing elders. Still, the intense stress of a divorce can cause physical, mental, and emotional problems for older people. Those with medical problems such as high blood pressure or heart conditions can be even more vulnerable to such difficulties. Fortunately, as demographics shift and the number of people of retirement age grows, more attention is being paid to the special issues that affect divorcing elders. Organizations such as AARP offer support and information on all aspects of life after fifty (see Appendix A). Local senior service providers also offer a variety of helpful services in most communities, ranging from transportation, meals, and assistance in applying for financial benefits, to social and recreational programs that can help combat isolation and loneliness.

5

Divorce and Property

UNDER TODAY'S PREVAILING system of no-fault divorce, the primary issues to be decided include the classification, valuation, and distribution of property; spousal and/or child support; and child custody and visitation. Property division is supposed to be one of the "simple" issues in divorce, since all states basically require an even split of property acquired by both parties as a result of efforts expended during the marriage. Yet, despite this tidy legal theory, property division is often among the most complicated and wrathfully contested aspects of a divorce.

Legal Property Systems Today

Two systems of property ownership are recognized for divorce purposes in the United States. Eight states follow the community property system, with its roots in Spanish law, while the others use a system known as common law, or marital property. Although the two systems have substantial differences, the distinctions have lessened in recent years. To simplify the discussion, I will use the term "marital property" to refer to property jointly owned by both spouses under either system. Bear in mind that such property is identified by different labels in different states. Likewise, "separate property" refers to property solely owned by either spouse, which does not need to be divided upon divorce, because ownership is already established.

While community property states start with the assumption that marital property (called "community property" in these states) will be divided fifty-fifty between the couple, in practice the division is seldom precisely equal. In common law states, courts are supposed to apply equitable distribution standards to divide property "equitably," or as "justice requires." These rules give judges more latitude, and property awards tend to vary greatly, although a fifty-fifty split is considered the norm. Notwithstanding the differences between the two legal schemes, the goal is essentially the same: fairly dividing property that the couple owns together. Debate arises first in trying to identify what property should be divided, and second in deciding just what "equal" or "equitable" means in a particular case.

Classifying, Valuing, and Dividing Assets

The simplest way for divorcing couples to approach property division is to begin by identifying property that is clearly owned by each person separately or that would logically go to that person, such as clothing. Next, figure out what is jointly owned, including intangibles, and see what you can and cannot agree to divide. Many couples are able to reach agreement fairly quickly. For others, negotiation through lawyers or with the assistance of a mediator can lead to a fair solution on the sticking points. Charts and checklists found on websites or in books such as Violet Woodhouse and Victoria Felton-Collins's *Divorce and Money* (see the "Resources and Suggested Readings" section) can aid in streamlining this process.

A fair division requires consideration of such factors as whether a large, indivisible asset should be awarded to both the husband and wife according to percentage of ownership, whether it should be sold and the money divided, or whether one party should get full ownership. In the latter circumstance, one asset may be traded for another (say, one spouse keeps the home while the other keeps a vacation cottage and boat), or the person receiving the property may be ordered to buy out the other party's interest over time.

Such decisions may have a significant impact on the value of the property.

When preparing to value, classify, and divide marital property, remember that while the law varies from state to state, courts generally are influenced by the following specific factors, among others:

- Each spouse's contribution to the marriage, including homemaking and child rearing
- The economic circumstances of each party
- How long the marriage lasted
- Whether either partner interrupted a career or education, and whether one contributed to the career or education of the other
- Whether it may be more desirable to allow one party to retain any asset as separate property (for example, in order to keep a business concern going rather than selling it off piecemeal)
- What each partner contributed to producing income or incurring debt

The idea is to start with the presumption of a fifty-fifty split and then apply these extenuations to see whether adjustment should be made. For example, a wife who takes the primary responsibility for managing the home and raising the children but also makes valuable contributions to a family business may be found to be entitled to more than 50 percent of the marital assets. Today, this type of award is generally preferred to alimony when sufficient assets are available. However, a substantial property settlement does not exclude the possibility of alimony.

It is important to realize that, unlike spousal or child support, which can be modified if the parties' circumstances change, a final property division decree is just that—final. Unless the case is appealed, or one spouse can prove that the other committed fraud, the order dividing property—whether by a negotiated property settlement or by decree of the court after litigation—is generally not open to challenge. So, tread carefully and with eyes wide open in reaching the final resolution of property issues that are important to you.

Income and Benefits

All income earned by either spouse during the marriage is generally classified as marital property. On this point, though, some states distinguish between two types of income earned during a marriage—passive income and earned income. Passive income is that which accumulates as a result of property owned before the marriage, such as interest, appreciation, and rent. Earned income is money garnered through a job or other activity that goes on during the marriage. Typically, passive income remains separate, while earned income becomes part of the marital property estate. As in most other areas of matrimonial property law, however, these classifications are subject to confusion and frequent change. For instance, if passive assets are reinvested or otherwise actively used, they are often deemed to be earned income.

Each spouse's income (whether wages, salary, royalties, lump-sum payments to an independent contractor, or other funds generated by a person's work) earned during the marriage is usually classified as marital property. Income earned after the divorce becomes final (or, in some states, after the couple separates) is separate property. Timing can affect the classification of income, such as unpaid bonuses earned before the couple splits, so be sure to consider this in dividing income-based assets.

Employee benefits may also form a significant part of the marital estate. Assets such as employee stock options are becoming an exceedingly valuable component of many employment compensation packages, and they must be analyzed and valued carefully in a divorce proceeding. The help of a divorce financial analyst, CPA, or other financial professional may be required when complex benefits must be valued and distributed.

The Family Home

The home a couple has shared is a special piece of property that must be handled carefully, for several reasons. First, the home often has deep emotional meaning. Children may benefit from staying in a place that is familiar and stable. The home is also the biggest asset many couples own, and one that is subject to fluctuating value. Some states, reacting to problems that arose with the advent of no-fault divorce, will not allow couples with minor children all the options that may otherwise be available in dealing with the family home. Be sure you're clear on what your state's law does and does not permit if you own a home and have children.

Whatever may eventually happen to a couple's home, an up-to-date appraisal of its current value must be obtained. A real estate agent will estimate the fair market value of a house for free. This is a good starting point and may be all you need in some circumstances. Then again, if you are going to be refinancing a mortgage or getting a new mortgage in one spouse's name, a professional appraisal by a certified appraiser may be required. This can cost several hundred dollars. Don't forget to assess this expense and related refinancing costs in figuring out your settlement. Remember too that maintaining a home can be a financial drain. Factor in the total cost of the home, including upkeep, association fees, utilities, mortgages, taxes, appliances, and likely repairs.

Many married couples hold real estate in what is called joint tenancy. This is essentially a form of ownership in which each person owns all of a piece of property jointly with another person. If one owner dies, the surviving joint tenant automatically assumes the decedent's ownership interest. This arrangement can pose a problem during a divorce—but a quick fix is at hand. It is generally simple to transfer joint tenancy into a form of ownership known as tenancy in common, in which people share ownership of a piece of property but without the right of survivorship. In some states, this transfer happens automatically when a couple divorces. Another form of ownership, tenancy by the entireties, is similar to joint tenancy but can't be turned into tenancy in common unless both people agree. If you own any real estate together and anticipate a dispute regarding how it will be handled, talk to your lawyer for guidance as soon as you have decided to divorce.

If the home is likely to be sold at any time, you'll definitely want to consider possible liability for capital gains tax. This type of tax must be paid on profit accrued on real estate. It is assessed at variable rates, depending on the tax bracket of the individual or couple, in addition to other factors. The law provides for exceptions that allow people to escape the assessment of capital gains tax, but this area of tax law is complex and has undergone a great deal of change in recent years—and more tinkering with current laws is likely. Anyone involved in a divorce who owns real estate as either separate or marital property—whether a family home, vacation property, rental or other income property, or business location—should seek competent advice from an attorney, a CPA, a divorce financial analyst, or another expert well versed in the current tax laws. This form of tax may come back to haunt you years down the road—for example, if you move and rent out a home that you receive in your divorce settlement and then later decide to sell it. Discuss your future plans with your advisers, and learn the tax consequences attached to any property you receive. If any real estate will be sold before, during, or soon after your divorce, make sure that all anticipated tax liabilities are addressed in the divorce decree. Responsibility for taxes may be assigned to one person or apportioned between each.

Also, invest some thought in how you would manage other unavoidable costs inherent in selling a house. Repairs or refurbishing may be necessary to get it ready for the market. Real estate agents generally charge a commission of about 6 percent of the selling price. You'll also be on the receiving end of closing costs, escrow fees, recording fees, and other incidental expenses that can add up to thousands of dollars. Some locales require inspections and services such as termite treatment, which can also be expensive. You should have a clear overview of the total expense you will likely incur before you sign off on any final settlement agreement.

Pets

The law generally views pets as personal property to be treated like any other possessions when a couple divorces. In reality, though, many people consider their animal companions to be members of the family. The solace provided by a pet can be especially comforting when someone is enduring unsettling circumstances. Physiological studies have shown that petting a dog or cat can lower blood pressure and relieve stress. Pets also provide companionship to people who find solitude lonely after ending a relationship. And, quite simply, most of us love our pets and form strong emotional bonds with them—which makes the decision of what to do with the animals when a marriage ends all the more confounding.

If a pet was owned by one spouse before the marriage, it is usually his or her separate property, while an animal acquired by both is generally marital property that will have to be awarded to one spouse or the other. Partners who reach their own terms on what will happen to their pets should add the appropriate provision to the property settlement agreement filed with the court. Most often, one person simply takes a pet, or the pets are divided. However, some couples opt for shared custody or visitation, similar to parenting arrangements.

Whether a particular court will enforce pet-sharing agreements—or order visitation or shared custody when a couple can't agree—depends entirely on the court. Judges called upon to made a decision in "pet custody" cases may consider the best interests of either the animal, the people, or some combination of both in deciding what to do—and while some will order a sharing arrangement, most tend to shy away from such provisions, because they are not contemplated by the governing law. Therefore, as with any other disputed issue, it is best if people can work out their own arrangement regarding the family creatures.

Business and Career-Related Assets

As life in general has become more complex, so has our property. Future earning capacity, business holdings, or other career-related assets may represent some of the most valuable property a couple owns. These assets may include pension and retirement benefits, professional licenses, employee stock options, insurance, business goodwill, and miscellaneous discounts and perks.

Assess the value of these items and any other intangible property you own. From your perspective, some of these may not initially seem to be worth much, but the marketplace price may be more favorable than you think. For example, if you live in a rent-controlled apartment or co-op, or your apartment has an option to convert to condominium or co-op space, this may constitute a valuable asset. Even less obvious, if one spouse worked while the other acquired a professional degree, the latter's future earning capacity may be considered an asset that should be included in the pool of marital property to be divided, depending on the state. In some states, a spouse who pays for the educational expenses of the other may be entitled to reimbursement if the couple divorces before both have had time to enjoy the benefits gained by the degree earned.

Also, look into the potential value of such possessions as artwork, collections, and hobby equipment. That heap of marbles, baseball cards, old toys, or similar items collecting dust in the attic may be worth much more than you might imagine. A couple who spent years collecting the work of an unknown artist who eventually becomes highly successful could be sitting on a gold mine.

Intellectual property rights—copyrights, trademarks, patents, and similar intangible assets—may also be, or become, very valuable. Something a person creates or invents during the marriage may bring in royalties, licensing fees, or other income for years afterward. If you or your spouse hold such assets, discuss the details with your attorney (who may need to consult with a lawyer specializing in intellectual property), and see that they are cited in the final decree.

The Family-Owned Business. One of the most formidable property division problems to be tackled by the couple, attorneys, and financial advisers in a divorce is that of the family-owned business. Valuing and dividing such companies accurately and fairly can be a grueling undertaking, for several reasons. In addition to the difficulty of placing a value on a family business, its classification as marital or separate property may be equally vexing. The answers to the following questions can be instructive in determining whether a business enterprise or professional practice should be classified as marital property, in whole or in part:

- Was it established before the marriage or after the marriage?
- Did it grow substantially during the marriage?
- If so, was such growth due to any support of a spouse not working full-time in the business?
- Was the separate property of either spouse invested in the business?
- Was it a joint enterprise run by both partners?

If any part of the business is to be designated marital property, a value must be placed on it. As a rule, calculating the monetary worth of the hard assets such as buildings, inventory, and supplies will not be particularly troublesome, although there are exceptions to the rule, such as when a retail business carries a high level of inventory that turns over slowly. It's when you must move beyond these calculations that the waters become muddier. The most valuable component of many businesses is their goodwill, which refers to the value of the business above and beyond the worth of the tangible assets. For example, a store that has just opened its doors is far less valuable than an identical store that has been in business for twenty years, because the new store has not built up a customer base or a reputation for quality or demonstrated the staying power of the older store.

These determinations are always complicated, and the outcome depends on many variables, including the unique nature of the business. A medical practice, for example, may be severely discounted in the marketplace. Because its worth is so closely tied to the individual doctor, it would have few assets beyond its equipment and supplies if the doctor left the practice and sold the business. This is especially true for a highly specialized professional. It is often impossible to determine the actual, "real" value of an ongoing business until a sales contract has been negotiated between a willing buyer and a willing seller. Even then, there is no guarantee that the agreed price reflects the true market value of the entity.

Labor is also a valuable commodity. One partner in a marriage is often primarily responsible for running a family business, ranch, or farm. Many times, though, the other partner contributes a great deal to the growth and value of the enterprise, either by working for it directly with or without regular compensation, or by rendering work support, such as performing random errands, providing seasonal assistance, and filling in for absent workers. When personal and professional lives are so closely intertwined, it may be problematic to place a dollar value on this type of work. However, it is necessary to evaluate the contribution of a spouse who works, whether without compensation or as an employee, in terms of the person's total contribution to building a successful enterprise. If you did any work for a family-owned business, retrieve any records, schedules, or diaries that you have kept of your daily activities. If you didn't keep such documents, write out in as much detail as possible a synopsis of the work you did for the business, as well as any work to help improve property, such as maintenance or repairs. This information has practical application whether the business is jointly owned or is the separate property of one.

Different businesses require different approaches in valuation. When a business has limited assets but constant cash flow, as is typical of a professional practice, capitalized earnings is the favored method to use. On the other hand, when a business such as a manufacturing or retail enterprise has a large amount of capital tied up in assets but a more limited cash flow, the focus generally should be on the market value of the assets. Other types of businesses have a balance between assets and cash flow, and for these, calculation of value should be by an excess earnings method. IRS ruling 59/60 deals with methods of valuing closely held corporations such as a professional practice.

Confused? So are most people. This is why you shouldn't proceed without consulting professionals thoroughly versed in business valuation anytime this will be an issue in a divorce. A family-owned business will often need to be assessed by a certified business appraiser. See Appendix A for sources of referrals to these professionals through organizations such as the American Society of Appraisers. Be certain you understand the fee that will be charged and exactly what you will get in return for that payment. Taking this action does not mean that you should blindly hand over all your books and records to the appraiser and expect this person to figure it out, leaving you out of the loop. Qualified professionals should be able to explain their recommendations and assessments in terms you can understand. Likewise, they should be willing to delineate the alternatives available, explain why certain decisions are recommended, lay out the risks involved, and answer your questions fully. If you are uncertain about the validity of the appraisal, get another opinion.

Pension and Retirement Benefits. Two types of pensions or retirement plans are recognized in the law: vested and nonvested. A vested pension is one that is guaranteed to be paid, whether an employee remains with a company for a set period, retires, or leaves before retirement age. For example, if a person with a vested pension plan has worked for a company for ten years and then leaves, whatever is in the plan account will be paid out at that time. A nonvested pension, on the other hand, is not guaranteed; it will be forfeited if the employee does not meet certain requirements, such as staying with the company for a set number of years. Most states today recognize both types of pensions as marital property if the pension was acquired through the efforts of either person during the marriage as part of his or her salary or compensation for work.

A federal law passed in 1984, the Retirement Equity Act, deals specifically with distribution of private pension benefits upon divorce. Under this act, private pension plans such as those provided by individual companies or unions must be handled in a specified way in a divorce. A qualified domestic relations order (often called a QDRO, pronounced "quadro") must be included as part of a divorce decree if such assets are to be divided. A QDRO tells the person in charge of distributing the funds that a specific proportion of the benefits must be distributed to an "alternate payee," the ex-spouse. This protects against plan administrators who, in the past, sometimes refused or were reluctant to pay benefits under the plan to anyone other than the individual named in the plan documents. When a QDRO is entered, the plan administrator can take up to eighteen months to approve the order. During this time, the court may order that the spousal shares be kept separate so that the pension holder can't withdraw any money that would dip into the other person's allotment. The pension holder can also be ordered not to borrow against the ex-spouse's share, or the court may order that the ex-spouse be designated to remain listed as the surviving spouse. The order may also specify the age at which each spouse can withdraw from the fund.

Retirement benefits do not necessarily have to be divided between the spouses. In many marriages, the couple will decide to allow the person who earned the benefits to keep them in exchange for granting the other full ownership of equivalent assets. For example, one person keeps the pension fund, and the other keeps the house. In marriages in which both have jobs that provide retirement plans, couples typically specify that each will keep his or her own benefits. A QDRO is not required if the plan will not be divided. In any event, an accurate value should be placed on the retirement benefits to ensure that whatever agreement is reached is equitable.

Different types of retirement plans must be treated in different ways to satisfy the legal requirements that pertain. This aspect of the law can become complex, and you may need the assistance of a financial professional who specializes in pension and retirement planning. For example, QDROs can be used only to divide retirement plans subject to the Employee Retirement Income Security Act (ERISA). This act covers most plans but does not include government plans such as the U.S. Civil Service Retirement System, public employee pensions of state employees, or military pensions. Each of these requires a different type of order to divide the benefits. Fortunately, the procedure is similar for each form of pension. The appropriate order will assign a portion of the benefit earned by one spouse to the ex-spouse, the "alternate payee." Designing a QDRO or other appropriate order to divide retirement benefits is fairly simple for a qualified attorney who knows the ins and outs of the specific type of plan.

Individual retirement accounts (IRAs) also require special attention. A QDRO is not necessary to divide an IRA, but the tax consequences may be a hard pill to swallow. Again, your attorney should be sufficiently experienced in such matters or able to obtain expert assistance from a tax attorney, actuary, divorce financial analyst, or CPA. A further consideration is that a retirement plan owned by an employer or other entity may vanish if the company goes out of business, merges with another, or is otherwise changed over the years.

Anytime pensions or other retirement benefits are at issue, both spouses should become informed about the pros and cons of the "opt out" feature. With these benefit plans, a worker can either receive a reduced pension to provide a survivor's benefit for the spouse or elect to take full monthly checks after retirement during the worker's remaining lifetime. Under the Retirement Equity Act of 1984, a worker may not opt out of survivor's benefits without the knowledge and agreement of the spouse. Thus, a worker must obtain the written consent of the spouse—or ex-spouse, if a pension was split at divorce—before survivor's benefits may be effectively waived.

The question of how a pension should be divided at divorce may be sticky. Several approaches are possible. One is for the spouse who earned the pension to provide the other with a lump sum or an asset of equivalent value to buy out the value of the pension at the time of divorce. Sometimes pension payments are made to the ex-spouse before the one who earned them retires, according to the terms of a QDRO. Another alternative is to delay the division until the time the pension benefits are paid out, generally at retirement; then the pension will be divided and payments made to each spouse according to the terms of the divorce decree. Which method is better depends on the individual circumstances, with the age of the parties being a major factor. Younger couples often favor the buyout or present payment method, whereas those closer to retirement age may prefer the second method. Anyone choosing the buyout method should make certain that the future value of the pension benefits is accurately calculated.

Get qualified advice on anything you don't completely understand. Employers, plan administrators, trustees, or actuaries can furnish information. Your attorney will probably know professionals who can help and may even decide to hire them as experts in the negotiation process or at trial. As always, it is best if the spouses can agree on one expert. This will both save money and give that person more credibility in the eyes of the court.

Military Pensions. In 1981, a landmark U.S. Supreme Court decision called *McCarty v. McCarty* ruled that military pensions are not to be treated as marital or community property. This state of affairs gave rise to the organization of a nationwide lobby for federal legislation to guarantee divorced wives of current or former servicemen an equitable share in the assets accrued during a marriage under a military pension. A group called Ex-Partners of Servicemen for Equality (EXPOSE) (see Appendix A) was organized and made impressive efforts in advancing their cause, including picketing military facilities and garnering press attention to stories of wives who followed career military husbands around the world for twenty or thirty years only to be denied a share of the husband's military pension later. The efforts of EXPOSE and other activists who were outraged by the *McCarty* decision helped persuade Congress to pass the Uniformed Services Former Spouse Protection Act in 1982. This federal law overturned the *McCarty* decision and explicitly permitted state courts to treat military retirement pay as community or marital property if the court had jurisdiction over the service member. The law does not guarantee military spouses a definite share of these benefits, but leaves it up to the court of each state to award a maximum of 50 percent of the disposable retirement pay and related benefits such as medical care and commissary privileges under some circumstances. Thus, the exact manner in which this federal law is applied may be subject to the discretion of individual courts and the laws of the various states.

Other Benefits. Similar acts help protect spouses of other federal employees, such as foreign service officers, under the Foreign Service Act of 1980, and civil service workers, under the Civil Service Reform Act. Current Social Security law allows a divorced spouse to receive Social Security benefits drawn from the earnings of a working spouse if the marriage lasted more than ten years. This can be adjusted according to individual circumstances when both spouses have worked during the marriage. Your local Social Security office can help you compute the benefits to which you and your spouse are currently entitled. It also can furnish you with a form to complete that will help you ascertain your estimated future benefits.

Investments. If you have investments such as stocks and bonds, it's to your advantage to review your portfolio before you get divorced. What is a wise investment for a married person may change with the financial transformations of a divorce. This is an opportune time to review all your investments and get rid of those that aren't performing well or don't suit your future needs. Arm yourself with professional advice from your broker, attorney, or accountant regarding your portfolio holdings as well as the tax consequences of prospective decisions and alternatives.

If your spouse handled jointly owned investments, you will be at a disadvantage unless you gain a complete understanding of the nature of each investment and its risks, obligations, tax consequences, dividend policy, transaction fees, and other implications of ownership. In addition to stocks, the same type of analysis should be done for real estate investments, cash value insurance policies, limited partnerships, commodities, and any other valuable property that you own. All may have hidden pitfalls and require a thorough understanding of their true nature and value.

Other Property Concerns

Tax treatment must also be taken into account for other types of property or support, not just a home or business. Property division awards and child support are nontaxable, while alimony is defined as income and is taxed. For this reason, the label placed on a monetary property award can be crucial. It should be easy to see why the services of a competent accountant (and sometimes other financial advisers) are indispensable in any case in which substantial assets are part of the package. "It's far better for people to meet with an accountant before they sign the final agreement," says CPA Sandra Ricci. "People can cut their taxes so much by planning the timing of their divorce and the language of the decree."

Some accountants specialize in financial consulting on matrimonial cases. Any accountant or other financial adviser hired to work on a divorce should be familiar with the special demands of this type of case. Some, such as divorce financial analysts, specialize in division of assets and related issues in divorce actions. Also, a professional hired as an expert in a divorce case should be acquainted with the nuances of courtroom procedure if litigation is likely. An example is the need to protect one's credibility as a witness by rendering a neutral assessment of the facts provided by the client's lawyer, who is an advocate for the client. Here also, the ideal is often for both people to agree to use the same expert.

Remember, the settlement agreement is like a snapshot. It can resolve matters only as they exist at the moment the agreement is signed and filed. It is not up to the court to plan your future for you, and it is a heavy burden to undo provisions in the decree that later prove unwise. Sit down with your attorney, tax accountant, and other advisers, crunch the numbers, and get a thorough, detailed explanation that you fully understand before you make any final decisions. Don't be afraid to ask plenty of questions. I believe that the only stupid question is the one that doesn't get asked. This applies in spades when future consequences are at stake that could have serious ramifications on your financial well-being for years to come. Surprises are not good in this context. No one wants the financial detritus of an ill-conceived property settlement resurfacing months or years later in the form of an unexpected tax penalty, damaged credit rating, or depleted retirement fund.

Taxation Issues. Nearly every divorce requires mulling over some fine points of taxation. The IRS maintains a library of excellent, free publications that can help divorcing couples get an overview of the tax matters they will need to address. IRS Publication 504 is a well-presented reference with general tax information related to divorce or separation, including facts on alimony, filing status, exemptions, QDROs, retirement, legal fees, property settlement, and other topics. Publication 503 surveys child and dependent care exemptions. Information on contacting the IRS is provided in Appendix A.

Whenever significant taxable assets are divided in a divorce, both present and future tax consequences must be nailed down. Responsibility for paying all applicable taxes should be assigned to one party or the other, *before* the final order is signed, and *before* any property is transferred. In addition to real estate, taxable assets may include financial holdings, settlements or verdicts in legal claims, stocks, trust assets, and many other types of property. Some family attorneys are trained in such matters and can handle these issues on their own, but in other cases, a qualified tax accountant, divorce financial analyst, or other professional with expertise in tax issues should be consulted.

Divorce financial analysts can help forecast the short- and long-term effects of a proposed settlement, as well as provide information on tax consequences, division of pension plans, stock option elections, and related subjects. The Institute for Divorce Financial Analysts certifies individuals in this field who meet certain qualifications. Some are also trained as mediators or work with collaborative law teams, but they do not replace attorneys or give legal advice.

Tracing Assets for Classification as Separate or Marital Property

Most couples in a marriage combine at least part of their assets into a joint pool. Frequently, this involves the pooling of clearly marital assets, such as depositing two paychecks into the same joint account for the use of both parties. However, couples often add separate property (such as funds received by one person as a gift or an inheritance after marriage, or money saved before the marriage) to marital property for a major purchase, such as a home. This is called "commingling." This action makes sense during a marriage, but it can cause severe headaches if the marriage ends and the couple must try to sort out separate property that has been commingled with marital property.

Tracing consists of following the property that is claimed as separate back to the original source of ownership. Accomplishing this mission is uneventful with some types of property. For example, an antique table that a grandmother gave to one person may become a part of the total furnishings of the home, but because the table stays as it is—one piece of property—separating it from the rest of the furnishings is easy.

Such property as money, stocks, or even land can be harder to isolate, especially if it has been sold and the proceeds have been reinvested. In essence, as long as the property can be traced back to its origin without gaps in time, its classification will be fairly obvious. Otherwise—if one link in this chain is missing—the property will often be deemed too commingled to divide and will be treated as marital property. Take an example in which inherited stocks were sold, new stocks were purchased using additional money from one person's salary and later were sold as well, and then the proceeds were combined with marital income to buy a home. Here, the original investment has "transmuted" from separate property into marital property by the way the owner treated it.

The burden of proof in tracing separate property is on the spouse who is claiming that a portion of certain property is separate. States have different standards for tracing such property, but the key is always careful documentation. If the person can produce sound records showing what happened to the property at every step of the way, this is the best evidence available. States vary in how specific the evidence must be.

Proving separate property may be a vexing task, as when money has been invested and reinvested without a clear paper trail to record every movement, but it can be done. The assistance of experts, such as divorce financial analysts or someone in the relevant field of business, can be invaluable. Courts need concrete details, and experts can often assist in the preparation of flowcharts and other visual exhibits to show how the property moved around and changed during the marriage. Even if the case does not go to court, these materials can be persuasive in demonstrating proof and leveraging a fair settlement. A good settlement is always preferable because it is a sure thing, while any courtroom procedure carries some risk, not to mention a sharp increase in expense.

Hidden Assets. Old movies often depict a detective crouched in the bushes outside the bedroom window of an adulterous spouse, waiting to snap the photograph that will provide proof of adultery in a divorce case. While such antics still go on, most of the detective work in today's divorces is financial.

Attempts by one spouse to hide assets from the other occur with appalling frequency in divorce actions. The types of assets typically involved include boats, motorcycles, and similar vehicles; real estate; stocks and bonds; and bank accounts. Phony debts may also be claimed. The books, records, and accounts of a business may be manipulated to obscure assets and make a successful business appear less lucrative by padding of expenses, profit-sharing schemes, payments in cash, phony or temporary contracts with outsiders, and misuse of retirement plans. Sophisticated swindlers have even been known to hide the existence of entire businesses.

The legal discovery process, which is a part of any litigated case, is designed to ferret out such hidden assets. Remember: if anyone (including Internet websites promising to protect your interests) should advise you to hide or obscure the true value of assets, run. A party in a divorce action who is caught in such dishonesty may be subject to monetary sanctions levied by the court, a less favorable property division, and civil or criminal charges of perjury or fraud.

Some of the more common methods used in attempting to conceal assets are colluding with an employer; manipulating a business by paying salaries to phantom employees or paying contractors for services never rendered; asking a parent, friend, or paramour to hold money; depositing funds in accounts held in a child's name; cash skimming; delaying transactions; issuing payments on phony debts; negotiating business with traveler's checks; and concocting nonexistent securities or bonds. If you suspect your spouse of hiding assets, you will need to take action to thwart the maneuver. It may be necessary to hire an investigator or other professional such as a forensic accountant. There are as many devious methods of hiding assets as there are dishonest people.

Practical Matters

It is most beneficial to resolve and finalize any significant changes in your financial arrangements as soon as feasible after you and your spouse reach a property settlement agreement, before the final decree is entered. This way, you not only help streamline the process but also can preempt being handed an endless list of chores and details at the last minute—or worse, a decree that mandates a lot of behavior after the divorce that your ex may not be inclined to follow.

As soon as a couple has decided to divorce and the initial allocations are made pertaining to division of some property, the sequence of establishing separate ownership of that property or debt should begin. Joint accounts should be closed and assets put in individual names. This is the time to initiate contact with creditors to refinance loans, mortgages, and other debts in the name of one partner, if possible. Any related transactions that cannot be completed before the divorce is finalized should be put into a written agreement signed by both spouses and filed with the court, or stated clearly in the settlement agreement. For example, if the divorce will occur at a time when income taxes cannot yet be calculated, consultation with a tax professional can help you decide how you will file and how any refund or bill will be divided.

Money is always a loaded topic, even in a strong marriage. For most of us, money is an emotional issue, one that can be volatile during divorce. People are sometimes tempted to exploit the emotional side of financial transactions to get revenge on a spouse or force reconciliation. Others want to extricate themselves from attending to what was a painful issue in the marriage as quickly as possible, without regard for the future. These responses are as unwise as they are understandable. Having to make a series of logical, detailed decisions can compound the frustration if your spouse was the one who chose to end the marriage. Yet, even if you are hoping for reconciliation, the fact remains that, right now, your financial interests may be at risk. You owe it to yourself to be an active participant in the divorce process, even if you don't want it to happen.

Make it an ironclad rule that any agreement you reach with your spouse is put in writing—and that the attorneys are copied on all such documents. This practice may seem unnecessarily dismal, especially if the parting is amicable, but it's a good idea even if you trust your spouse completely. It avoids misunderstanding and confusion that can turn a friendly relationship unpleasant.

If you own a joint safe deposit box, inventory its contents and remove any items that are clearly yours as separate property, such as inherited jewelry. A bank officer can review and sign an inventory of a safe deposit box. The same type of inventory should be taken of all your valuable belongings. This does not mean that you have to write out a description of every piece of Tupperware in the house, but articles such as coin collections, marbles, baseball cards, hobby equipment, and similar items may be more valuable than you assume. It is smart to get such things appraised also. Remember too that children's property is their own. It stays with them wherever they go and is not divided in the settlement.

Further, you may have to anticipate what would happen to property if either spouse were to die before the divorce is final. Review all property held in joint tenancy and life insurance policies. Your attorneys should be able to advise you or put you in touch with an appropriate expert to help you cover your bases.

If you have a large amount of money in a joint bank account, an interim agreement to be filed with the court should spell out the terms regarding who has access to the account and how much of it. If you need funds immediately, you will usually be entitled to withdraw up to half of the balance in any jointly held account. In reality, however, whoever gets there first can legally withdraw the entire amount. Although the person may be ordered to reimburse the spouse's share later, by that time the money could be long gone. Clarifying these points not only avoids this type of risk but also prevents argument and hostility.

Most experts advise getting property settlements in the form of cash or specific property rather than any future promise—with some exceptions, such as when the specter of bankruptcy is looming over either partner or both. If a payment or property transfer owed to you must be delayed, you are entitled to be compensated for having to wait, in the form of interest or another type of increase in the payment.

Financial Planners

Financial planners are a specialized type of expert who can help people contemplating divorce identify potential risks in a settlement, understand tax consequences, get an accurate picture of assets and liabilities, plan for future needs, and determine what and how much support may be necessary. Some people who simply sell investments refer to themselves as financial planners, but a true financial planner is an analyst who is familiar with all types of assets and liabilities. The Financial Planning Association can provide a list of members who have met rigorous requirements. As previously noted, a subspecialty among financial planners has developed to address the financial issues involved in a divorce. The Institute for Divorce Financial Analysts maintains a list of these specialists who have met the requirements for certification. Contact information for these organizations is provided in Appendix A. Take care to hire the right kind of expert who is qualified to handle your needs.

Certified Public Accountants

As with lawyers, various types of CPAs specialize in different facets of the accounting field. If you need a tax specialist, you may want to verify that the person you are contemplating hiring is an enrolled agent who is qualified to practice before the IRS. Call the National Association of Enrolled Agents at (800) 424-4339 for more information. Some professional fees are deductible on your tax returns, such as attorneys' fees to collect or secure alimony. Any fees for advice on tax consequences of your divorce from an attorney, accountant, broker, financial planner, or other professional may also be deductible if they are itemized and meet other requirements. Check with your professional advisers about this provision.

If you do not have copies of old tax returns, you can obtain them by calling the IRS at (800) 829-1040. Ask for Form 4506. Be sure to give your current address if you have moved; otherwise, the form will be sent to the address on the latest return. The IRS also maintains an excellent website providing forms and information in an easy-to-understand format (see Appendix A).

The Recalcitrant Spouse

It is human nature for people entwined in a divorce to want to get it over with quickly. In conformity with this goal, many final decrees contain orders to accomplish unfinished business, such as selling a home, refinancing a debt, or transferring title to property. It is generally better to complete as many of these transactions as you can before the decree is signed, but both practical concerns and personal desires to get on with a new life can make a certain amount of unfinished business unavoidable.

Leaving a few chores until after the final decree is filed is not an impediment if both parties are responsible, satisfied with the agreement, and eager to get things squared away. Often, though, the path to the final exit is not so smooth, and one party will drag things out for any number of reasons—a desire to cause trouble for the other, hope of reconciliation, lack of concern, or simple laziness.

That said, family attorney David B. Riggert cautions against the common inclination to agree to an unwise or unfinished property settlement in order to expedite the divorce. "Clients often want the attorney to solve their problem immediately; they just want the divorce over and done with," he observes. "Husbands, especially, often don't care what the wife gets in the property settlement—they just want out. This is understandable, because people in the midst of a divorce are under tremendous stress. But later, when they're feeling better emotionally, they will be more concerned about financial matters. I have to remind them that if I do as they ask, two years from now, when the smoke clears, they may see things differently—and, all too often, blame the lawyer. It's my job to do my best to satisfy their current needs as well as their future needs."

For matters that may take time, such as the sale of a business, various methods can be used to ensure accountability, including mandatory reports to the court on the efforts the person is making to accomplish the task. If the problem boils down to simple laziness, recalcitrance, or a desire to be irritating, the solution may be a gentle reminder, in writing, that if one person has to go to court to enforce the agreement, the costs and attorneys fees can be charged against the other.

Throughout this book, I have underscored the importance of setting accurate values on property so that any division is fair to both parties. It's also true that people sometimes don't want to go through extensive analysis—especially when both have other priorities, can agree on property division, and are committed to moving on. This is an individual choice, and the emotional equation, plus the normal desire to bring a quick and clean resolution to a divorce, deserve as much recognition as the financial aspects. At a minimum, do enough analysis to know the effect of your choices, particularly with regard to matters that could have a negative impact after the divorce, such as the tax consequences of relinquishing, taking, or selling the home. Certainly, nonfinancial considerations such as a strong sentimental attachment to a piece of property are equally germane and should be given due thought.

In short, be confident that you understand what you have accepted and what you have relinquished. A final property settlement executed with a firm understanding by both parties of what they actually received helps both of you turn your focus on the future. The bottom line in reaching a fair property settlement, as in any other aspect of your divorce, is to figure out not only what you're legally entitled to receive but also what is truly important to you. Finding a solution with which everyone can live with is always a higher priority than insisting that all of your legal rights be satisfied regardless of the human consequences. While you must guard against selling yourself short under the influence of guilt, depression, or bullying tactics, it's equally advantageous to distinguish what is truly important to you, and to your children, from what is not worth a battle. On this subject, a friend of mine once stated, "All I wanted when I got divorced was my dog and my truck." As a childless, employed young woman who had shared an apartment with her husband, she recognized that this was all she really needed. She got what was important to her, and she was content.

Insurance

American insurance laws and the types of plans available are in constant flux, so it is difficult to characterize how these assets should be treated upon divorce. What is clear is that insurance rights are valuable and must be handled carefully when a marriage ends. Start with the agents or administrators who currently manage your insurance needs, and then bring in other financial advisers if necessary.

If you are receiving alimony or child support, be sure that your settlement or decree requires your spouse to keep you as the beneficiary on a life insurance policy sufficient to cover your needs if anything should happen to him or her. The person paying support can deduct insurance payments from taxes under certain circumstances. Your broker or agent should be able to advise on how this may be structured. Disability insurance is a must and shouldn't be overlooked. In reviewing your insurance, check all of your policies. Divorce may affect auto, property, business, and other domains in addition to life insurance.

Health Insurance

Under a federal law known as COBRA (Consolidated Omnibus Budget Reconciliation Act), a divorced person whose former spouse is employed by a company with twenty or more people and is a medical plan participant must be allowed to remain on the spouse's insurance plan for up to thirty-six months after the divorce. You are required to pay for your own coverage according to the terms of the plan. Contact the personnel department or plan administrator for specific information. Your lawyer should also advise you about this type of coverage. You can contact your local office of the U.S. Department of Labor for a booklet entitled *Continued Health Care Coverage*, which outlines the specifics of this law.

Some states also have laws providing for conversion of insurance policies to cover the former spouse and any children upon divorce. While conversion policies can satisfy certain needs, they may offer less coverage and lower benefits, as well as higher costs, than the original policy. People who are not covered by either COBRA or a conversion policy also may be able to keep a spouse's employment-related coverage for a limited period, depending on both the property settlement and the employer's plan. Individuals, especially parents, who are covered under a spouse's insurance policy should get qualified guidance regarding their options.

On a more positive note, additional insurance alternatives are now becoming popular. Good coverage frequently can be obtained through sources other than an employer. Professional organizations, private clubs, health maintenance organizations, and other groups may sponsor group insurance plans. The type and cost of coverage vary widely, so any person shopping for insurance is wise to look into all the offerings that could fit the bill.

If you feel that you could benefit from mental health counseling or therapy to help you cope during this stage, check to see if your medical insurance will pay for some or all of the cost. If you're not covered, call your local mental health association or family services agency. Your state or county may provide free mental health assistance through contracts with local clinics, centers, or providers. Many types of outreach exist; make sure you get the type of help that is right for you. The majority of people going through a divorce do not need long-term psychoanalysis but only short-term counseling, stress management therapy, or a support group. Most agencies that extend mental health services will screen clients to determine the appropriate treatment program. If you are unsure what type of assistance would be best for you, explore the available options and talk to a qualified professional for guidance.

Debt and Credit Issues

Divorce is not only hard on the emotions but also a pain in the pocket. Discussions of property divisions and settlements are often somewhat deceptive when applied to the reality of the average American. The fact is that the majority of divorcing couples do not have substantial assets to be divided; instead, the question at hand is who will be responsible for paying off the debts. This is a major component of the property settlement in most divorces.

Debts are classified in the same way as property: separate or community/marital. Any debt that a couple incurs during the marriage is presumed to be a marital debt, with both people responsible for payment. Debts that existed prior to the marriage are usually separate. In general, debts that are incurred after a couple separates but before the final divorce decree is entered are declared separate debts, except for items that are understood to be necessities, such as clothing, food, shelter, and maintenance of children. This formula may vary according to the state and any agreements that have been made with creditors.

Keep in mind that a property settlement agreement covers only the relationship between the spouses. It is not binding on creditors. Thus, if a couple buys a car in both their names, and the lender that finances the loan relies on the income and credit history of both people, the fact that the divorce decree says the husband will get the car and be totally responsible for payment of the loan does not mean the creditor can collect only from the husband. If he refuses to pay, goes bankrupt, or disappears, the lender can legally look to the wife for payment, no matter what the divorce decree says.

Therefore, it is best to try to negotiate new, separate loan contracts with creditors before signing the final papers. If this is not possible, the person no longer responsible for making payments on a debt under the terms of the decree should take other steps. One possibility is to keep a security interest in the property until it is paid off, as many businesses do when selling merchandise on credit. For instance, if there is still quite a bit of money owed on a car that is going to the wife, and she is assuming the debt, the husband may want to keep his name on the title and indicate in the decree that he will retain an interest in the car until it is paid in full. Other provisions to ensure compliance with the decree can also be added to its terms, such as an agreement to indemnify one party for any money he or she has to pay a creditor if the other fails to follow the terms of the agreement. Still, it's preferable to get all obligations separated before the decree is final, in case the other spouse vanishes or goes broke.

One strategy for coping with debt is to sell jointly owned property before the divorce to pay off, or at least reduce, the debt load. Ideally, the time to clarify exactly how your debts will be paid and how your credit options will be handled is before you and your spouse separate, or immediately afterward. Home equity lines of credit, margin accounts from stockbrokers, charge accounts, and other such instruments may be closed, frozen, or adjusted so that both spouses must sign for any advances or withdrawals.

Cash flow statements can be instrumental in assessing where your money goes on a day-to-day basis. This information will suggest likely areas where you can cut costs and how much you will need in the future. Cash flow charts, personal financial statements, and other financial work sheets for people going through a divorce are available from various sources, such as banks, financial planners, and books or websites on money management. One good book full of such work sheets is *Divorce and Money*, by Violet Woodhouse and Victoria Felton-Collins (see the "Resources and Suggested Readings" list at the back of this book). Financial advisers, classes, credit counselors, and other sources of assistance are also available in most areas.

It's not uncommon for people to experience a severe letdown when they see their financial lives spread before them on paper. If you find yourself in this position, take comfort in the knowledge that many people today do live beyond their means and still maintain a fairly stable financial life. Focus on your monthly obligations, not the total amount you owe, and try to come up with a realistic analysis of what you are going to need to make ends meet.

Credit

Under a federal law called the Equal Credit Opportunity Act, every individual has the right to apply and be fairly considered for credit without discrimination on the basis of sex or marital status. Even so, it is always best to negotiate new credit terms in a separate agreement with each of your creditors following a divorce. Default by your ex-spouse on a marital debt that he or she was supposed to pay can leave a black mark on your credit record as well.

If your creditors won't agree to refinance a debt in your name alone, don't give up. Creditors who were unwilling to change an account to the name of one person at the time of divorce may be willing to do so later, after each person has had an opportunity to establish an independent track record. If you can't negotiate a change now, check again in a year or so. Also, strive to keep all joint debts current during the divorce proceedings, even if one party has to pay more than his or her fair share—compensating adjustments for this gesture can be included in the final settlement. If any payments are late, creditors are less likely to let go of joint liability and reestablish the account in one name. As soon as any accounts that remain in both names are paid off, they should be closed.

What if you never had credit in your own name or had credit problems during your marriage? Your recourse is to pursue a good credit rating as soon as possible in your name alone. Start by setting up bank accounts and applying for credit cards that are easy to obtain, such as gasoline company and department store cards. Another tactic is to take out a bank loan for a reasonably small amount, say $1,000; put the money in a savings account, and use it to make timely payments on the debt. These actions can help you build a solid credit rating and become eligible for additional forms of credit. If you have never had credit of your own, but you and your spouse established a good credit rating, try to establish credit in your own name before the joint accounts are closed.

Before the divorce is final, get a copy of your current credit report. There are local credit reporting agencies in most cities, as well as national agencies (see Appendix A). Various sources provide free access to a person's credit reports from three of the largest credit reporting agencies—Equifax, Experian, and Transunion— once per year, free of charge. The reporting agencies usually offer an additional free report if a person has been denied credit. Otherwise, a modest fee is imposed. It's a good idea to take a look at your credit report at least annually, to be sure there are no errors or surprises, especially if any aspect of your financial life remains entangled with that of your ex-spouse after your divorce.

Credit ratings are a different matter. These "magic numbers" are used by creditors to determine such things as a person's interest rates on mortgages or other loans, and they vary in both accessibility and the cost to get them. Sources of free annual credit reports or the reporting agencies themselves may offer to provide your credit rating for a small fee—but the number you're quoted may not be the same one that potential lenders use in their calculations. Still, it can give you a ballpark idea of how your credit stacks up, which can be both illuminating and useful in assessing your credit options.

Creditors are often willing to make adjustments in their current payment plans for an individual who has been through a divorce or other change with financial ramifications. If you believe you may have trouble meeting your current credit obligations, call your creditors to discuss the possibilities. Many will be willing to work with you if you are up front and are diligent about keeping your payments current.

More options are becoming available each day for people with a problematic or nonexistent credit history. Talk to local banks, savings and loan companies, credit unions, or nonprofit credit counseling agencies. As you do, beware of "no-questions-asked," 900-number credit companies, as well as the ever-increasing gaggle of online schemes promising to vanquish your debt at the stroke of a pen for one "low" fee. Offers that seem too good to be true usually are, and consumers who fall for them often end up paying exorbitant interest rates or other outrageous fees for services that are either useless, detrimental, or available elsewhere for free. Unfortunately, there are a lot of scams out there. Make sure you know the source and full terms of any credit agreement you enter, or you could end up with more problems rather than solutions.

Credit Counselors. The only person I know who hasn't experienced some sort of debt overload at least once is a very meticulous

CPA. Virtually all people are at risk for falling into the deep waters of debt, particularly since the cost of living keeps going up while credit is easier to come by every day. Fortunately, there are also many people who can help consumers get their financial lives back under control.

Many credit counselors are affiliated with nonprofit organizations such as the United Way, YMCA and YWCA, and even churches. The National Foundation for Consumer Credit sponsors consumer credit counseling services, with offices nationwide (see Appendix A). These counselors can help you tackle immediate crises, negotiate a more realistic payment plan with creditors, learn better ways to manage your finances to make your money go further, set up a budget, and avoid problems in the future. The service is sponsored by various creditors who realize that it is in their best interest to cooperate with debtors in reworking payment plans, rather than having to go through the headaches of foreclosure or simply not getting paid.

The credit counseling service works only with clients who are able to pay their bills on some type of monthly plan. It does not assist debtors who need the protection of bankruptcy. The counselors charge only nominal fees, which usually come out of the monthly payment that is set up to meet the client's debts. The counselor reviews the total debt owed by the client, interacts with the creditors to formalize a payment plan, and then collects direct payments from the client once or twice a month and in turn pays the creditors. This service can also help get late charges, wage garnishments, and other legal actions dropped.

Private, for-profit credit assistance or "credit repair" services are another possible avenue. Some are entirely legitimate, while others are highly suspect. All charge a fee, which is generally absorbed into a set monthly payment that they formulate with your creditors, similar to the nonprofit agencies. Again, with any credit service you contemplate using, insist on receiving a full explanation of what it will do for you and what the total cost will be. Using any such service, whether nonprofit or commercial, may adversely affect your credit rating, so take all of the consequences under advisement before you sign on.

Bankruptcy

For a couple in a financially troubled marriage, divorce is often the last step that leads them over the brink and into bankruptcy. A couple who is still married can file jointly for bankruptcy, and anyone, whether married or single, can file individually. When one spouse files individually, however, the effect on the other can be devastating if the couple is still married or if there is unresolved business, such as debts that have been divided by decree but not refinanced with creditors.

Illinois attorney David B. Riggert, who maintains a bankruptcy practice as well as a family law practice, confirms that the two fields frequently overlap. "The big issue," he states, "is that people must realize early on that they will have higher household expenses and only one income to meet them." Riggert stresses that no matter how the divorce decree divides the couple's debt, both spouses will often remain liable to their creditors on joint debts unless the debts are refinanced through a separate agreement with each creditor. The language of the divorce decree, he points out, may be a controlling factor if one spouse later declares bankruptcy. Most debts can be discharged by a bankruptcy action, but child or spousal support cannot. Therefore, the language designating property division versus support must be clear and specific. Riggert advises, "Spell it out cleanly to make it stick."

Changes to Bankruptcy Laws

Significant changes to the federal bankruptcy laws were enacted in 2005. The new law revises the rules and qualifications for filing bankruptcy, restricting the ability of an individual to file a Chapter 7 bankruptcy, which wipes out all or most unsecured debt. Only debtors who meet specific criteria, focused on income and other factors, are permitted to file under Chapter 7.

Chapter 13 bankruptcy is strongly preferred under the new system. In a Chapter 13 bankruptcy, the debtor pays back a portion of his or her debt in installment payments, over a three- to five-year period. With either chapter, the debtor must complete an approved course of credit counseling and financial management, as well as meet other requirements, before the bankruptcy may be filed or discharged. State laws may affect how a bankruptcy works, as well.

Special Concerns for Divorcing Couples

Several aspects of the new law raise special concerns for divorcing couples. The homestead exemption provisions have changed, and a person's right to keep a vehicle may also be affected. In addition, the test to determine whether a debtor will qualify under Chapter 7 looks at family income for the six-month period prior to filing—which often changes drastically when a couple separates or divorces. If you are contemplating bankruptcy—or if you believe your spouse may file, either before or after your divorce—get advice from a qualified bankruptcy attorney or have a frank talk with your divorce attorney to determine whether he or she is well versed in bankruptcy law. If necessary, ask for a referral to an attorney who specializes in this area.

Filing any form of bankruptcy will reflect negatively on your credit rating for years to come and may afflict your life in areas far beyond the financial sphere, since potential employers, landlords, and others with whom you do business may check your credit history. As long as you and your ex still have both your names on bank, credit, or other accounts, your financial affairs remain entangled. If he or she files bankruptcy or experiences other credit damage, you can be hit by the fallout. The safest course of action is to establish separate accounts before the divorce is final, or immediately afterward.

Bankruptcy can also wreak havoc with a property settlement that has not been completed. Property settlement obligations are usually nondischargeable (meaning they can't be wiped out in the bankruptcy proceeding), but there are some exceptions. Therefore, if you are concerned that your spouse may declare bankruptcy before all of your property transfers are complete, consider taking a lien on the property (which will make you a secured creditor) or structuring the settlement so that the property is transferred as spousal support. These undertakings require expert assistance.

A former spouse's bankruptcy can also interfere with efforts to collect unpaid child support or alimony. While these debts are non-dischargable, the automatic stay provision (which kicks in to stop all debt collection efforts from the time the bankruptcy case is filed until it is discharged or the stay is lifted) may apply, depending on the type of bankruptcy filed. Generally, a parent's obligation to pay ongoing child or spousal support is not affected by a bankruptcy filing, but actions to collect back support may be.

David Riggert says it is imperative to assess the practicability of bankruptcy early on in the divorce process. "One of the first things I do," he relates, "is to analyze the ability of each spouse to maintain payment on the debts that are likely to be assigned to them. This is a vital consideration and, in most cases, not too time consuming or difficult. If I see that either party is likely to file bankruptcy, I immediately open discussions with the other attorney about his or her client's ability to handle the debt." Riggert also tells all divorcing couples for whom bankruptcy may be on the horizon to consider filing a joint bankruptcy petition. It is usually simpler and less expensive to file jointly before the divorce.

Spousal Support

Alimony is now called "spousal support" in most regions. Not only the name but also the purpose and character of this type of support changed during the latter half of the twentieth century, as social roles evolved and states adopted no-fault divorce laws. Today, the majority of women in America have employment other than (or in addition to) homemaker and mother. In fact, in many families, the woman is the primary breadwinner, while the man makes less money or stays at home with the children. It is generally expected by the court system that all adults, unless they are unable to work, will be self-supporting. Thus, instead of the "permanent" alimony that was once common, support awards today are designed to be temporary and to better match the individual circumstances of the people involved.

Since more women spend substantial periods of their married lives working outside the home, fewer women nowadays seek or receive long-term support, with alimony (if awarded at all) usually designed to cover a relatively brief interval in which a wife who has been out of the workforce may get the training or education she needs to be self-supporting, or until small children reach school age. Additionally, as it has become more customary for men to take time off work to stay at home with a couple's children, or to be the secondary breadwinner in the family, more men are seeking spousal support when a marriage ends.

The current law and practice of spousal support are controversial. As discussed in Chapter 4, temporary awards have been criticized for ignoring the real-world environment of most working women. In general, women still earn less than men in most fields. Furthermore, although the court may see a strong, intelligent, forty-year-old woman who appears capable of doing many types of work, this woman might in fact have been a homemaker and mother since she was twenty and is thus entering the workforce in the same position as a much younger, inexperienced worker. Therefore, a woman (or, in some cases, a man) who needs spousal support is obliged to present a detailed summary of her capabilities, plans, and needs to her attorney and, if necessary, the court.

This may require the use of a vocational expert, either hired privately or appointed by the court. As discussed earlier, vocational experts can help people who are facing a change in circumstances to identify what type of work they want to pursue, what additional education or training they will need, their chief capabilities and limitations, how long training will take, realistic expectations as to starting salaries, and perhaps whether outside guidance such as mental health counseling will be necessary before the person will be fully capable of self-support.

Alimony does not always end when the recipient remarries. In most states, this depends on whether the decree specifies that support ends on remarriage or cohabitation, or on whether the payer goes back to court and asks for the decree to be modified due to this change in circumstances. Other states, however, do have statutes providing that alimony automatically ends on remarriage or cohabitation.

Whatever the situation, remember that support awards are never written in stone. They can be modified when the circumstances of either party change in some way so that the support is no longer necessary or fair. For example, if a woman expects to spend two years training for a job that pays a modest salary, but she unexpectedly gets a job after one year that pays much more, her ex-husband can ask the court to modify the award. Conversely, a person who received little or no support may be able to seek an increase later if he or she loses a job or suffers other financial hardship. In some states, though, spousal support is waived if it is not awarded in the original decree and cannot be requested later.

Additionally, a person paying support who suffers financial setback can ask the court to lower the payments. The support system is designed to be flexible, in accordance with the reality that people's plans and circumstances are not fixed in time. The court exercises broad discretion in this area. If the paying spouse decides to change careers from surgeon to surf bum just to get out of support payments, the judge will not be amused. So, while modification is flexible, it will only be granted for good cause.

Be Aware of Your State's Laws

Partially as the result of demographic shifts, alimony laws are subject to ongoing revision, so if spousal support will feature in your divorce, update yourself on where you stand. The states are about evenly divided between those with statutory schemes setting specific requirements for support awards (with some, such as Texas, having unusually restrictive laws) and those that allow the courts broad discretion in awarding spousal support, based on the intricacies of each case.

Generally, under either of these statutory schemes, judges will look at the duration of the marriage and the age, health, occupation, income, skills, needs, and overall situation of each party. A few states, such as North Carolina, still consider marital fault in making an alimony award. Most, however, focus on the "reasonable need" of the spouse seeking support. Alimony may be either short-term (generally called "rehabilitative" or "transitional" support), designed to help a spouse who has been out of the workforce to get the education and training required to qualify for suitable employment, or it may be permanent, which is usually available only to older or disabled people who are unlikely to become fully self-supporting. In the latter instance, the reality is that the money to provide support may no longer be available when the former spouse retires, so this should be taken into account when older couples divorce.

Some states are leaning toward adoption of alimony guidelines that use standard formulas and work sheets, much like those used to calculate child support. In New Mexico, guidelines have been developed as a pilot project of the courts. The guidelines and a corresponding work sheet are available for divorcing parties, attorneys, and mediators to employ in settlement negotiations. They serve as a tool for use with the existing statute, which lists factors applicable in making the initial determination of whether an award of alimony is appropriate. The committee that developed the guidelines is currently collecting feedback from users of the guidelines to see how well they work. It will then issue recommendations as to whether they should be adopted in a court rule or statute, continue to be used only as a settlement tool, or abandoned. Other states are studying similar innovations. Opinion is growing that methods such as these can reduce litigation over spousal support (one of the most frequently contested and appealed issues in divorce litigation) and help to bring predictability to an inherently unpredictable arena.

Don't Hesitate to Insist on Support If You Need It

According to Lester Wallman, a leading matrimonial attorney and coauthor of *Cupid, Couples, and Contracts*, there are four important words to remember about alimony: Don't count on it. All the same, Wallman's view is that anyone who needs spousal support, especially older homemakers, should fight like hell to try to get it. Even if alimony is not awarded, it can be a valuable negotiating tool to leverage a more equitable property settlement.

Emerging evidence indicates that the courts are beginning to pay more attention to the value of a homemaker spouse who contributes to the success of a partner with a demanding career. In 1995, General Electric executive Gary Wendt asked his wife, Lorena, for a divorce. During the course of the couple's thirty-year marriage, Lorena had taught to help put her husband through

Harvard business school and then became a full-time homemaker, mother, and hostess (including serving a lavish business dinner eight days after delivering her first child). She argued that in light of her contributions toward her husband's success, she was entitled to half the couple's estimated $90 million net worth. The court ultimately awarded Lorena assets worth more than $21 million, two of the couple's five homes, plus lifetime alimony of $21,000 per month. She has since established a foundation called the Equality in Marriage Institute, with the goal of advancing recognition of the contributions of stay-at-home spouses who make meaningful commitments to the success of both partners (see Appendix A).

Alimony Tax Concerns

Alimony is separate and distinct from the property settlement. It is also separate from child support, although sometimes when a spouse is paying both alimony and child support, the sums will be lumped together in one payment called family support. This can cause problems with tax classifications. The IRS may not agree with how the parties say they have divided this payment between child support and alimony.

The size, character, timing, and structure of alimony payments can also have imposing tax consequences. Seek the assistance of a qualified tax accountant, divorce financial analyst, or attorney with specialized training in tax law if you are contemplating any type of alimony. Also, alimony is sometimes characterized as part of the property settlement in order to manipulate the tax consequences. The tax impact must be considered whenever someone is contemplating a lump-sum alimony award.

Tying Up Loose Ends

Before your divorce is final, all those who may be indirectly affected by the divorce should be informed of the terms of the property settlement. These include insurance agents, stockbrokers, bankers, personnel at children's school, accountants, pension fund administrators, and others involved in your financial affairs. Timing is essential. It's best to notify everyone who needs this information after the settlement is tentatively finalized but before it is signed and filed with the court, if possible.

After you have taken the steps to divide and refinance your debts, change title documents, and review other records, check with the corresponding companies and agencies to verify that the changes were made as directed. This measure can provide reassurance that your spouse kept up his or her end of the agreement and that no mistakes were made. As we all know, errors are excruciatingly common in large companies and government bureaucracies. Check wills, trust documents, records of debt, credit cards, any documents of title, deeds, bank accounts, stock documents, and any other records you can think of. This activity will usually involve no more than a phone call, an e-mail, a letter, or a quick stop at company headquarters, the recorder of deeds' office, the tax assessor's office, and title companies. Such steps can be tiresome and time consuming, but most people can accomplish it all in a day or two. And it can be well worth the effort if a problem crops up somewhere along the line.

Once the divorce is final, don't fail to attend to any remaining paperwork. Have you acquired all of the important papers reflecting the terms of the settlement or order? These may encompass deeds to property, evidence that bank and credit accounts have been closed or transferred to one name, and car titles. If anything has fallen through the cracks, take it upon yourself to finish this business. Look over your divorce documents before filing them away: Are all the loose ends taken care of? For example, if you were awarded the family home in the divorce settlement, your spouse should have signed a quitclaim deed relinquishing legal title to the property.

In many states, divorce will automatically change certain aspects of your personal business arrangements. For example, in California, a final decree of divorce cancels spousal rights under a will, trust, retirement beneficiary plan, power of attorney, joint tenancy real estate, vehicle registration, and similar property. California law does not cancel a spouse's status as beneficiary under a life insurance policy—but the laws of some other states do. This can loom large if such rights and benefits were intended to be a part of the property settlement or otherwise intended to survive the divorce. Even where the law does not make these automatic provisions, you should review your insurance, estate planning, retirement, and similar documents, and know what your spouse has arranged as well, so that any required changes or clarifications with third parties can be made. Insurance, retirement, and investment documents should all be revised with the assistance of the agent, trustee, or administrator to reflect the provisions of the decree.

Even if you're fairly well organized on your own, the time that follows a divorce is a prime opportunity to regroup and verify that you know the location of items you may need for various practical purposes. If you do not already store your important documents in a safe place, organized so that you can quickly put your hands on what you need, the interim after a divorce is an ideal time to get these files in shape. Vital documents should be stored in a safe deposit box at your bank, or in a fireproof box or filing cabinet at your home. If you have children, maintain the basic information on your former spouse such as Social Security number. You may need to tap this information for tax matters, children's school records, or support enforcement.

6

Family Law and Children

Divorcing parents face numerous challenges and concerns regarding their children. Legally, two primary issues must be decided: child custody and child support. While a divorce is always traumatic, children bounce back and readjust in nearly all cases—*if* the parents focus on their love for them, and love them enough to put aside their animosity toward each other and behave in a civilized manner. Ideally, parents should try their hardest to reach an accord and move on to a place in which each can treat the other with decency and respect, so that they can maintain their ongoing relationship as parents in an atmosphere of peace. If they cannot, then simply calling a cease-fire and limiting contact to essential exchanges on the business of parenting may be the next best alternative. No matter how the feelings between the parents pan out, the child's need to be allowed to love both parents must be kept at the forefront. Many believe that ongoing hostilities between parents is one of the most harmful occurrences for a child to endure, second only to direct abuse of the child.

Child Custody

Perhaps the most fruitful way to begin a discussion of child custody is by looking at some of the common misconceptions about custody law and how custody decisions are made. According to

135

Anne Kass, a family court judge for many years in Albuquerque, here are three of the most popular myths:

- Courts favor mothers over fathers.
- Children over a certain age can choose where they live.
- Equal time between parents solves custody problems.

None of these notions is accurate.

Judge Kass points out that the parents themselves make the decision on custody, often unknowingly and unintentionally, long before the divorce process is initiated. Parents begin when they establish patterns of looking after the child's basic needs, such as who gets up for 2 a.m. feedings, who stays home from work when the child is ill, and who takes the child to the pediatrician. If only one parent assumes these responsibilities, she reasons, the other should not be surprised when a court recognizes and affirms the decisions of the parents, maintaining the status quo. This does not mean, of course, that the other parent is completely eliminated from the child's life—and this is another reality that some parents are slow to accept.

Children do have some say in the custody process. Many states have laws requiring the court to consider the wishes of a child who is over a set age, usually twelve to fourteen. In fact, courts usually listen to the preferences of all children. However, Kass emphasizes, judges do not automatically accept the children's wishes, for numerous reasons. Children are sometimes influenced by inappropriate promises, such as a new car or no curfew. Some may try to stay with the parent who they feel needs them, may have unrealistic expectations that a parent they hardly know will be better than the parent with whom they have been living, or may take the materialistic route and choose the parent with more money. "In other words," she says, "what a child wants is often not what a child needs." Judges hope that the parents will come up with an agreement allowing the child to spend time with both of them and that both parents will abide by it.

Reaching your own child custody agreement is always the most effective course. It can save years of turmoil, thousands of dollars, and immeasurable amounts of grief for all involved. The first action called for in nearly any case in which child custody or visitation is contested is for the parents to sit down and clearly and concisely state what each would like to see happen. Family court judges accentuate the need to be specific in such discussions, whether in preliminary negotiations, mediation, or litigation. Articulate exactly what you want; for example: "I want the children to reside primarily with me and to spend alternating weekends from after school Friday until they return to school Monday morning, plus Wednesdays from after school until 8 p.m., with their father." Even if your spouse has a much different result in mind, when you both declare your desires in precise terms, you have a place to begin.

One California judge reports that airing such straightforward requests increases the likelihood that the parties will form their own agreement—although he has handled plenty of cases in which no clear proposal is offered until the parties are in the courtroom, at which point a prompt agreement is reached that obviously could have been accomplished much earlier. When the relationship is hostile, face-to-face meetings or other direct contact may be inadvisable, but the same type of negotiations can be carried on by mail or e-mail, or through the attorneys.

When courts are called on to decide custody arrangements, they look at various factors, sometimes set out in a state statute that specifies what must be considered. Additionally, judges do listen to the preferences of the children and often ask professionals such as psychologists and social workers to make recommendations. Courts are supposed to base all custody decisions on one bottom-line factor: the best interest of the child. Nevertheless, often the situation is inherently "no-win," because any decision will hurt someone.

A parent seeking custody or increased visitation rights must be prepared to demonstrate, with concrete examples, why he or she is a good and devoted parent. As in all other legal cases, evidence is powerful in a custody dispute. Parents will benefit by compiling a well-organized, detailed collection of information on their relationship with the child, the goals and responsibilities they are prepared to face in parenting, how they would encourage the child to maintain a good relationship with both parents, and as many related issues as pertain. Unfair as it may seem, parents must also be certain that their own behavior is above reproach and be willing to avoid actions that could be used against them by the other parent, such as living with a new mate during the custody proceeding. While judges are supposed to base decisions on how a behavior actually affects the child, many can't help but be biased by their personal opinions.

It can't be stressed enough that it is always favorable for parents to reach their own agreement—often called a parenting plan—rather than litigating custody at trial. Child custody suits are agonizing for parents and children, and they can cost tens of thousands of dollars. "Both the pain and the expense have a huge, negative effect on children," Judge Kass warns.

Erica Jong, writing of her daughter Molly and her current relationship with former husband Jon in her book *Fear of Fifty*, describes what can be achieved when parents put down their swords and work to become at least civil co-parents: "I was always either flush or broke, but somehow I was able to pay the bills and raise my daughter. I even learned how to be a decent mother. Eventually Jon and I stopped suing each other and began to talk. Sometimes we even reminisce about old times and remember why we loved each other. And Molly's face lights up as if with a thousand candles."

Joint Custody

The predominant type of child custody today is called joint legal custody. In theory, at least, joint custody means that both parents share responsibility for raising the child and actively participate in the child's life—that both maintain "frequent and continuing contact" with the child. It does not necessarily mean joint physical custody, and it may encompass any type of time-share arrangement. In most situations, one parent still has primary physical custody—that is, the child spends the majority of time at one home. The label of joint custody may be significant in itself, no matter how a child's physical custody is actually divided.

According to the Joint Custody Association, a group based in Los Angeles, fathers in joint custody arrangements are less likely to be late in making their support payments than fathers who have only visitation rights. The group, which advocates for joint custody rights, cites another study showing that joint custody fathers contribute voluntary extras beyond child support, such as paying for camp and music lessons, 60 percent of the time, compared with

20 percent for visitation fathers. Furthermore, they return to court requesting custody changes or support adjustments only 16 percent of the time, versus 31 percent for visiting fathers, according to the study.

Sole Custody

Sole custody refers to the situation in which one parent, still most often the mother, keeps the child nearly all the time, with visitation rights held by the other parent (unless the court has found the other parent unfit or dangerous to the child, in which case there is no contact). In a sole custody arrangement, the primary parent has virtually all the decision-making authority as to how the child will be raised. While sole custody may not differ all that much from joint custody in its day-to-day arrangement, the label can affect how the parents and children view the visiting parent's role, as the studies cited by the Joint Custody Association reflect. Some psychologists criticize the usage of *visitation* as casting the noncustodial parent in the role of a guest in the child's life, although the term is commonly applied in both joint and sole custody arrangements.

Divided or Split Custody

Divided or split custody refers to a situation in which two or more children are "split up" between the parents. For example, in a family with two sons, one parent may be primarily responsible for the older, and the other parent for the younger. This type of arrangement seems to work well for some families, especially if the two households are not far apart and the divorced parents get along well. However, it is controversial, because it divides siblings who may be close and poses the risk that the siblings will drift apart or become alienated from the noncustodial parent, particularly if the parents remain in conflict. Some judges require approval by a psychologist or other professional before agreeing to split custody.

Fifty-Fifty Custody

In a fifty-fifty arrangement, which is a species of joint custody, children spend approximately half of their time at each parent's home, with each parent actively participating in all facets of the children's lives. Equal sharing of time is viewed by many people as a cure-all, yet psychological studies have shown that it is stressful for most children. It takes an enormous amount of energy for children to cope with both the practical aspects (such as having their things in the right place) and the emotional challenges (constantly shifting gears to adjust to the different rules and expectations) of an equal custody arrangement. They often feel a sense of divided loyalty and shoulder a heavy burden of inconvenience and confusion to avoid hurting either parent, more so if the parents do not get along.

Judge Kass recalls the angry comments of an eighteen-year-old boy who had spent the past five years of his life shuttling between his parents' homes each week. "When my parents divorced, my mom got a new house and my dad got a new house. I got a suitcase," he remarked. "This fall, I'm going to pack my suitcase and go off to college. I do not plan to visit either of those houses again anytime soon."

"Unfortunately, he had never told his parents how he felt, and they were shocked at his reaction. Equal time is fair for parents, but it is rarely fair for children," says Kass.

However, in other cases, especially if the parents live close together, communicate well, and are equally dedicated to making it work, a fifty-fifty time-share arrangement can work beautifully. "The kids don't always like going back and forth so often, but they also see the advantages," says Johanna Robinson, the mother of three children, now teenagers, who have successfully navigated a fifty-fifty custody arrangement for nearly six years. "None of the children had a strong desire to live with one of us instead of the other when we divorced, and they all maintain a close relationship with both of us. Their father and I agreed to stay in the same community, so this made the most sense." Robinson feels the arrangement has been beneficial to everyone in the family. "The kids have learned to be responsible with their stuff and to manage their schedules, which are incredibly busy. And just as they get tired of one of us, they get to go spend time with the other," she says with a laugh. "My ex and I each have time to live our own lives, too, so when the children come back after several days with the other parent, we feel refreshed and ready to focus on them."

Robinson emphasizes that both parents' commitment to maintaining positive, businesslike communication has underpinned the family's success. "The kids do try to play us off each other sometimes—as they did when we were together—but we're both aware of it, and we don't let them get by with it. The minute I hear, 'Well, Dad said we could . . . ' I reach for the phone and tell them I'll just have to call Dad and see what he has to say. That puts a stop to that!"

Robinson believes that fifty-fifty time shares also require flexibility, in both practical and emotional matters. "My ex and I still have issues with each other, but we've had to learn to be mature enough to put them aside," she explains. "We don't make it about the kids—we keep our business separate. We respect each other as parents and people, and we adjust our schedules when necessary. We cooperate so that the kids get what they need. It hasn't always been smooth sailing, but no arrangement will be—and this really works well for our family."

What Type of Custody Is Best?

Any type of custody arrangement can be wonderful or disastrous, depending on the players and how they interact. Also, custody arrangements may be modified when circumstances change. The court that makes or approves the initial custody arrangement retains jurisdiction, and the case may be reopened if a request for change is made by one or both of the parties, within limitations set by state law and court rules.

Mental health counselor Kathryn Lang feels that stability is a particularly important issue for children. "I have a personal bias in favor of one parent having primary physical custody, with visitation by the other," she says. She adds, "If parents are going to try to do a fifty-fifty split of the child's time, it should be large blocks of time such as one week, two weeks, or a month, rather than half a week with one and half a week with the other. That would be very disruptive and hard on the child. It may meet the needs of the parents, but it usually isn't best for the children."

Echoing many of her colleagues, Lang contends that joint legal custody, in which the parents share decision making, is fine, if the parents can agree on major tenets and each defers to the decisions of the other. "The success of joint custody depends on the maturity of the parents," Lang explains. "If there is any kindness in the marriage, then there can be kindness in the divorce. People who are inherently cooperative do better in divorce. There is a lot to be said for recognizing the fact that the other person is a good parent, has the best interest of the children at heart, and can be trusted not to do things that are detrimental to the kids."

Lang has seen many parents get trapped in minor disputes, and she notes, "People often get caught up in the petty stuff, start yelling and screaming, and proceed to work out their own issues with each other supposedly in defense of the kids. The best thing parents can do is to agree to try to be pleasant to each other and to recognize that they have a vested interest in the mental and emotional health of their children. This is essential if they care about the kids."

According to a study conducted in the late 1980s, judges tend to believe that joint custody has not necessarily worked well in cases in which custody is disputed, despite its being the preferred plan according to the law of most states. Some of the reasons given by these judges were poor cooperation between parents, the instability for the child created by frequently shifting from home to home, the distance between parents' homes, and the parents' acrimony or vengefulness. Most of the judges preferred limited joint custody, in which one parent has primary physical custody while the other has liberal visitation and shares in decision making. Notably, the judges' reservations were limited to cases in which custody was disputed between the parents, as opposed to custody decisions that were made amicably between the parents or with the assistance of mediators. Joint custody, the study suggests, may not be the best arrangement when the parents have a history of emotional disagreement. Australia was the first country to allow a judge to impose joint custody when parents could not come to an agreement on their own, but it later became the first to forbid it unless both parents agreed.

The more time during which divorced parents are required to be in contact with one another, the more opportunities those in an acrimonious relationship find to fight. Some of the states that jumped onto the joint custody bandwagon early on have even modified their laws so that joint custody does not get automatic preference over sole custody. Also, some fathers who fight hard for more time with their children are later unwilling or unable to accept the responsibility that this type of arrangement entails. Courts are hearing more and more actions by mothers who ask the judge to order the father to spend the amount of time with the child that he requested and that the child expects.

Parents often perceive custody decisions by a court as punitive or unfair, and some decisions certainly are. Yet whatever the decision may be, it is essential to remember that a grant of primary custody to one parent is not tantamount to a finding that the other parent is unfit or in any way inadequate as a parent. Courts have to weigh all the evidence that is placed before them against that impossibly subjective standard: the "best interest" of the child. It's obvious how imperfect this exercise can be, how errors are sometimes made, and how painful the outcome will inevitably be for some or all of those involved in a custody dispute, especially the children. The trauma may then be aggravated if one parent pushes for a change of custody years after the divorce.

Visitation

Despite criticism of the term, *visitation* is still the word most commonly applied to the time a child spends with the parent who does not have primary physical custody. In most families, both the children and parent look forward to this time and make the most of it, but in others, problems come with the territory. Often these hitches are tied to logistical fine points, such as trying to make sure that both parents are aware of the child's scheduled activities, or that the child doesn't forget schoolwork, favorite toys, or other high-priority possessions when transferring between homes. A little more attention to organization can usually ease these problems, and tools are available to help. For example, mediator and author Roberta Beyer has developed a special calendar for children of divorced parents called "My Two Homes." The calendar is bright and cheerful, with stickers the child can use to mark upcoming events such as school activities and birthday parties, as well as the days when the child changes homes. Beyer made a point to use engaging colors and positive images in her design, so that the premise of living in two homes is presented as perfectly normal.

More ideas on helping children cope with visitation are provided in Chapter 7.

Children may balk at visiting a parent simply because they don't want to be away from the more familiar home, activities, and friends. These dilemmas can be resolved if the parents and children can all communicate and look for creative solutions. Insight can be gleaned from books such as *How to Go to Visitation Without Throwing Up*, written by Joshua Shane Evans, a boy who learned how to overcome the stress of visitation, with the help of his stepmother (see "Resources and Suggested Readings"). However, if a child exhibits strong resistance or fear as the scheduled visit approaches, this response could be a sign of more serious parental alienation, which often requires therapy and always needs to be handled with care.

Psychologist Judith S. Wallerstein, who has conducted social science research on child custody, found that the quality of visitation, not the quantity, is the critical element in a child's development. Her studies indicated that as long as a child has regular communication and contact with the parent that is extensive enough to sustain their relationship, the child's interests are served. Wallerstein also concluded that the most important factor for positive development was a strong, well-functioning relationship with the custodial parent; so, what's good for that parent is generally good for the child—and, in turn, for the noncustodial parent. The interests of all are fundamentally interrelated.

The Custodial Parent's Duty to Facilitate Visitation. Parents have an affirmative duty under the law not only to comply with the terms of the custody and visitation order but also to encourage scheduled visitation between the child and the other parent. Custodial parents are sometimes unaware of the weight and seriousness with which courts view the other parent's visitation rights. In fact, any parent—custodial or noncustodial—who maliciously or vindictively thwarts the parental rights of the other (for example, by consistently failing to return the child at the scheduled time) may be fined, ordered to pay related attorney's fees incurred by the other, or even held in contempt of court if a valid court order is repeatedly disobeyed. In extreme cases, the violator may even lose custody rights.

When Parents Do Not Honor Visitation Rights. While parents typically battle for more time with their children, some, especially those who were deeply hurt by the divorce, feel the need for time alone, completely away from their family, in order to sort out their emotions and regroup. When the noncustodial parent refuses to spend time with the children according to the time-sharing plan—or refuses to see the children at all—the effect on them can be devastating. There is no real judicial remedy for this type of neglect. As a practical matter, the custodial parent can try to explain the situation to the children while at the same time maintaining nonthreatening contact with the other parent, such as sending occasional cards or letters with updates on the children and recent snapshots. Many absent parents do come around after a period of isolation.

Visitation Rights of Grandparents and Others. Some of the people most integral to a child's development and sense of stability are classified by the law as "legal strangers"—that is, having no legally recognized relationship with a child that would entitle them to seek custody or visitation rights. Children often form strong, loving bonds with grandparents, uncles, aunts, stepparents, and other adults in their lives, connections that are all-important to both the adult and the child. When parents divorce, these people are often rocked by the impact as well, particularly when the parent with primary custody does not want to maintain a relationship with a member of the ex's family. Traditionally, grandparents and other relatives had no legal rights to maintain contact with a child, but this began to change as legislators recognized the benefits of preserving such relationships. Today, all states have some type of statute allowing grandparents (and sometimes other relatives or caretakers) to ask the court to grant them visitation rights with a child. While all of these laws focus on the best interest of the child, they vary widely in how they work. Some are narrow, restricted to use by a grandparent when one parent has died or the parents divorce, while others are more permissive, allowing various relatives or others to petition the court for visitation rights—in some cases, even when the parents are still married.

These laws, in turn, have been challenged by parents who contend that the statutes infringe on their right to raise their children as they see fit. In a 2000 case entitled *Troxel v. Granville*, the United States Supreme Court struck down a Washington State law that allowed "any person" to petition the court for child visitation at any time. The court's decision was complex but essentially found the particular statute to be an unconstitutional infringement on the fundamental rights of parents to make decisions concerning the care, custody, and control of their children. However, the Troxel decision did not hold that grandparents and others may never be granted visitation rights; it was limited to the particular statute that was challenged and others like it.

In the wake of the *Troxel* case, some states amended their statutes, and the law remains in flux regarding the visitation rights of "legal strangers." Generally speaking, grandparents will almost always be legally entitled to preserve a relationship with their grandchildren when parents divorce. In some states, the parties are required to mediate if grandparents petition the court for visitation rights and one of the parents opposes the petition. Most states likewise now have laws addressing the rights of stepparents. Since these laws are always changing, you should check the current law of your state or consult a legal professional if nonparent visitation may be a wrinkle in your case.

Virtual Visitation

The explosive growth of communication technology over the past few decades has had a far-reaching effect on nurturing relationships between children and noncustodial parents. Cell phones and family wireless plans have become more affordable, so even young children may now have their own phones. Digital cameras and DVD recorders allow parents to share images or films of special events in a child's life. And the Internet has revolutionized all areas of communication.

A new phenomenon called "virtual visitation," in which noncustodial parents and their children maintain regular contact via the Internet, has influenced several aspects of child custody in recent years, including parental relocation. The term itself was coined in a New Jersey relocation case (*McCoy v. McCoy*) that suggested that trial courts in the jurisdiction must consider virtual visitation in determining whether to permit long-distance relocation by a custodial parent. Other states have begun to address this burgeoning trend, with Utah enacting the first statute citing virtual visitation in 2004. Legislation in several other states is pending.

Online technology can enable parents and children who live in different cities, states, or even nations to engage in regular contact through e-mail, instant messaging, websites, and real-time audio and videoconferencing media. Parents and children can interact directly through live webcams and microphones, for both general communication and shared activities. Many play online games, do homework, scan and send drawings and photos, and share hobbies. For example, one father and son use Web technology to participate in a fantasy sports league, research their genealogy, and work together on constructing a family tree. Another father remarked that while it had been hard to hold his ten-year-old daughter's attention for more than a few minutes when they spoke on the phone, Web interaction permitted longer and more relaxed contact. The two routinely play checkers, practice multiplication tables, and talk. The girl said she enjoyed being able to see her dad and also to play her piano for him, since he had not been able to attend her recitals.

Some detractors have lambasted virtual visitation as a second-rate substitute for physical contact and express a fear that it may prompt more frequent judicial approval of parental relocation. Meanwhile, advocates—including the legislators who draft the laws allowing virtual visitation—assert that it is a supplement to live contact, intended to help sustain the parent-child relationship between visits. As in any other custody matter, parents are urged to reach their own agreement on how virtual visitation should be handled. For example, in the *McCoy* case, the mother designed an interactive website for the child, which the court praised as "creative and innovative."

Early feedback from families using virtual visitation gives every indication that the medium is being used appropriately, generally in cases in which children spend significant portions of their time (such as summer vacation) with a noncustodial parent. Both parents are usually required to maintain the necessary equipment so that the children may communicate with the other parent from either home. Reliable technology is a prerequisite, since frequent breakdowns, interruptions, and similar glitches may only add to the family's frustration. Some court orders are fairly general in stating the technological requirements, while others are highly detailed and include specifications regarding what kind and quality of equipment will be provided, upgrades, requirements for digital subscriber lines, even furniture.

Advocates enumerate several matters that should always be addressed in a parenting plan that includes virtual visitation. One is that privacy of the parties must be assured. It is best, when financially feasible, for the child to have his or her own computer and/or telephone line, usually located in the child's bedroom. In addition, who pays for the required equipment (as well as repairs and upgrades) should be specified, and usually a third party (rather than one parent) is designated to perform installation and troubleshooting. Further, parents should agree in the written order that they will not use the child to communicate messages between them and that the privacy of all parent-child communications will be absolutely respected. Many agreements also add penalties for noncompliance, such as requiring a parent who fails to maintain computer equipment to pay for the other to have an extra weekend of live visitation.

Of course, such endeavors are easier if the parents can keep their relationship positive, but virtual visitation can also be useful in high-conflict situations when parents need or want to avoid contact. Moreover, some proponents have suggested that it may bolster a weak relationship between parent and child that would otherwise worsen.

The conventional wisdom is that anything that can lighten the burden on parents and children who must be geographically separated, and help bridge the emotional distance when the family can't be in close proximity, can only be an asset. "A video image can't take the place of a hug," said one father, "but it's better than nothing."

Parental Alienation

Even when parents do their utmost to prevent children from taking sides in a divorce, the children may do so on their own. Such reactions occur more often among children of certain ages. Nine- to twelve-year-olds frequently blame the parent they believe "caused" the divorce and side with the one they see as the innocent victim. However, alienation from a divorced parent can occur among children of any age, including adults. "I had a really hard time being civil to my dad after he left my mother, especially when I saw how miserable she was, watched her cry at Thanksgiving—it was so difficult to see his side, or to forgive him," says one woman, whose parents divorced when she was twenty-eight. "He left her for someone else, and that made it really rough," she recalls. "It was only after my mother found someone and was happy again that I could truly rebuild a good relationship with my father. I know that seems juvenile, but it's how I felt. I forced myself to be decent to him and his new wife, but that was all I had to give. Now we're all close again, but it took a long time."

Some younger children cannot, or will not, affect a facade of civility, and custodial parents often wonder whether they should insist that the child spend time with the other parent when the child strongly resists or outright refuses. Virtually all mental health professionals agree that it does no one any good to force a child who is furious or terrified to spend time with the object of that anger or fear, even if the basis for the emotion is irrational. Instead, the custodial parent should try to maintain and encourage open communication to root out the cause of the discord.

Such resistance also should be brought to the attention of the court, particularly if it is ongoing or if the other parent is excessively upset or angry, since failing to produce a child for court-mandated visits may equate to child abduction. Bringing the problem to light helps quell any concerns by the court or other parent that the child is being concealed or that access is being obstructed without legitimate cause. Consult your attorney, as well as a mental health professional, if your child displays such behavior. An alienated child may need to be seen by a qualified therapist, and if any visitation is continued before the feelings are resolved, it should be supervised—especially if any allegations of abuse have arisen.

A few loud advocates claim that in such cases, alienated children are usually coached by a custodial parent to make false charges of abuse. Their position is that in such circumstances, the children should be removed from the parent's custody and placed in the sole care of the other parent in order to "deprogram" them. While false accusations do happen occasionally, this is an extraordinarily cruel and dangerous theory of how an alienated child should be "cured." A child may be subjected to continued abuse if the charges are true, and even assuming the noncustodial parent is a kind and loving person who would never hurt the child, cutting the child's bonds with the parent who has been the primary caretaker during an already stressful time is extremely damaging. Children as young as eight years old have committed suicide in such circumstances. Also, it often happens that children make up stories, for a variety of reasons; depending on the individual situation, it may take time and counseling before the truth is sorted out. Until it is, parents must act with extreme caution.

Plainly stated, this is nothing to mess with. Once again, the rights and well-being of the children—not the parents—must be the paramount concern in all custody matters. Needless to say, if a parent has coached a child to make false accusations of such a serious nature against the other, the consequences may—and should—be severe and may indeed culminate in a change of custody. Until the truth can be elicited—most likely through therapy—any child's charge of abuse must be taken seriously.

If you are falsely accused of any kind of abuse, seek an attorney's advice immediately. It is also advisable to contact a social worker at your state family services agency, a parents' advocacy organization, and any family therapist involved in the case. If you and your child are not seeing a mental health therapist, both of you should begin—as should the other parent. It will be vital to both your future well-being and that of your child to insist that appropriate mental health intervention is initiated right away. Gather a team of professionals who can assist you in setting the record straight without delay.

Custody and Relocation

One of the thorniest issues that divorced parents may confront, either at the time of divorce or years later, is how to manage joint custody and/or visitation when one parent wants or is required by work obligations to move a considerable distance away from the other. Even a short move can cause a slew of problems when parents have an ongoing conflict. All too often, one parent's intention to relocate breeds extreme upset or even hostility in what until then had been a friendly, civilized co-parenting relationship.

Relocation always is a tricky issue due to the competing rights involved. Courts have acknowledged the constitutional rights of all individuals to travel and live where they choose. Some jurisdictions, such as California, hold that courts may neither prohibit a parent from relocating nor require proof of the "need" to relocate (although a parent whose move is primarily motivated by a desire to keep the child away from the other parent may lose custody). Concurrently, under modern constitutional theory, both parents also have an equal right to the custody of their children. So, the competing rights blur in a case involving custody and relocation, especially given that the rights of the parents—even fundamental rights guaranteed by the constitution—must take a backseat to the best interest of the child.

Ideally, a parent who is contemplating a move of even a short distance should discuss with the other parent how this will affect the current arrangements and what, if any, changes will be required. Parents who are able to communicate well and maintain a good rapport in the interest of their child are usually able to work out a solution that both can accept, through changes in visitation schedules, sharing of transportation costs, and other compromises. If you must go to court for approval of the move, be prepared to show that it is in the best interest of the child and that it is being done for a legitimate reason and not to vex your former spouse. If the children are in favor of the move, note this as well.

Changes in the Law. The brouhaha surrounding relocation has become such a headache that some states are changing their laws to be more specific about what is and is not allowed without court approval. Yet the law may not make sense in every case. For example, Illinois law currently allows the custodial parent to move anywhere within the state without specific approval by the court or the other parent, but approval is mandatory for an out-of-state move. Under this system, a parent could move from Chicago to Cairo, a six-hour drive, but a parent living in the Quad Cities straddling the Illinois-Iowa border could not move across the river. In California, the law holds that a parent cannot be prevented from choosing to move, but the choice may affect time-sharing or custody arrangements.

Relocation can obviously fall under the category of "changed circumstances," triggering the court's scrutiny and allowing the other parent to ask for a change. Courts that have the power to approve or disapprove relocation by a custodial parent will generally consider numerous factors, including whether the proposed move will yield benefits such as improved employment opportunity for the parent, a safer or healthier environment for the child, and better schools. If a spouse can prove that the other chose to move primarily to thwart the agreed access to the child, a change of custody may be ordered. Courts will look at all the pertinent circumstances—for example, the distance of the move, whether the custodial parent is moving to an area where job opportunities are better or worse, and basic elements of fairness, such as whether one parent is in the military and cannot choose where to live. Furthermore, a parent who does not inform the other of his or her whereabouts may be subject to civil and criminal penalties for parental kidnapping.

This area of family law is currently evolving as the states grapple with efforts to balance the competing rights of family members in our increasingly mobile culture. If relocation may be a ticking bomb in your case, be sure you understand your jurisdiction's perspective.

Unique Solutions to Custody Dilemmas

Although traditional patterns of custody still predominate, many parents are trying innovative arrangements. Those who form a cooperative parenting relationship after the divorce are often able to devise flexible, creative systems that suit everyone involved. Couples living a great distance apart have still managed to share joint custody by extending the child's stays in each place and reducing the frequency of the switches accordingly, even alternating years. Others have taken the opposite route: the children remain in the family home, and each parent alternates between living in the home and living in another residence nearby. This setup is sometimes called "bird nesting."

Individual judges may or may not be amenable to proposals for such unique scenarios, but where all parties favor them, this unity can carry the day. Judges tend to take a positive view of anything that promotes harmony among members of a divorced family.

How Are Custody Decisions Made?

There has been some limited scientific study of the inherently subjective processes used by judges in reaching child custody decisions. Judges characteristically give great weight to each parent's demonstrated sense of responsibility, overall mental stability, and maturity. One study found that judges attach more significance to evidence that comes from impartial sources not aligned with either parent, and to the desires of older children. The opinions of psychologists hired by one party were given less weight than the findings of court-appointed psychologists (or one whom both parents agree to use).

On the whole, judges and mental health professionals agree that when considering joint custody versus single-parent custody, the most meaningful criteria include the age of the child, the willingness of the parents to cooperate in a joint custody situation, the quality of the child's relationship with each parent, the level of anger and bitterness between the parents, and the psychological stability of the parents. Least relevant factors include the gender of the child, the wishes of a young child, the ages of the parents, economic and physical characteristics, the marital status of the parents, religious beliefs, the necessity for day care, and the parents' economic stability. Again, a key criterion is whether the parents can refrain from displays of hostility. A parent who uses the child as a pawn, openly incites battle in front of the child, or poisons the child's mind against the other parent not only hurts the child but also may—and should—risk losing custody.

Some of the ugliest cases are those in which parents resort to false accusations of abuse to try to "win" custody. Family law attorney David Riggert reports that he is seeing an increasing number of false charges of child or spousal abuse by parents trying to gain leverage in the divorce proceeding. "An often-used practice is to apply for an emergency order of protection charging the other spouse with domestic abuse, in an effort to get immediate physical custody of a child," he recounts. "I have clients who actually suggest this as a strategic move. I try to explain to them that not only are such false charges illegal and a waste of everyone's time and money, but also they are terribly destructive to the child."

Even worse, says Riggert, are the cases in which both parents wage a war by firing false and damaging accusations at one another. "People who do this fail to realize that if both manage to convince the judge that the other parent is unfit, the child may be placed in foster care, and neither will get custody. When a client appears to be ready to start a war, I ask, 'What is the worst thing that could happen?' Invariably, clients acknowledge that it would be far worse for both to lose custody than for the other to be the primary custodian."

Equally ugly are the cases in which a parent threatens to seek sole custody without really wanting to care for the children, but only as leverage to gain a more advantageous settlement with respect to property division or support. This vicious game has become less common since the advent of mandatory mediation in custody disputes and broader use of psychological evaluations, but it still occurs. If you suspect your spouse of contemplating such a strategy, tell your lawyer, gather your evidence, and take a firm stand.

One Woman's Story

"You don't know them until you divorce them," says Cynde Goyen, whose divorce in 1986 involved a bitter child custody battle. "We thought we had settled the property issues; then he would use the custody battle to try to manipulate me into agreeing to a less favorable settlement," she says. "It took more than a year and a half until all the dust settled, and then he ended up with sole custody of our children. This was very unusual in the mid-1980s, and I felt the decision was a horrible judgment against me. It was devastating emotionally, personally, and socially."

Goyen says her husband was emotionally abusive during the marriage but grew much worse when it ended. "After I had stayed home for nine years raising three children, I asked him for a divorce. He couldn't stand the idea of rejection, so he did all he could to try to hurt me back. He knew that taking the children away and denying me access to them would be the worst thing he could do to me," she explains.

Even after Goyen's husband "won" custody, he kept trying to poison the children's minds against their mother. She recalls, "When I got an offer for a better job and had to move one hour away from the home, he made it really difficult for me to see them. He made the children believe that I was abandoning them and tried to turn them against me. But I'm glad I made the move, because I needed the space to sort things out."

Goyen is quick to add that she does not believe that primary custody should automatically go to the woman. The man to whom she is married today received sole custody of his three daughters after his own divorce. "What is interesting is comparing his situation and mine. There are similarities and differences," she says. "Brad is a good father and got custody for the right reasons. He actually raised his children, and he was the parent primarily involved with them during the marriage."

While Cynde Goyen and her ex-husband still have unresolved differences, he gradually stopped denying her visitation and has allowed the children to spend longer periods with her. Her oldest son eventually came to live with her and her new family. Even so, she worries about her children's upbringing and her ex-husband's influence on them: "Men who are good parents should absolutely have the equal right to get custody of their children, like Brad. But some men are misusing their rights and seeking custody for the wrong reasons. This isn't fair to anyone, especially the children."

Professional Custody Evaluation

When parents are unable to agree on custody issues, or when they request an unusual arrangement, a judge, a mediator, or the parents themselves may decide to hire a mental health professional to conduct a custody evaluation. In many jurisdictions, courts maintain a list of neutral mental health professionals with the required qualifications. If parents cannot agree on whom to hire, the court will appoint someone from its bank of experts. When parents can work together to choose a neutral professional, courts generally accept any candidate who meets the state's criteria for custody evaluators.

The evaluator usually begins by meeting with the children and parents. He or she may also speak with other important people in the child's life such as grandparents, potential stepparents, babysitters, and teachers. Another source that should not be overlooked is close friends of the child, who often have insights into the child's feelings and thoughts that are not shared with adults. The evaluator may also visit the homes and workplaces of the parents and may conduct various psychological tests on the parents and on the child.

While a parents may be tempted to recite a litany of the other parent's faults, this is not the focus of the professional's assessment and may even be detrimental. Rather, the evaluator will pay the most attention to the relationship between that parent and the child, and to each individual's parenting contributions and skills. Parents hoping to impress an evaluator should concentrate on demonstrating an ability to provide a positive, stable living environment; qualified supervision for the child while the parent is not at home; nourishing food and adequate clothing; sensible discipline; and strong, genuine affection. The quality of education that the child will receive is becoming increasingly important in custody determinations as well. Of course, if there has been abuse or other serious wrongdoing by the other parent, this should be brought to the professional's attention, but any display of unwarranted hostility toward the other parent is likely to be viewed as a negative factor.

The findings of the evaluator can be used in various ways. Generally, a report including custody recommendations is prepared for the judge. A highly qualified professional who completes a comprehensive evaluation at the behest of the court may sometimes testify as an expert witness. Those who conduct more limited examinations are often made available as fact witnesses who offer information on their findings but do not state an expert opinion as to what custody arrangement would be best. The recommendations of such experts may be helpful outside the courtroom, too, in private settlement negotiations or mediation. In any context, the professional evaluation is usually far more valuable if the person conducting it is neutral—that is, appointed by the court or agreed on by both parents.

Custody Modification

Broadly speaking, child custody arrangements may be modified when one party shows that "changed circumstances"—whether economic, logistical, or otherwise—make an adjustment necessary to serve the best interest of the child. While judges are reluctant to bounce children around through frequent switches of custody and visitation arrangements, a child's life can change a lot in three or four years. It isn't unusual for custody or visitation arrangements to be modified as a child gets older and becomes involved in different activities. Naturally, such changes are more easily accomplished if the parents can communicate amicably and remain focused on the needs of the child. Judges have been known to chastise parties who rush into court without first making a conscientious effort to work it out with the other parent, as well as those who come to court too often. Some states limit both how often someone may seek modification and on what grounds. In Illinois, for example, if less than two years has gone by since the time of the divorce, the parent seeking to change custody or visitation rights must prove a substantial change in circumstances.

To avoid frequent bickering over the details of a custody arrangement, the initial order should be thorough, precise, and carefully thought out. While flexibility is a plus, specificity also has a place. I once read a custody decree that stated the father was to pick up his son from school several evenings a week and then return him to the mother's home at 8:00 p.m., but on Wednesday nights he could return the boy later, so the child could watch the end of his favorite television show. Such items may seem trivial but can be an important part of maintaining some stability and continuity in a child's routine. Documenting these fine points in no uncertain terms prevents the kind of petty disputes between parents that can escalate into a battle royal.

Parents who have taken extraordinary steps to spend time with their children, such as moving or rearranging a work schedule, make a strong impression on judges and their professional advisers. A willingness to have a mental health professional monitor any change and periodically report to the court, especially in a potentially difficult situation such as a fifty-fifty living arrangement, can also score points with a judge.

Family attorney David Riggert believes that a lot of postdecree problems derive from a failure to address all of the issues at the time of the divorce. "People need to ask their attorney to formulate a plan that will keep them out of court, so they can avoid the trauma and expense of constant litigation."

Working Mothers and a Catch-22

As a general rule, judges are given broad discretion in the area of child custody decisions. While most do their best to apply appropriate criteria to reach a decision that is both fair to the parents and in the child's best interest, some let their inappropriate biases creep into the process.

Divorcing mothers often find themselves in an impossible fix: Under today's no-fault law and preference for rehabilitative alimony, women are expected to support themselves after a divorce and, in most cases, to provide the bulk of the support for their children as well. Women who work full-time, though, especially those who place their children in day care in order to further their careers or education, may be vulnerable to change or even loss of custody for following the very course the law says they must. Author Erica Jong has described custody suits as "my generation's cruel and usual punishment for daring motherhood and a career at the same time."

An example is the highly publicized 1994 case of Jennifer Ireland, a Michigan mother who lost custody of her young daughter after she placed the child in day care while she attended university classes. The father worked, but his mother volunteered to look after the child during the day. The trial court awarded custody to the father, and the mother appealed. The Ireland case dragged on through more than four years of protracted litigation, including an appeal to the Michigan Supreme Court. By the time the case reached that level, the court of appeals had overturned the trial court's award of custody to the child's father, and the supreme court affirmed this decision. It emphasized that the parties had been found to be equally qualified as parents on all but one of the factors listed in the Michigan statutes that courts must consider in a child custody case—"permanence, as a family unit, of the proposed custodial home." It said that the trial court had incorrectly found in favor of the father on that factor. Jennifer Ireland was in college, and the court had focused on the likelihood that she would move and make other changes in her life when she completed her education. In comparison, Steven Smith, the father, lived with his parents and had no definite plans for his future. The Michigan Supreme Court acknowledged that the father's situation could arguably be characterized as the stabler for the moment, but it added, "It would be ironic, indeed, if the uncertainty of Mr. Smith's plans regarding education, employment, and the early years of adulthood worked to his benefit." It remanded the case back to the trial court for still more litigation, admonishing the court to weigh all the facts that bear on whether the mother or father could provide the child a greater sense of permanence. After another protracted trial, the parties finally reached a settlement.

Some working mothers have found that a reluctance to remarry may be seen as a strike against them in a custody dispute. Nicky Whelan was devastated when the court shifted primary custody of her son to her ex-husband because, she believes, she was single, working, and living in a small, two-bedroom townhouse, while he was remarried and could offer the child a larger home. "I was found guilty of committing single motherhood," she says. "Imagine what the courts would be telling me if I was on welfare. I didn't even receive child support when my son lived with me. I have a bachelor's degree, I have a full-time job, and I volunteer in my community. I am, however, single and below average in pay. After nine years, the judge changed custody because my ex-husband lives at an address the judge considered preferable, and he is married. I call it the 'fungible mother theory'—the notion that one 'mother,' or stepmother, will do as well as another."

Whelan saw an ironic flip side to her situation, as well: "The psychologist that was brought into our custody battle let me know that if I were to find a man, she would reconsider her custody recommendations. Not only is this idea that I should 'find a man, any man' in order to be a good mother outrageous, but also it ignores the reality of being a single parent. In our culture, the growing pressure on women to support themselves and their children leaves little time to build a real relationship. Yet, when I did not take her suggestion and find a man, I paid the stiffest of penalties: a judge took away custody of my child."

Fathers and Legal Bias

Over the past twenty years, the law has almost universally adopted the idea that fathers and mothers should have equal rights to custody of their children. For example, the controversial "tender years doctrine," a presumption that gave marked preference to mothers in custody disputes involving young children, has now, at least in theory, been rendered defunct. As of 2002, there were approximately 2.2 million divorced fathers with primary custody, constituting about one-sixth of the single parents in America—up from around one-ninth in 1970. In most states, any gender preference in custody cases is prohibited by statute. Yet parents of both genders still encounter unfair stereotypes far too often.

"Fathers should have rights fully equal to those of the mother," says attorney Judith Finfrock. "Children need fathers as role models, and this is as important for daughters as it is for sons. Psychological studies show that daughters learn the level of respect and care they should expect in their relationships with men from observing the way their fathers treat their mothers. So, it's essential that parents maintain a civil, respectful relationship after the divorce and that fathers set a good example for their daughters to observe. For the same reason, fathers who are abusive to a child's mother should not be allowed to influence the child until they clean up their act."

While fathers are faring better in custody matters, Neanderthal attitudes nevertheless persist. In one New York case, a female judge refused to allow a father to keep his infant child overnight because she assumed he would not know how to take care of a baby. Consequently, there has been a growing movement by fathers seeking better laws, fairer custody and visitation determinations in the courts, and public support for the rights and responsibilities of single male parents. Many organizations have been founded to assist divorced fathers (see Appendix A).

What does all this mean? It means that pockets of gender bias still exist in too many courtrooms. Parents of both sexes who are unable to work out custody arrangements on their own should get expert legal representation if any custody dispute arises. The lawyer should be not only well versed in the nuts and bolts of the law but also very familiar with all local judges who could be assigned to the case.

Sexual Orientation and Child Custody

Unfortunately, some courts still consider sexual orientation as a factor of parenting fitness in determining custody issues. In 1995, the Virginia Supreme Court ruled that a lesbian mother was unfit because her gay relationship would bring a burden of social condemnation on her child, and it granted custody of the child to his grandmother. However, other states have developed laws specifically prohibiting consideration of a parent's sexual preference in determining parental suitability or child custody.

While the cases are still all over the board, sexual orientation is no longer considered an automatic reason to deny primary custody in most courts. Also, an increasing number of attorneys specialize in the rights of gay individuals.

In most places today, parents are free to live their private lives as they see fit, as long as the child is not directly harmed. Any sexual behavior between consenting adults will usually not affect custody, unless it is flaunted in front of the child.

Child Support

Unlike spousal support, child support is mandatory in nearly all cases, until the child reaches the age of majority, generally eighteen or twenty-one. A few states are changing their laws to require that child support be paid until graduation from college. The amount of support a court orders depends on state guidelines, how custody is arranged, and the earnings of both parents. Child support orders are always subject to later modification as the circumstances of the parents and children change.

State Support Guidelines

In 1988, Congress passed the Family Support Act, which required all states to adopt a uniform, statewide formula to set child support payments. All states now have guidelines written into their child support laws that estimate the basic expense of raising a child and determine how much support will be paid by the parent who does not have primary physical custody. The guidelines are essentially based on the income of both parents and how much time the child spends in the custody and care of each. These guidelines are considered just that—guidelines—and not mandates. Courts will look at other factors such as the individual needs of the children, alternative plans proposed by the parents, and new children to be supported. Some states apply different formulas depending on custody arrangements or other factors.

In most jurisdictions, couples may depart from these standards if they mutually agree to do so. However, a judge has to review and approve all custody and support agreements to verify that the child's needs will be met, especially if the amount set by the couple is below that recommended by the guidelines. Both parents have a legal obligation to support the child, so an agreement for zero child support will seldom, if ever, be approved. While child support has no tax consequences in that it is neither deductible to the payer nor taxable to the recipient, custody arrangements generally state who gets to take the dependent deduction for the child.

Child support may take other forms besides monetary payments. "Indirect support" refers to items or services a parent purchases directly for the child. If these expenditures add up to a significant sum, they may offset the amount of child support owed (for example, when the non custodial parent starts paying private school tuition or buys the child a piano). In states that don't allow for payment of college tuition as child support after the child turns eighteen, parents may agree in a private contract to extend payments. If their agreement is properly drafted, it can be enforced in court like any other contract. In some jurisdictions, the family court presiding over the original parenting plan and child support order can enforce the agreement if it is filed and made an order of the court.

Child Support Enforcement

In the 1980s it was estimated that only 58 percent of single-parent households had current child support orders in place and that, of these families, only half received the support due. In response to this national crisis, state, federal, and local governments initiated various efforts to make parents take financial responsibility for their children.

Under the federal Family Support Act, all child support orders must include an automatic wage withholding provision. If the employer of the noncustodial parent receives a copy of the court order, a portion of that parent's pay will be withheld and sent directly to the custodial parent. Other income such as Social Security may also be withheld and sent directly to the custodial parent by using the court order. Payments do not have to be late before wage withholding can begin, and an employer must follow this method for any child support order if the payer is one month late.

States have various laws and methods to deal with child support enforcement when parents don't pay. Parents who are self-employed must sometimes pay a state's child support enforcement agency directly. The agency then pays the custodial parent. That way, the agency can monitor payments and take steps to enforce them if any are missed. In other states, a court trustee or clerk collects payment from the noncustodial parent and pays the custodial parent. This allows the same court that issued the order to monitor payment. In 1996, the U.S. Postal Service announced that it would coordinate with states to assist in the identification and apprehension of deadbeat parents by displaying "Wanted Lists" in post offices of parents who had failed to pay child support.

Parents who refuse to pay may also be denied passports. An innovative program established in Racine, Wisconsin, gives deadbeat parents two choices: go to the county jail or get a job, keep it, and pay child support. The program assists the parents in finding work and developing the skills to keep the job. Child support payments are automatically deducted from paychecks.

Courts, too, are taking a harsher stance toward those who refuse to pay child support, in particular repeat offenders. Judges will not hesitate to issue such tools as writs of seizure to impound and sell businesses or tools of trade. Filing for bankruptcy will not get a person off the hook for child support, nor for alimony, taxes, or mortgage payments. Even imprisonment may not end the obligation to make support payments. The same applies to youth: sixteen-year-old fathers have been ordered to pay child support. In Massachusetts, a person who does not pay child support faces losing professional or business licenses and even a driver's license.

The U.S. Department of Health and Human Services' Office of Child Support Enforcement, a federal agency serving all fifty states through regional offices, oversees various efforts to enforce child support orders (see Appendix A). In addition, all states have agencies to help collect overdue child support, locate parents, get child support orders established, garnish wages and tax refunds, set up automatic deductions from paychecks, obtain liens against property, and file reports (on those who owe more than $1,000) to credit bureaus. State and local agencies often work in conjunction with the federal Office of Child Support Enforcement to track the whereabouts of missing parents.

Welfare reform legislation signed by President Clinton in 1996 included strong new measures against noncustodial parents who fail to pay the support they owe. The law added tough penalties to those already available, including driver's license revocation and seizure of many more types of assets. The legislation also recognizes the importance to children of having access to the noncustodial parent.

To assist in this effort, the Child Support Enforcement (CSE) program is a federal/state partnership that promotes family self-sufficiency by securing regular and timely child support payments. State CSE programs locate missing parents, establish paternity, set and enforce support orders, and collect payments. CSE services are available automatically for families receiving assistance under the Temporary Assistance for Needy Families programs and to other families who apply for the services. During fiscal 1996, an estimated $12 billion in child support payments was collected, and paternity was established for a million children. Almost 1.1 million new child support orders were established in fiscal 1995. Income tax refunds, lottery winnings, retirement benefits, real estate, and other property of nonpaying parents may be seized or encumbered by lien to satisfy unpaid child support.

The "teeth" provided by this law have proved sharply effective at the state level as well. In New Mexico, for example, child support payments collected by the state's Human Services Department increased by 27 percent in a single month after the state revoked the driver's licenses of nearly 11,000 people who had failed to pay child support and had not responded to a six-week amnesty program that gave parents an option to pay what they owed before the penalties were invoked. The message is clear: parents must assume responsibility for the support of their children, or else they'll suffer serious consequences. State offices involved with this program are listed in Appendix B.

In 2001, Congress passed a new law called the UIFSA (Uniform Interstate Family Support Act) to make the nationwide child support system even stronger. This new act includes more expansive long-arm jurisdiction and relaxed rules of evidence, so that most interstate child support cases can now be heard in one court, in one state. It embodies a policy of "one order, one time, one place," so that the state that issues the controlling order retains continuing, exclusive jurisdiction over the case. That way, any child support modification requests will be heard in this court as well, subject to some exceptions. Additionally, the federal Child Support Recovery Act now makes it a federal crime not to pay court-ordered child support.

The Internet is an entryway to a variety of resources to assist both individuals and agencies seeking to enforce child support orders. The federal Office of Child Support Enforcement maintains a website that links to the website of each state, as well as providing forms, reports, and handbooks. The site offers general information applicable to all cases, as well as specialized information on military, tribal, and international laws affecting child support enforcement.

Most states have a long statute of limitations so that parents may collect back support at any time, including after the child reaches majority, even allowing a suit for back support to be brought ten to twenty years after payment became due. If a parent is required to sue for back support, interest may also be collected at the statutory rate, which is frequently higher than current market rates.

Child Support Modification

Child support orders or agreements can always be modified by the court that entered or approved the original order. Parents who reach their own agreement simply file a written document reflecting the change with the court. Unless the judge believes that the change may harm the child, the agreement will generally be approved and incorporated into a new court order. (Remember, parents can and often do change their custody or support arrangements informally, but if the court is to enforce the agreement, the documentation must be in the court file.) When only one parent wants a modification, he or she must request that the court make the alteration and show "changed circumstances."

The following changed circumstances may justify lowered child support by the noncustodial parent: a legitimate and substantial decrease in income; a reasonable increase in expenses such as a new child in the home; a windfall by the custodial parent; or a decrease in the cost required to cover the child's needs (for example, both parents agreed to take the child out of private school). Similarly, for a custodial parent, support may be increased if he or she can show either a substantial decrease in income; increased expenses such as another child; a windfall by the noncustodial parent; or increased expenses to cover the child's needs. Specific criteria vary by state. Laws in many states are becoming more specific as to what qualifies as an appropriate change in circumstances to increase or decrease child support; many now provide that a new spouse's income cannot be considered.

Most people agree that anyone who accepts the responsibility of parenting a child must be held accountable for the child's financial support. Beyond that level lies an area with conflicting realities and no easy answers. With serial marriages and blended families becoming increasingly common, many parents are daunted by the financial obligations of supporting children from both former and current relationships.

The key to reaching a workable solution—and avoiding huge debts and severe penalties—is communication with the other parent and the court. Parents who cannot meet their support obligations will have a much better chance of fair, favorable treatment by the court if they take the initiative to request a reduction in monthly support payments and keep paying something each month, even if they can't pay the full amount.

Family attorney David Riggert has found that a yearly review of finances and support can be an effective mechanism for avoiding litigation over child support. "An agreement can be drafted in which parents volunteer to exchange information once or twice a year and then complete their own analysis of that information by a certain date. Then, another period is provided within which the parents must come to a decision if they want to request any changes," he explains. "If neither asks for a modification, the whole thing flips over to the next year. In this way, couples can negotiate a fair compromise and take the results of what they decide to their attorneys, who can draft an order for the judge to sign."

This type of agreement can be especially useful if a change in current salary or another aspect of the present situation is anticipated by one or both parents. "In this community, there is a Mitsubishi manufacturing plant that is one of the largest employers in the area," Riggert comments. "They often change their production line based on marketing trends. One year, an employee may work a great deal of overtime, and then the next year, the overtime stops and his or her income drops by as much as a third. The judges in our community have to deal with this in support modification agreements all the time. If parents know that something like this is expected to happen, it can be dealt with in advance."

How to divide uninsured medical expenses is another question that is often ignored when the couple or judge formulates a final decree, and it's one that Riggert frequently encounters in his practice. He advises that the parenting plan specify how these costs are to be handled.

Beyond the Child Support Guidelines

In trying to establish a support plan that can work for a period of years, it is important to consider factors beyond the state guidelines. People often disregard the everyday details and uncommon expenses that can throw a budget into disarray. Judy Lawrence, a budgeting counselor and author of several books on financial planning (see the "Resources and Suggested Readings" section), notes that people involved in a divorce often don't take the time to look at the real, total cost of living, especially children's expenses. Although calculating the expenses of very young children may be straightforward enough, the older a child gets, the more complex such planning becomes.

In Lawrence's experience, most parents readily identify such costs as tuition, day care, orthodontia, and karate lessons, but a complete profile requires a much more detail-oriented approach. She reviews with her clients each of the child's school programs, sports, hobbies, lessons, and general activities and then figures out all the expenses entailed by each activity. Also added are school-related expenses such as yearbooks, class rings, photos, uniforms, accessories for proms and homecoming, and graduation gifts. Many extracurricular activities carry hidden expenses such as entry fees, banquets, and equipment that parents typically don't anticipate in assessing the cost of participation. Even if the expenses do not occur every month, Lawrence urges parents to calculate a monthly average, which may be substantial. Parents need to have an accurate projection of the expenses in order to plan how to meet them and avoid having to take the child out of cherished and worthwhile activities.

Parents Who Misuse Support

Another encumbrance to enforcing child support is the sad fact that custodial parents occasionally misuse the money they receive. Tom Murphy is the devoted father of two girls. He has never missed a child support payment in the twelve years since his divorce, and he has been generous in providing extra benefits and gifts for his daughters. All the while, he has been continually frustrated by his ex-wife's refusal to abide by the terms of the custody and support agreement, combined with constant demands for more money.

"I kept up my end of the bargain, but she didn't," he declares. "For instance, I agreed to pay extra at the time of the divorce so the girls could have a private parochial education; I later found out that she was using the tuition money for other things, mostly to benefit her rather than our daughters. Child support should be viewed as child support, specifically for the good of the children, not another source of income to be spent any way you please. She used the money for herself, on summer cottages and vacations with her boyfriend, while the girls did without. I had to buy them things such as gym shoes and glasses on my own, in addition to paying child support, if I wanted to be sure they got what they needed. I would advise anyone in a similar situation to keep very careful records, including receipts and accounts for everything bought directly for the children." Such expenditures, as mentioned earlier, are sometimes called "indirect support," and if the parent can prove the sums spent were significant, the court may offset support that is due to even things out.

Parenting Through—and After—the Divorce

Even under the best of circumstances, divorce makes children afraid and anxious. They lose their sense of security and protection. While parents often see the divorce as primarily occurring between themselves, children perceive it as something happening to them. They see the family splitting apart and their own identities changing. Many states have modified their laws to impose constraints on divorce or require a longer waiting period when minor children are involved, in an effort to lower the rate of divorce among couples with children. The motive behind such efforts is noble, but it's debatable whether they actually promote stronger families or only prolong the pain of families trying to end an unworkable situation.

One certainty is that it is not the divorce itself, but rather exposure to hostility between the parents, that is most damaging to children. Study after study has shown that one of the worst things children can experience is ongoing conflict between the parents, whether before or after a divorce. In a home where argument and discord define the prevailing atmosphere, it is far better for children if the parents split, provided the end of the marriage results in the end of the fighting. One woman, whose parents divorced when she was in high school, remarks, "It was really upsetting when my parents divorced, but it's worse to grow up in a home filled with constant conflict. I think it would have been easier if my parents had split when I was younger, because there would have been fewer years of conflict overall."

The lesson, to put it both harshly and simply, is that conflict between parents absolutely must be defused. If parents can't do it on their own, they need the expertise of a mediator, therapist, coach, or other professional. As one psychologist stated, when parents in a high-conflict divorce cannot find a way to put their anger aside, and insist upon bringing their children into the conflict, they are abdicating one of the primary parental duties—protecting the children from harm.

Parenting with an Ex

Coping with, or even acknowledging, the fact that you must maintain a continuing relationship with someone you want only to vanquish from your sight can be agonizing. Attorney Judith Finfrock is surprised at how many of her clients with children have no concept of the relationship they will need to carry on with the other parent after the divorce. "People come in, for example, with two children, aged nine and seven. When I tell them they will have to deal with their husband or wife for the next ten or eleven years, they are shocked. They thought they could just eliminate this person from their lives."

Some enlightened parents who utterly hate each other but nevertheless love their children have used a unique type of couples counseling, which has proved effective in helping them to establish a civil, businesslike relationship. This type of assistance is becoming more common and is often available through marriage counselors, mediators, or family therapists. In some places, court-annexed clinics offer communication classes for divorcing parents. With help, most people can become proficient co-parents who can get along at least well enough to deal with the essential interactions without overt unpleasantness.

Psychologist Constance Ahrons, author of *The Good Divorce*, stresses the benefit of maintaining a "limited partnership" when couples with children divorce. She urges parents who have trouble communicating or cooperating after a divorce to look for common ground and to try to keep sight of mutual goals for the children. Sometimes this calls for setting limits and stating boundaries in an explicit manner, all the more when the balance of power between the parents is unequal or a subject of struggle. Counseling or mediation can help parents who clash to establish a cooperative arrangement. As Ahrons states, "A good divorce does not require that parents share child care responsibilities equally. It means they share them clearly. Whatever living arrangements and division of responsibilities parents decide on, they cooperate within those limits."

Parents who manage to build a child-centered, cooperative relationship may even discover that they can enjoy their children's achievements together. Career counselor Kathy Potter and her former husband were committed to keeping the focus on their mutual love for their children, and they remained friends after they divorced. "We would go to the kids' soccer matches together, and people thought that was strange," she remarks. "But we both care about them, and we will always have that in common, so why not?"

When Exes Just Can't Get Along

When parents absolutely cannot be civil to one another—or when one parent poses a danger to the other—solutions can still be reached that allow the child to have a relationship with the noncustodial parent. In many communities, there are drop-off locations where parents may exchange children in a safe, nonthreatening environment, such as the YWCA or YMCA. Some communities have places such as the Neutral Corner, in Albuquerque, specifically for this purpose. These locations are becoming more common. Some also provide space for supervised visitation, when the court has made such an order. Your local family court office or clinic can refer you to such resources in your community.

Child Abduction

According to statistics produced by the U.S. Justice Department in 2002, more than 200,000 children were kidnapped by family members during 1999 alone. The most common reason for such abductions is that a person feels that a custody decision was unfair or wants to avoid becoming further embroiled in a custody dispute and decides to take the law into his or her own hands. Sometimes desperate parents view a custody battle as too risky, too expensive, or too time consuming. Some blame the legal system as contributing to the problem by its cost, inflexibility, and inability to address the emotional issues involved.

An earlier Justice Department study, commissioned by the department's Office of Juvenile Justice and Delinquency Prevention, found that most children abducted by family members were back home in a week or less. Still, even a brief abduction can cause anguish and terror for both the parent and the abducted child, who may suffer long-term emotional trauma. When a child is abducted and forced to live on the run for a longer period, the trauma can be severe.

Many parents who kidnap their children believe they are justified. They feel they were forced into doing so by a system that denied them their rights or by a spouse who deliberately isolated the children and prevented them from maintaining contact. Often they have an idyllic fantasy of creating a perfect new life with a child who will adjust easily, freed from the former spouse once and for all. Needless to say, this is virtually never the case.

In the past, there might have been some legal basis for such high hopes. When the parents lived in different jurisdictions, and one parent brought the child into the area where he or she lived, judges felt obligated to hold a custody hearing to protect the rights of the citizens they served. Many sincere judges believed they had a duty to fully investigate the welfare of a child brought into their jurisdiction, even if another court had already held a full custody hearing. Today, all states have adopted some form of the Uniform Child Custody Jurisdiction Act, which was designed to eliminate such incidents. The act requires courts to defer to legally binding custody orders from another court in a different jurisdiction.

Recently, increasing attention has been given to the plight of all kidnapped children, including those abducted by family members. Both greater media coverage of individual stories and broader social concern overall have made finding missing children somewhat more likely. Numerous organizations exist to help locate missing children (see Appendix A). Most children who disappear are eventually located.

Penalties for Child Abduction. The penalties faced by a kidnapping parent vary from state to state. Nearly all states now have their own laws, in addition to the Uniform Child Custody Jurisdiction Act, making child abduction a felony. Federal legislation went into effect in 1988 to enforce the Hague Convention on International Child Abduction, a treaty that set up a system to be followed by member countries to guarantee the prompt return of children taken across international boundaries. This law, called the International Child Abduction Remedies Act, is aimed at reducing international child snatching. If a parent takes a child into a country that is not a signatory to the law, the other parent's remedies may depend on the justice available in that nation.

A parent who abducts a child may be subject to serious criminal penalties, such as charges of felonious concealment, as well as a civil lawsuit by the other parent to recover legal fees and expenses for locating and recovering custody of the child. In one international case that required more than four years of effort to locate a child abducted from Spain by his American father, the mother won a civil judgment for her legal and investigative fees to locate her son, which totaled more than $76,000.

Anyone who conspires to assist in a child kidnapping, such as a grandparent or another family member, can also be subject to civil and criminal penalties. Those who assist indirectly may suffer consequences as well. In 1983, the Donahue Television Production

Company was ordered by a court to pay $5.9 million in damages to a mother whose child had been kidnapped by the father. The father had appeared, in disguise, on the "Donahue" show while an employee of the company babysat the little boy backstage. The mother happened to be watching the program and sued the company for assisting in the criminal behavior of the father.

Resources and Support. Numerous individuals and organizations continue to fight child abduction, including the Office of Children's Issues, Overseas Citizens' Services (a division of the U.S. State Department Bureau of Consular Affairs), in Washington, D.C., and the National Center for Missing and Exploited Children, in Arlington, Virginia (see Appendix A). The center also provides advice to parents on how to help prevent a kidnapping, such as emphasizing to children how much they are loved no matter what anyone else may try to tell them, and teaching children how to telephone them or someone else who is close to them, both locally and long-distance directly or as a collect call. It also advises parents to notify schools and day care centers about custody and visitation arrangements and to keep basic information regarding the spouse, such as Social Security number, passport number, automobile information, and bank account numbers, in the event it is ever needed by law enforcement authorities.

Also, parents should keep an up-to-date written description of each child, with photographs taken at least every six months. Under the Federal Missing Children Act, parents can register descriptions of missing children into the FBI's National Crime Information Center (NCIC) database, even if no crime has been charged. Furthermore, many local organizations sponsor fingerprinting, identification cards, and other programs designed to help keep children safe and locate them if they are abducted.

The Internet has developed into an exceptionally valuable tool in locating abducted children. The National Center for Missing and Exploited Children, the nation's largest private agency devoted to locating missing kids, has an outstanding website that posts photos, acts as a clearinghouse for information, and provides additional resources for parents, law enforcement, and others seeking to locate children. Additionally, the NCIC helps law enforcement agencies share information to locate children.

If you believe your spouse or someone else might have abducted your child, you can turn to many sources of help, which are increasing in both number and efficiency all the time. Begin by contacting your local law enforcement agency. Make sure that both a child abduction report and missing person report are filed and that they will be entered on the NCIC files. Also contact the National Center and your local district attorney or state's attorney (prosecutor's) office; many have special units to help locate missing children. Also check your telephone directory or the Internet to see if there is a local agency, such as Los Angeles's Find the Children, that can help. With the rapid growth of information-sharing technology, more tools to locate missing children are assisting in more happy endings than ever before.

Many parents want nothing more to do with a former spouse and feel that nothing good can come of continued contact between their ex and their children—sometimes with good reason. Remember, however, that concealing or keeping a child away from another parent who has a legal right to see the child under a custody or visitation order (or before such an order has been entered) is both a crime and a sure way to incur the wrath of the court. Of course, there are exceptions to the general rule when a parent reasonably believes that the other poses a danger to the child, but these are narrow. If you fear for your child's safety, it is best to contact an attorney, law enforcement, the district attorney's office, a social services agency, or another source of expert advice before you take steps to deny access to the child.

Final Thoughts from a Family Court Judge

When parents quarrel over their children or criticize each other in the presence of the kids, children receive the subtle message that they must choose between the parents, picking one to love and the other to reject. Judge Anne Kass has compared such parental behavior to the movie *Sophie's Choice*. Sophie, the mother of two small children, was sent to a Nazi concentration camp. An especially cruel soldier told her she had to pick one child to live; the other would die. When she replied that she could not choose between her children, the soldier said that if she didn't, she would lose both. So Sophie made a choice and suffered lifelong anguish as a result. Her life after the war becomes aimless, nonproductive, and alcoholic.

Judge Kass says that parents often force their children into a similar decision that may be nearly as painful. Sometimes the message is blatant, as when a parent makes a child tell the judge which parent he or she wishes to live with. In others, it's subtler, with one parent moping or acting annoyed when the child tries to enjoy the company of the other parent. "Divorcing parents need to know that the most loving gift each parent can give their children is permission for them to love—and accept love from—the other parent," Kass adds.

When parents battle over custody, they often do not give their children this permission and may eventually force them to make "Sophie's choice." Says Kass, "These children often self-destruct, as Sophie did in the movie. Theirs is the lifelong anguish of being denied what should truly be an inalienable right—the right to love both parents."

7

The Emotional Challenges of Divorce

EVEN THE MOST amicable divorce is seldom entirely painless. Society still places heavy pressure on everyone to be a part of the perfect, happy, stereotypical family: Mom, Dad, and 2.5 kids securely nestled in their home with the white picket fence. This ideal is held up as a symbol of personal success, and those who do not meet it often feel a sense of failure. "I never felt like a loser because I got divorced," one man remarked, "but I definitely felt like I had stepped out of the winner's circle."

In reality, only about 10 percent of American families today fit the traditional mold, and nearly 50 percent of all marriages eventually end in divorce. Given the obvious shift in society, the children of tomorrow are likely to feel less pressure to achieve this supposed norm as they grow up surrounded by many versions of the secure and successful family. But for most people now old enough to be contemplating divorce, the stigma remains, in particular when a comfortable, familiar role is traded for one that is not only new but awkward to boot. "I was no longer among those the fictional heroine Bridget Jones called the 'smug marrieds,'" one woman said. "Now I have a better idea of how she felt as the only single in a group where everyone else is paired off and being single is seen as an affliction."

All humans harbor a population of resident demons, and divorce brings them out at their most sinister. Grief is unavoidable. There are messy emotions. There is fury, rage, and anger of a degree that truly can be called madness. Both the partner who leaves and the one who is left—and even those who mutually and amicably agree to part company—will suffer on some level, though the form and timing of their torments may differ. No one gets out unscathed. People who have survived war, disabling injury, disease, terrorist attacks, and all manner of tragedy have been heard to remark that their divorce was the worst thing they had ever been through—and yet they made it.

Erica Jong, in her memoir *Fear of Fifty*, described an experience that many find typical: "What happens when your partner and best friend becomes your enemy? You scream and hang up the phone in the middle of the night, throw yourself at cars and at men, drink too much, sue and get sued, discharging money—and rage. You can't skip all that—even though it seems so useless at the time. Unlike childbirth, it only ends in emptiness. As with war, you are happy simply to come out alive."

Despite the trauma that inevitably accompanies the transition from married to single again, numerous studies of divorced people have shown that the vast majority are happier after the divorce or, at least see that, in retrospect, it was the right decision. As those who study human behavior and development learn more about the progression of the human life cycle, it is becoming clear that stable people with strong values may simply change from stage to stage in life. People are living much longer than they used to, and it is increasingly considered a normal option for people to have several careers, as well as several mates, over the course of their existence.

Making the Decision to Divorce

Deciding whether to end a marriage that is no longer working is the first and often the most agonizing step in the divorce process—and many people spend years waffling before they make a final decision. Contrary to what many people believe, most American divorces occur after seven or more years of marriage. Nearly one-third of people divorcing have been married fifteen or more years.

By this time, the people in a marriage have formed strong habits, identities, patterns, and emotions associated with the marriage. Even if they are terribly unhappy and divorce ultimately proves to be the right choice, changing these patterns results in upheaval and requires a great deal of personal adjustment.

This does not mean that divorce should not occur. On the contrary, most mental health professionals believe that the pain and misery of a divorce is much less detrimental than the damage of remaining in an unhealthy, miserable union. What it does mean is that the decision to divorce should not be made lightly or in haste, and that it is better to get a realistic picture and make preparations for life as a single person rather than expect either automatic bliss or inevitable devastation as soon as the divorce papers are signed.

It is not unheard of for one spouse to ask the other for a divorce when what he or she is really asking for is major changes and improvements in the marriage. For many people, this overture leads to marriage counseling or similar professional intervention. Janice Parker, for instance, had been growing increasingly unhappy in her marriage over a period of nearly ten years, but whenever she tried to discuss her feelings with her husband, Bill, he tuned her out or discounted her concerns. She finally hired a lawyer to prepare divorce papers, with every intent of ending the marriage. When she presented them to Bill, he immediately heralded the wake-up call and committed himself to doing everything within his power to save the relationship. He proposed counseling, and Janice agreed. With the intervention of their therapist, both made adjustments in the way they communicated and worked with each other to address their problems. Six years later, the marriage remains on solid ground, and both partners are convinced it will last a lifetime.

For couples like Janice and Bill, who are uncertain, counseling is often the most sensible first step, whether it restores the marriage or not. Some discover that miscommunication, extreme stress from outside factors, or other solvable problems distorted their perception, leading them to believe that the marriage was to blame for their unhappiness. Therapy may help them see that the marriage is still supported by a foundation of love, mutual respect, equality, friendship, and a shared desire to rebuild the joy that was there in better times. For others, counseling clarifies what one or both suspected: that the marriage is not salvageable, and the kindest result is to end it.

Counseling can be of use in rebuilding a marriage only if both partners truly want to try to forge a new relationship, are willing to accept some responsibility for the problems, are prepared to work to change behaviors that are detrimental to the marriage, and can put aside anger and misunderstanding to make a good-faith effort to save the marriage. If one partner resists counseling and is determined to leave or participates half-heartedly, expecting failure, this can be an indication that the marriage is already over. Divorce is determined not by the signing of the final decree, but by the certainty in the heart and mind of one or both partners that the bond that formed the marriage is gone.

"The hardest part of getting a divorce is making the decision," says counselor Kathryn Lang. "People waver back and forth before the final conclusion, and many start going through the steps of grieving even before the decision is made." Lang, a licensed professional mental health counselor, works with many people who are at various stages in the divorce process.

Many people are surprised to learn that the decision to divorce commonly takes several years. According to Lang, two to three years of uncertainty before making the decision to divorce is about average. "People barter, bargain, and make excuses to avoid coming to the final decision. For someone who has been married before, the process is somewhat easier in the second marriage, simply because you've been down the road before. Often, the process that leads up to the decision to divorce is not even conscious," Lang explains. "Something is a catalyst, and then the person starts thinking about what he or she can do and can't do. Once one person or the other decides to leave the marriage, the nuts and bolts of the decision start to fall into place."

Lang emphasizes that while the process of coming to a decision to divorce can be painful, the amount of time invested can have a significant effect on the person's future emotional state. "It's best to be sure you have no doubts before you leave. Some people leave a marriage without thinking things through and find that they have traded one set of problems for another. You don't want to look back and say, 'If only we tried counseling, if I'd been more assertive, if we had tried harder to communicate.' If you have doubts, try these things first. Don't leave before taking away all of the 'what ifs.' Otherwise, you'll be beating yourself up over your uncertainty, along with everything else divorced people have to experience."

Noting that single life is not easy, Lang favors proceeding with caution: "I'm more apt to counsel people who aren't sure about a divorce to try to work it out, to recognize their own issues, as opposed to blaming the spouse for everything that is making them unhappy. First, I advise them to look at how they could change their own lives. For some, there is nothing they can do, and they know then that divorce is the right choice. If you can look back and say, 'I did everything I could,' then you'll know that divorce was the right thing to do."

Even when a person has given the divorce careful consideration and determined that it is the only reasonable choice, it is still tough on everyone involved, she contends. "When you get divorced, your life is displaced," she says. "This is especially true for the person who leaves the home. The one who retains the home, usually the woman, keeps some familiar structure. In a new home, everything is new. It's especially helpful if children can stay in the home they know."

Lang also says that things go a bit more smoothly when the decision to divorce is unanimous, but she acknowledges that this is seldom the fact. Both parties in a divorce go through a grieving process, even the person who makes the decision to leave. "The one who files for the divorce often feels an initial sense of freedom and elation but will usually go through an emotional transition about six months later. If you have someone else waiting in the wings or begin dating someone right away, this can prevent the grieving process or delay it, which only makes it more grueling and painful in the long run. I believe that you don't go through this essential process unless you spend some time alone. You don't get a real feel for the pain you need to work through. Everyone needs to come to terms with aloneness, to learn to be a one before you can be a two. You need that time to learn who you are."

Divorce and the Emotional Roller Coaster

Many men and women have described the period during and after a divorce as an "emotional roller coaster," and it's hard to imagine a more accurate term. It would be a fine thing to deftly complete the legalities of a divorce and walk away unruffled, but this is rarely how it happens. Nearly everyone experiencing a divorce feels some combination of shock, elation, misery, and confusion. These emotions occur at different times in different people, sometimes in perplexing combinations.

Emotional upheaval during divorce is to be expected, with the degree of severity depending on the individual. "People walk a fine line between being sane and insane during a divorce," Lang explains. "Most people feel fragile, like a china doll that would shatter if you touched it too hard. The emotional roller coaster is universal. There are, inevitably, a lot of ups and downs." Lang, who is now remarried, went through a divorce as the mother of two young daughters. She relates, "I was shocked by the feelings I had. I consider myself an extremely stable person. Not much shakes me. But divorce shakes everybody severely. I honestly had no idea what people felt until I went through it myself. Now I have a much greater appreciation for the pain that both people suffer."

When you make the decision to leave your marriage, you may have a clear conception of why it is ending or only a vague certainty that, due to some combination of factors, the marriage can no longer work. No matter what the perspective, the actual act of separation is always a discomforting and emotionally charged episode. In the book *Divorcing*, psychologist Mel Krantzler identifies "seven deadly emotions" that can turn the decision to separate into a nightmare. They are fear, guilt, self-pity, failure, anger, self-flagellation, and hatred of the spouse. Krantzler warns that these emotions may overwhelm a person.

Adding to the confusion, these emotions commonly erupt in combinations that seem to be directly conflicting. For example, hatred toward your spouse may bring about guilt for feeling that way. The key is to understand that such feelings are normal and not let them paralyze or control you so that you are impeded from making good decisions. The fact that such threatening, complex emotions prevail helps to explain why many people get stuck and cannot come to terms with feelings of failure, bitterness, and anger for years after the divorce has technically ended. This is why most professionals, as well as laypeople who have been through a divorce, recommend some form of professional counseling during this tough transition.

Krantzler emphasizes that no emotions are inherently good or bad; they all should be seen as signals alerting you to insights about yourself. He stresses that his "seven deadly emotions" inevitably appear in some form during the early stages of any divorce and are a natural part of mourning the death of a relationship with a person who was, at one time, the most important adult in your life. What can make them deadly is if you attach yourself to them rather than letting them go. If this happens, they can stunt your life permanently. So if you can't move forward on your own, get assistance. Remember, it is the strong person who seeks out counseling, rather than the weak one.

Counseling and Therapy

Genevieve Clapp, author of *Divorce and New Beginnings*, believes that those who are the most devastated at the breakup often recover more quickly and completely. This phenomenon may be due in part to the willingness of people who are in extreme emotional pain to seek professional help. According to counselor Kathryn Lang, different types of mental health counseling, or combinations of types, work for different people. "Individual therapy is usually more important at the beginning," she says. "Many people need to heal on their own first, to take time to recover from their anger and pain. Then group therapy can be very helpful. There are different types of divorce adjustment groups and divorce recovery groups available; but many people right out of a divorce are too angry, emotional, and self-absorbed to benefit from the group process. They can't see beyond themselves. Also, different types of therapy work for different people. Some of my patients, especially older women, find it hard to be in a recovery group. They may be ashamed that their marriage ended. Others, especially those who are deeply religious, believe that marriage was supposed to be for life. They simply are not comfortable sharing their feelings in a group, at least not until they have had some individual help first."

Stephen Feher, Ph.D., is a family psychologist whose practice has focused extensively on couples trying to work on their marriage or come to a decision about divorcing. Feher concurs that the emotional reactions to divorce vary by individual. "The absolute worst comes out in people," he also notes. "Many of us don't deal with conflict well. We put things aside over and over; then divorce opens the floodgate to all those things that haven't been dealt with over the years. Tremendous anger, bitterness, self-doubt, grief, loss, and depression often pour out."

Feher believes that while some people are able to reach a well-reasoned decision to leave a marriage and carry out the necessary steps to end it and move ahead on their own, some form of therapy is helpful for most. "It's a painful process for most people," he says. "A few come to a decision and know it's right, and they don't really have any problem with it. But especially when there are children, it's difficult not to have a divorce that's troubling in significant ways. It requires a major adjustment in identity for everyone involved. It's like a fabric that's been woven together: you can't just take the scissors and cut out a piece and expect what's left to be whole; you have to pull out the threads one by one and weave a new tapestry from them."

Feher emphasizes that different types of mental health services work for different people and that a variety of programs are available, he points out. "There is individual therapy, couples therapy, and groups or seminars. The main thing is to talk to others who are going through or have gone through the same thing and had similar feelings and experiences, and to get some objective input."

Some people Feher has counseled did not realize they were facing unresolved problems until long after what appeared to be an amicable divorce. As Feher recounts, "Denial and repression are common in a divorce. People push their feelings aside, but the feelings don't just go away. I worked with one couple who did very well for five years after the divorce, worked together as parents, and were friendly enough that they had lunch together on a regular basis. Then, out of the blue, everything hit the fan. It seemed they had been pushing things down the whole time, ignoring negative feelings in their efforts to have a good relationship."

Feelings may often become confused, with unfamiliar emotions coming out as anger, for example. "So many people are able to express only a few emotions. They feel powerless and help-less—they have a sense that they can't do anything about what is happening to them—and these feelings manifest as anger. This sometimes happens when people believe they were treated badly by the court system, especially in custody matters. They feel helpless against a system that can affect their lives in such a big way, and it manifests as extreme anger," he states.

One of the main goals of the therapy process is releasing blame. Feher observes, "As long as the couple keeps blaming each other, they will stay stuck. They need to look at themselves, too. The place to get to is forgiveness—of others and of themselves." Reaching this point, he says, takes time. "You can't just jump into it. There's a rejection factor that makes divorce, in some ways, harder to cope with than the death of a loved one. For children, especially, it takes a long time to come to terms. They see the parent as not wanting to be with the family or with them. Death and divorce are both tumultuous, and there's a grieving process for both."

Looking back years later, Jane Foster, who was introduced in Chapter 3, values the importance of both personal and professional support for anyone going through a trying divorce. "I've always made sure I had good friends in my life, and their support was absolutely essential," she says. "I was seeing a counselor too, who told me about the stages of grief and pain I could expect to experience. At first I told her, 'No—that won't happen to me.' But everyone goes through it. Naturally, you don't want to endure pain, conflict, and bad decisions, but you can't avoid it. At least if you know what to expect, then you can remind yourself that you're normal—there's nothing wrong with you. Absolutely everyone should get some kind of counseling, group therapy, or other outside support."

Feher is concerned that sources of mental health assistance for people and families at lower socioeconomic levels are diminishing in some areas. He recommends that people with limited resources talk to clergy, if they have a religious affiliation, or contact a local hospital with a mental health department, many of which operate referral services. Feher says, "I would strongly advise anyone in distress during a divorce to keep trying until they find some professional support. There are agencies that provide services on a sliding scale according to income. Friends and relatives are important, but they're not enough. You need to look at what's going on within yourself as well, with the help of a more objective person. Most people need to find some resource they can utilize, before they really get over it."

Professionals also caution that some sources purporting to help actually do more harm than good. "There are some bad therapists out there who only contribute to the hostility and pain of a divorce," mediator Roberta Beyer says. Avoid anyone who tells you that the divorce is all your fault, that you are a failure, that you just need to work harder on the marriage, that you should fight harder against your spouse, or, especially, that you should accept unkind or abusive treatment.

When Help Becomes Essential. While the emotional roller coaster is perfectly normal, up to a point, beware if it appears to be reeling out of control. One danger sign to watch for in yourself or your children is a persistent sense of hopelessness. People who feel this way are at the greatest risk for suicide, either directly or indirectly through high-risk, self-destructive behavior. If you notice hopelessness, ongoing depression, or persistent lack of caring about yourself and your future, or if you go so far as to seriously consider hurting yourself or someone else, seek professional counseling immediately. Every county has an emergency mental health service provider.

Self-destructive behaviors that serve as a red flag for serious problems may appear abruptly, or may creep slowly. Be wary if you notice your own behavior changing in negative ways, such as increased drinking or drug use, sexual promiscuity, overeating or undereating, workaholism, or extreme expression or suppression of emotions. Also monitor any changes in your physical health. People suffering from the stress of the divorce may experience symptoms ranging from headaches and lethargy to serious physical illness. Your medical doctor can help you attend to your physical health as well as recommend counseling or therapy.

Common Feelings During the Divorce

Kathryn Lang describes some familiar feelings that anyone in a divorce is likely to encounter: "Both people participate in a divorce, so there is often anger at yourself that you allowed it to happen. Anger, grief, depression, crying episodes, remorse, panic, and anxiety attacks are common symptoms."

Lang explains how these emotions are logically related to the context of a divorce. "For example, anxiety is tied to specific future fears. People are afraid they will be alone for the rest of their lives, which is a big reason many people don't leave unhappy marriages in the first place," she says. "Those with low self-esteem may think an unhappy marriage is all they deserve. This is especially true for somebody who is left by his or her spouse. They often feel rejected, whereas the person who initiates the divorce will feel empowered and experience an initial high for six months or so. But eventually, that person too will go through an emotional crash." She recalls, "When I left my first marriage after fifteen years, I was walking on air. I felt unchained after being trapped, like I could finally do whatever I pleased. Then about six months later, the depression hit. There was no looking back or questioning my decision, but I still had to go through the grief of this ending."

In addition to the stark, raw pain that characterizes nearly every divorce, many people either experience severe guilt, in which they feel solely responsible for the divorce, or heap all the blame on their partner, believing he or she is entirely responsible. Seldom does either of these extreme perspectives reflect the truth. Of course, there are exceptions, as when one partner has been abusive to the other. In most situations, however, it takes two to make a divorce, just as it takes two to make a marriage.

The emergence of no-fault divorce has led to the easing of much of the hostility that occurred between spouses when one, "the winner," had to prove the other was a bad person, a "loser." Many psychologists believe, however, that the emotional realities of divorce remain essentially the same. Psychologist Mel Krantzler, who has written extensively on divorce and founded one of the first divorce-recovery seminar programs in the early 1970s, observes that certain psychological reactions to divorce are universal and transcend nations, cultures, and social differences.

Krantzler reports that he sees virtually every client, male and female, experiencing many of the same feelings he went through during his own divorce. Fear is one such universal emotion, since even those well equipped for single life are up against change and uncertainty. Divorcing parents always suffer anguish over the upheaval they are causing in the lives of their children and worry about how the relationship with them will continue. A sense of failure, or perhaps that the marriage was a mistake, is also nearly universal.

Krantzler and other psychologists emphasize that people in the midst of the divorce not only need to accept that such feelings are normal but also need to forgive themselves and look at the divorce as a learning experience leading to a better future, rather than a personal failure. They also must realize that every marriage that eventually ends in divorce was not a "mistake." Most involved a wonderful, healthy, positive relationship for at least a part of their duration. "It would help every divorced person to realize that because a marriage doesn't last a lifetime, it doesn't mean it was a failure," says mediator and divorced mother Frances Webb. "How could you conceive of a twenty-year marriage that produced two beautiful, happy kids who are doing just great as a failure? Every couple should be able to look back at what they achieved and say to each other, 'Didn't we do good?' "

It is entirely normal to feel overwhelmed during a divorce, even if everything else in your life is running smoothly. If other problems crop up, as they often do, involving family, health, work, or money, it may seem utterly impossible to cope with all the chaos. Remind yourself that it can be done, and people do it successfully every day. This, too, shall pass. "After my divorce, I realized that for the first time in my life, it was all up to me," said one woman who had gone straight from her parents' home to living with her husband. "If the car broke down, the money ran short, or the sink backed up, I was the one who had to deal with it. And so I did. Now that I know that I can cope with whatever comes my way, I have a new sense of strength. While I'd always considered myself a resilient and capable person, now I have proof."

Depression. Clinical depression is common among people going through the divorce process. Almost everyone feels blue or bereft at some point along the way. But if your spirits don't eventually lift or, worse, continue to plummet, you may need professional assistance. The symptoms of depression, as well as the disease itself, can be debilitating. However, many forms of effective treatment are available today, and depression can be successfully managed in most instances by counseling, medication, or a combination of both.

In his practice, psychologist Steven Feher has seen many people suffering from depression during a divorce. "It's very common," he says. "There are many types of depression, and divorce often brings on reactive or exogenous depression. This type of depression can occur due to some circumstance or situation in a person's life that affects the brain in a way that causes the symptoms. Fortunately, this kind of depression is generally temporary and responds well to treatment, with the best treatment often combining therapy and medication." As a clinical psychologist, Feher cannot prescribe medication, but he can refer patients to a psychiatrist or their own physicians for recommended drugs.

Finding help takes on greater import when symptoms of depression don't go away. "Sadness and grief are normal, but people have to assess their symptoms, which can be hard with clinical depression," Feher says. "It's an insidious illness, because it attacks our sense of self. Notice that people don't say, 'I have depression'; they say, 'I am depressed.' This tells a lot about the nature of the problem."

Feher advises those who don't seem to be progressing to be on the alert for symptoms that can indicate serious depression. Common maladies include loss of energy, change in sleep patterns, withdrawal, isolation from others, changes in eating habits, an inability to enjoy things that used to give you pleasure, and waking up too early and not being able to go back to sleep.

Nearly everyone suffering from depression has trouble sleeping. Difficulty in maintaining concentration, impaired reasoning, and a limited attention span are also experienced by many people. The trouble brought on by these symptoms can be magnified when you need to be functioning at an even higher level than usual, in order to cope with your everyday duties as well as the added stress and responsibility of dealing with the divorce. "Depression is especially problematic during the divorce process, because people have to make extremely important decisions," says Feher. "Yet, at the same time, the inability to make decisions is a characteristic of depression. Intense emotions cloud judgment. And the pressures that come to bear to make good decisions are immense. People feel as if they're in a pressure cooker—the stress is horrible. They're being asked to make decisions that will have an impact for years to come, under circumstances that are not conducive to decision making. People must get the help they need and do whatever it takes to get clear with their situation and overcome the symptoms so that they are making good decisions, instead of letting the symptoms make decisions for them."

It is important to seek treatment for depression right away. Some people start with their medical physician, while others look to a psychologist, psychiatrist, or other mental health professional. Often, the two professions will work together, with the physician providing medication and a counselor conducting therapy.

Some people are hesitant to use antidepressant drugs, either out of fear of becoming dependent or because they see medication as a sign of weakness. Others are concerned that drugs may mask the symptoms that need to be dealt with in therapy. Nevertheless, drugs can be valuable aids that are safe when administered and monitored by a physician, and many people suffering from depression have found them to be, quite literally, lifesavers. Most therapists emphasize that drugs are best used on a short-term basis in combination with counseling to address the underlying causes of the depression.

Stress. Divorce can also bring on severe stress. Not only is this an emotionally miserable condition, but also it can lead to physical disorders. Headaches, abdominal problems, chest pains, dizziness, and other symptoms may be caused by stress, or they can signal a more severe physical problem. These symptoms should not be ignored. Anytime you suffer from recurrent or serious physical symptoms, you should see your physician and tell him or her everything that is happening in your life. If you do have a serious health problem, this will need to be taken into consideration as you structure a divorce settlement and plan for your new life.

Most stress-related problems can be treated successfully by medication, counseling, changes in lifestyle and diet, or some combination of approaches. In a divorce, many of the outside factors contributing to stress will disappear eventually—and keeping this knowledge at the forefront can help ease the anxiety. But life is full of the changes and frustrations that produce stress, and it is valuable to learn skills for coping with stress both in the present and in the future. Professionals say that such simple actions as having a good cry, practicing deep-breathing techniques, getting physical exercise (especially outdoors), and writing in a journal can help appreciably.

Lorraine Parker, D.C., a chiropractor and nutritionist who teaches classes in stress management, explains that certain physiological reactions occur when a person experiences stress from either positive or negative changes in life: "People are surprised to learn that the body goes through the same reactions when a person gets married, gets divorced, experiences a birth or death in the family, or wins or loses a million dollars. Stress is not a thing; it is a process that happens inside the body because of an outside influence, which can be perceived as either negative or positive. The body doesn't differentiate."

The physiological reaction to stress involves the entire body. "It's a throwback to cave people," Parker says. "At the time modern humans were developing, people would encounter something such as a wild animal and have to prepare to either fight or flee. They would follow through with one behavior or the other, expending tremendous physical energy. Afterward, they were exhausted and would sleep for a long time and then awake restored."

In the 1970s, Dr. Hans Selye identified the steps that occur in the body in response to a "fight-or-flight" reaction. "The adrenal glands release hormones, heartbeat increases, muscles tense, digestion slows, breathing changes, blood flows to the extremities, and the blood clotting mechanism becomes more active," Parker explains. "In primitive societies, these physical reactions served an important purpose for survival, and people nearly always went through the usual steps of fight-or-flee and rest that we're programmed to follow. But in modern society, we can't go through these steps because we need to maintain our lives according to the norms and practices of today. This tension builds, but we don't get the opportunity to expend the energy and then rest and recuperate. Plus, primitive people faced this reaction on only an occasional basis. People today encounter stressful situations that can trigger the fight-or-flight reaction up to twenty times a day."

Single parents may repeat this process even more often. "For example, a mother may have to get the children up and ready for school, and then rush to drop them off, and then fight traffic to get herself to work, deal with the pressures and stresses of the job, and then the child support check doesn't come. People under these circumstances don't have the opportunity or take the time to react to the stress. It would be healthiest to drop everything and run around the block a few times, but instead, we keep the energy all inside," Parker remarks. "This causes enormous wear and tear on the body. In my stress management classes, I use a rubber band as an example: Stretch it a little at a time, farther and farther, until it's stretched out to the maximum. Then when you let it go, it flies around the room, in the same way people can fly off the handle."

Parker also notes that while the outside factors that can trigger stress change all the time, the internal reaction is always the same. "Stress is caused by changes or frustrations in life, and divorce is full of both," she says. "The people who suffer the most from stress are those who feel they have no control over their situations. Some people are surprised to find that it is not so much the high-powered executives who get severely stressed as it is their secretaries. The executive can go to the secretary with a report he has been mulling over all night and say, 'I need this typed in an hour.' But the secretary has no control and has to accomplish a lot of work under high pressure. People going through a divorce often feel a similar loss of control over their circumstances," she points out.

Tips for Managing the Stress of a Divorce. Parker emphasizes that exercise and good nutrition are imperative for people in stressful situations. "Exercise is important both psychologically and physiologically," she says. "It's important to dissipate that buildup of energy from the fight-or-flight response so it doesn't stay in the body and cause physical wear and tear. Therefore, everyone needs to find a physical outlet. It's essential for good health."

Additionally, she explains, "High stress compromises the immune system. As stress accumulates, white blood cells and other immune system cells don't function as well to protect the body. This increases the likelihood of illness, just at a time when people can least afford or cope with being sick. It doesn't mean that a catastrophe is inevitable; it simply means that people need to be more diligent about caring for their health. This includes eating balanced amounts of protein and complex carbohydrates, and avoiding excessive junk food. Rewards and treats are good in moderation—if I couldn't have cheesecake or Häagen-Dazs ice cream once in a while, there would be no point in living! But the key is moderation. It may be tempting to eat a whole pint of ice cream instead of dinner, but this can really set a person up for problems. Plus, eating a lot of sugar causes that familiar sugar rush that can make you feel flighty and irritable. This can add to the sensations that are already there with stress and can aggravate the negative feelings that people are trying to avoid."

People facing stress from a particular source, such as a divorce, can benefit greatly from a regular dialogue with people enduring similar challenges. "Support groups can help deal with the problem head-on," Parker remarks. "It helps a lot to discuss your feelings with those who have experienced the same thing. Support groups can be very worthwhile for kids, too. There are groups of different sizes and formats—prayer groups, classes, all types of programs to help people learn to cope with their stress. And that's the key. You can't avoid stress; it happens in a situation such as divorce. But you can develop positive coping mechanisms. Some people turn to negative coping tools, such as alcohol, drugs, escaping into excessive television, or overeating. It's important to channel the stress energy into more positive directions. This can also give a person a sense of gaining control over his or her life—something that really helps when you're going through a divorce."

Parker also advocates exploring new hobbies and activities, provided they are not related to daily work activities, which may contribute to the overall accumulation of stress. "For example, I wouldn't advise a person in the computer field to take a computer-related class—I would suggest a class in something like painting or swimming. People need to think about something else, to get a respite from the rest of their life." She emphasizes that a wealth of opportunities to learn new hobbies and skills, as well as classes specifically addressing stress management, are available in most communities today: "I teach a stress management class through a continuing education program at the local university. Some corporations offer stress management programs for employees, as do hospitals and HMOs." She also points out that many books and self-help programs offer assistance. Simple day-to-day activities such as journal writing can be therapeutic as well. "Writing gets feelings out," she explains. "Also, meditation and other simple relaxation techniques can be easy, free, and effective tools to reduce stress. These activities quiet the mind. Just as with stress, relaxation is cumulative. Tapes for guided relaxation are available in most bookstores."

Don't forget the positive effect of enjoying simple pleasures. Parker says, "Buy yourself flowers or something else that makes you smile. Do something silly. People don't play enough anymore. Taking a few moments to pet a cat or dog can be calming. Anything pleasant and simple can break the tension of the moment. I keep a jar of bubbles from the dime store—the kind that comes with a little wand—on my desk. When I start to get overwhelmed, I just sit back and blow bubbles for a few minutes. One of the best ways to relax when you have a little more time is to take a long, warm bath, with candles and a glass of wine. There are many simple and inexpensive ways to deal with the stress that we all have to bear. It's often just a matter of getting into the habit of doing this for yourself, but it's really essential. It's a major part of taking care of your health."

Also remember that you're not required to be perfect. None of us behaves ideally all of the time, even when life is running smoothly. "You have to realize that it's OK not to be 100 percent all of the time when you're going through this," says Becky Ralston, reflecting on the difficult time after her divorce several years ago. Perfectionism breeds stress, and it is particularly detrimental to set unrealistic standards for yourself during an unavoidably tough period.

"Tend and Befriend." While both men and women initially react to acute stress with the "fight-or-flight" response, recent research suggests that women (typical of female creatures of other species) move on to a second phase, in which they form alliances with others to protect their offspring and take advantage of the safety provided by a group. This "tend-and-befriend" reaction, a phrase coined by UCLA researcher Shelley Taylor, Ph.D., who studied the phenomenon, may be the result of different hormones produced by women versus men in response to stress.

In modern life, this means that women under stress frequently nurture themselves and their children, and talk or socialize with their friends to relieve tension. Men who are under stress, particularly during a divorce in which they detach from familiar ties, may be more likely to continue to "flee" their stress and may therefore be subject to a greater risk for isolation and loneliness.

Mental health professionals counsel men and women to seek the support of friends and family when experiencing severe stress—and divorce certainly qualifies. If you have lost touch with people important to you, reconnect. With the advent of e-mail and the ubiquitous cell phone, keeping in contact is easier than ever today. If you need to build a new network of friends, get out and meet people, even if you have to push yourself to do so. Check out a club or another organization that sponsors group activities you enjoy. Even hobbies that you pursued only as a solo or couple—such as hiking—can be enjoyed with others. Reconnecting with humanity is both healing and enjoyable. Perhaps the words of English metaphysical poet George Herbert say it best: "Living well is the best revenge."

Avoid the Siege Mentality During the Divorce

Couples trying to reach a divorce settlement often get stuck on one or more issues of custody, property, or support. Sometimes couples enter into a siege mentality in which one or both will become entrenched and refuse to budge, often over something seemingly trivial. This sticking point is actually a symbol of the battle for emotional control, a desire to hurt the other party, or an attempt to cover up sadness with anger and blame.

This type of stalemate never accomplishes anything positive. Results of the siege can range from mild irritation to ludicrous posturing to heartbreaking tragedy. Sometimes both people refuse to leave the family home and draw literal battle lines to mark territory. Others become embroiled in elaborate, destructive vendettas, as in the movie *The War of the Roses*. The film was a satire, but it scarcely exaggerated the warfare that some couples wage and the degree of destruction that can result. When custody is the sticking point, the innocent victims suffer the most.

While there are few universal truths in matters as individually varied and emotionally charged as a divorce, virtually everyone, including those who have been through a divorce, agrees that hostile and vituperative behavior toward the other party accomplishes nothing good. This does not mean that you should not be assertive and insist on your rights to a fair property settlement and good custody arrangements, as well as reasonable support if required. Assertive does not mean aggressive, though. Calm, persistent, mature behavior by both lawyer and client encourages a favorable outcome in any type of legal case, far more than anger and bitterness.

Renowned trial attorney Melvin Belli, himself divorced four times, states in his book *Divorcing,* "As a general principle, the way you act toward your ex-spouse will determine whether or not you will be scarred with hate and vengefulness or feel renewed as a better person, and this is something you should be seriously concerned about."

Based on his personal and legal experience, Belli advises clients, especially those with children, to cool their anger and never let it show in front of the children. Instead, they must reassure the children that both parents still love them and will continue to have a regular relationship with them.

Substance Abuse and Divorce

It is undeniable that alcoholism and drug abuse play major roles in the demise of many marriages. The stress of divorce also may lead those who tend to overindulge in alcohol or drugs to lean more heavily on a convenient chemical crutch. If you are concerned that you may be misusing intoxicants, talk to a private counselor or someone from a group such as Alcoholics Anonymous for information, assessment, and help (see Appendix A).

Self-Help Resources and Support Groups

Those who do not feel that they need or want to seek therapy or counseling, or who simply wish to do some solo work on personal growth, can avail themselves of a vast array of self-help resources. These include DVDs, books, hotlines/help lines, informative pamphlets, websites, live or online discussion groups, classes, magazines, and newsletters. Live groups and support organizations such as Parents Without Partners have the added benefit of providing new social contacts and often host social events for participants.

Self-help groups can be conducive to sharing feelings, experiences, and solutions to problems. On the other hand, therapists caution that self-help groups without a trained leader sometimes deteriorate into blaming and complaint fests, which can make participants feel worse. "Groups need to be facilitated by someone who can help the participants work through what they're feeling and move beyond where they are stuck," says counselor and former group facilitator Kathy Potter. "They are a great place to share both emotional issues and practical information."

More support groups for people coping with divorce are cropping up all over the country, as well as online. Some focus on one particular stage of the divorce process, such as recovery afterward, or on one issue, such as parental custody rights. Others deal with a broader range of topics at all stages. As divorce has become more common, some schools and churches have formed adjustment groups for children.

Group seminars often address topics as diverse as communication skills, anger management, intimacy, self-esteem, trust, friendship, self-discovery, stress, health, grief, forgiveness, sexuality, living single, letting go of old patterns, freedom, fear, and parenting. Many place heavy emphasis on learning to build healthy new relationships.

Information on groups available in your area can be found through local help and information hotlines, the Internet, mental health organizations, churches and synagogues, attorneys, counselors, college catalogs, and ads or community information bulletin boards in the local newspaper. Some of the organizations listed in Appendix A make referrals to local affiliates. Others provide materials and assistance to people wishing to start a self-help group.

Life Coaches. The last few years have seen a boom in the field of "life coaching," including the advent of coaches who specialize in divorce and related issues. Analogous to coaches who guide teams or individuals in sports, coaches in other fields provide strategies, game plans, pep talks, and other forms of advocacy to help individuals achieve a goal or make a transition. Specialized divorce coaches help their clients cope with the emotional side of divorce, clarify their options, make informed decisions, build communication skills, and move through the process to formulate a plan of action for the future. They may also help the client rebuild a support network or gather a team of other professional advisers. Some assist with investigation, asset location, financial evaluation, or other specialized issues. In some instances, coaches work with attorneys to help negotiate settlements, act as liaisons between parents in settling custody or support issues, or serve as sounding boards when clients simply need to vent. However, coaches do not take the place of lawyers, mediators, or therapists unless they also possess those credentials.

Divorce coaches may be especially helpful when one partner feels he or she is powerless or at a disadvantage in the process, or when parents are experiencing a high level of conflict but remain committed to their children. Some coaches specialize in particular issues or phases of the divorce process, or its aftermath. Stepfamily coaches are even available in some areas of the country.

Coping with Divorce Through Spirituality

Religious faith or other forms of spiritual foundation can be one of the most important sources of comfort and stability for a person facing any major life trauma. Until fairly recently, many religious groups forbade or condemned divorce. A few still do, in varying degrees. A few fundamentalist sects still prohibit their members from divorcing except when one spouse has committed adultery, and counsel even those in a violent marriage to stay. However, most churches today have a more enlightened and humane point of view, and many now offer divorce recovery assistance through counseling, workshops, group sessions, and self-help materials. As counselor Kathryn Lang observes, "There are good counseling programs through various churches, focused on both saving marriages and helping people whose marriages end. The Catholic Church has a program called 'The Beginning Experience' for people who are at least one year out of a divorce or the death of a spouse. This group sponsors weekend retreats, which can be extremely valuable and healing."

In fact, religious congregations and organizations are often at the forefront in helping families cope with divorce and begin healing. Many provide direct counseling services, as well as more indirect help through discussion groups and classes, in an atmosphere that encourages spiritual growth. Most open their doors to all who wish to participate in these services, regardless of membership or faith.

The Importance of Ritual

Rituals have been followed throughout history to symbolize major transitions: to highlight the exit from one phase of life and the entrance into another, and to provide reassurance to the person facing a difficult change that it is a normal part of life. While modern society has abandoned many of the ceremonies that were once common in nearly all cultures to mark an important life passages, we still follow social customs to celebrate birth, marriage, and graduation, to observe holidays, and to mourn death. Other rituals survive to a lesser extent, such as housewarming and retirement parties.

Unfortunately, there are no established rituals to mark either divorce or the beginning of a new family after the structure of the family has changed. Many people report feeling bereft or a sense of letdown. "No rites of passage exist to help mourn the losses, to help healing, to help solidify newly acquired roles. Entire sections of greeting card stores are given over to reminding couples and those around them that it is time to celebrate another year of togetherness, but only a few stores offer cards designed to cheer up those who have parted ways," Constance Ahrons points out in *The Good Divorce.*

Perhaps part of the reason for the lack of attention to this extremely important transition is the discomfort and uncertain feelings that usually accompany the news of a divorce. I have often asked acquaintances who told me they had been divorced whether

I should say "Congratulations" or "I'm sorry." Responses varied, but many people said, "Both." Divorce is, if nothing else, a situation in which some ambiguity and mixture of feelings are almost inevitable.

Many therapists who attempt to help people heal after divorce believe that ritual can be a crucial part of the process. Ahrons states, "I'd like to see us get to a time when a parting ritual for divorce is part of our culture." There does appear to be a growing trend, as divorce becomes more common throughout the world, to mark the occasion, not with mourning but with the recognition that it is a meaningful life passage that can lead to positive new beginnings.

There are many creative ways to survive divorce and heal through personal ritual. M. Carol Curtis, whose husband always cooked her a special dinner on her birthday, revived the tradition by re-creating the event with her daughter. She also held a "wake" on her wedding anniversary. She lit incense and candles, put on music from the era, and donned clothing from the time of her marriage. The fact that the clothes no longer fit comfortably, she says, added to the theme: "For me, this was a good physical reminder that many aspects of the marriage and the old life were restrictive and did not fit the new me."

Ritual and Recovery: One Woman's Story. Rituals may be in the form of a shared ceremony or of a private event. Lynn Peters, a jeweler and the owner of a graphic design company, came up with a unique idea several years ago when she noticed her old wedding band collecting dust in a drawer. She now runs a business called Freedom Rings: Jewelry for the Divorced. "The idea came from my own divorce," she explains. "The ring sat in the drawer for three years. One day, I realized what a waste it was—I should recycle it." She decided to invite a group of friends to join her in a ceremony to smash the old ring, which she would then fashion into a new piece of jewelry.

Thus a tradition was born, complete with humorous yet encouraging words, supportive friends, and champagne to celebrate the new beginning. Peters was so transformed by her own experience that she decided to offer the same ceremony to others. Her clients gather with friends and then smash the ring with a sledgehammer on an anvil. The ceremony prepares the ring for meltdown into a new design to be created by Peters, and the participants generally exorcise a few emotional demons in the process.

Levity and laughter are invariably a part of the event, but Peters is quick to disabuse those who accuse her of trivializing divorce. "It's a fun way of dealing with a serious issue," she explains. "The humor is very healing, and the jewelry becomes a symbol of recovery, confidence, and feeling good about being single. Some clients say a few words of their own before the ceremony, and sometimes there are tears. But in the end, the focus is always on making a fresh start with a positive outlook."

Clayta Spear was an early client. She recalls, "I still had both wedding rings five years after the divorce when I saw Lynn on television in an interview about her business, called Freedom Rings. I knew instantly that was what I wanted to do with them." She describes what transpired: "Going through the Freedom Rings ceremony with my friends present was really an experience. It provided a ritual that was therapeutic for me and the opportunity to do something creative with my anger and sadness. I wanted to turn it into something positive, entirely new and beautiful. We designed a pendant using the gold from both rings and a pearl from the Philippines. The rings and the pearl represented the two most dramatic and important times in my life, and I love the final product—it's an original, and people always notice it."

Recovery Takes Time

Even the most amicable divorce will have unpleasant aspects and leave a residue of hurt over everyone involved—partners, children, and those who care about them. Still, in almost every case, healing comes sooner or later. Most therapists estimate the time required to recover completely at one and a half to five years. Psychologist Genevieve Clapp, author of *Divorce and New Beginnings*, an excellent book on divorce recovery, states that on the average, it takes people about two years after a divorce before they even feel that they have regained their equilibrium. More time is often required before a person will feel completely detached from the divorce and enjoy a real sense of stability and satisfaction.

Disentangling a family is a complex undertaking that inevitably gives rise to unexpected feelings. Any change in the routines of a household generates stress and upheaval, even when the basic structure of the family remains intact. For those divorcing, the little things, such as the added responsibility of car care or cooking, can be almost as frustrating as the larger changes, such as no longer having daily contact with your children.

The practical aspects of dealing with a divorce—all the ten thousand little chores and papers and details—demand time and patience. Don't let the magnitude of what awaits you leave you paralyzed. Some people are so intimidated that they feel immobilized and can't imagine ever being rid of all the tasks and emotionally trying responsibilities hanging over them. If this happens to you, try to make realistic lists and schedules, rather than contemplating the mountainous responsibilities. Break big tasks down into small steps, and assign yourself a few chores to tick off each day or week. A professional counselor, organizer, or time management consultant may be able to help ease the perceived load. And remember, it's natural to feel flummoxed when virtually all areas of your life are immersed in chaos and change.

The Good News

Constance Ahrons, Ph.D., is a professor of sociology and associate director of the marriage and family therapy program at the University of Southern California. The title of her book *The Good Divorce* may sound like an oxymoron, but Ahrons believes that while no divorce is actually "good," we must accept that divorce is a fact of our society that acts as a safety valve for bad marriages. Nearly everyone seems to agree, particularly if he or she has been through an unpleasant marriage, that the temporary pain of a divorce is more bearable by a long shot than the endless suffering of a bad home life. Ahrons believes that a "good divorce" is one in which couples part without destroying their lives or the lives of those they love, especially the children.

Ahrons was the first social scientist to study normal divorced families. She coined the term "bi-nuclear family" to refer to a family that spans two or more households. Her study included both ex-spouses and the relationship between them, again a first. Ahrons found that the relationship between divorced parents often improves over the years, especially if both people are committed to the loving support of their children. Fortunately, among all those she studied, this group was the largest. And there is every indication that these peace mongers are becoming a silent majority. In 1997, Nailah Shami, of Redmond, Washington, launched the first "National Get Along With Your Ex Month." A newspaper advice column called "The Ex-Files" is cowritten by Jann Blackstone-Ford and her husband's ex-wife, Sharyl Jupe. The two also collaborated on a book entitled *Ex-Etiquette for Parents* (see Resources and Suggested Readings) and maintain a website for step-families called bonusfamilies.com.

According to Ahrons, in a recent study of divorced, middle-aged women, more than half reported feeling better about themselves after the divorce was over. Many also reported an improved relationship with their children. Adolescents in particular can appreciate what their mothers and fathers go through in starting a new life after a divorce and often gain a new admiration for their parents. Attitudes have begun to change, albeit slowly. It is a healthy reflection of our society that most people have come to accept that a family restructured after divorce is much healthier than a family that stays together despite misery, abuse, or general unhappiness in a home.

Looking Ahead to Your New Life

A basic function of therapy is to help people take a realistic look at their lives and future. Counselor Kathryn Lang speaks to this point: "I often ask my patients, 'What's the worst thing about his leaving?' When they say, 'Being alone,' I ask them, 'What's the worst thing about being alone?' People come to see that now when they are alone, they can do something about it and change what they're doing if they want to."

Lang explains that the fear of abandonment and betrayal tend to be universal themes that span the life spectrum. "Marriages are made in the unconscious, and often people who are the most afraid of abandonment or betrayal marry someone who won't give them what they need. Going through a divorce can actually make people become more flexible, learn how to communicate, raise their self-esteem, and, from this vantage point, realize that they overlooked traits that now seem obvious in their mate. They change in positive ways along with the negative changes of the divorce."

Many of her divorced patients feel they have no identity of their own when they leave a marriage. According to Lang, "Many people can't see the future, can't visualize any new partner who would want them. Their perceptions are distorted by the past relationship, especially if they were put down by their former spouse. They can't look at reality as it is now. When people realize they have already been alone for years, by being with a person who is emotionally and sometimes physically unavailable, the light turns on."

Lang believes it is important to reinforce the notion that one parent and children living in a home does constitute a family: "Over and over, I hear clients say, 'We don't have a family now.' People must realize that, yes, one person or two people can be a family. I have to remind people that they don't have to put their lives on hold until another partner comes along. One, two, or three of you can go on and enjoy life on your own. During my own single years, I did plenty of things with my daughters. We traveled through Europe, drove across the United States, and took trips to New York City. Some of my friends were horrified and shocked. They were so unfamiliar with the idea of a woman traveling without a man. They would ask, 'Aren't you afraid?' I told them there was nothing to be afraid of."

Women often have a difficult time shaking this preconceived notion. "I ask them to consider what they want to do in life," says Lang. "Men, to some degree, have different fears. Many are afraid of not being good single fathers, especially if they never took on an active parenting role during the marriage. Yet, some become better fathers after the divorce as a result of this, because they are actually more available to their children," she points out.

Lang agrees with other professionals who contend that the language we use to describe families who have been through a divorce needs to be changed. She proudly describes her own daughters' response when their friends commented that they came from a broken home. "They would say, 'What's broken about us? We're not broken.'"

The Stages of Recovering from Divorce

Over and over, people enduring a divorce and its aftermath are advised to expect the unexpected—especially as applied to the feral realm of human feelings. Emotional upheaval may come at peculiar times, sparked by the most seemingly insignificant occurrence. "I thought I was doing fine. We had been miserable together for a year and a half, and it was a relief when my husband moved out and we started planning the divorce," said one woman. "But when I got the papers in the mail, it really tore me up. I don't know why, but that really got to me." Such reactions are commonplace, and different events trigger different emotions in different individuals.

Many of the same stages that are necessary to mourn the death of a loved one are also necessary to move beyond the grief of the divorce. They encompass protest and denial, often accompanied by physical upheaval; despair, in which you are hit by the reality of what has happened; detachment, in which an apathetic, zombie period makes you isolate yourself from others and simply go through the motions of living; and recovery, in which you become detached from the old self-image of a married person and begin to rebuild your life with a new outlook.

This mourning process is integral to healing. Some people take longer to go through it than others. This is just fine as long as the person does not become fixed in one stage and unable to move on to complete the process. Some people go through all the stages before the divorce is final—in some instances, even before separating from the spouse. For others, especially those who were adamant about escaping the marriage, the painful feelings may not arrive until the initial exhilaration wears off.

Yet, as psychologist Mel Krantzler puts it, divorce can be an adventure instead of a disaster. Krantzler says that from his own experience, he learned that the valuable components of the marriage are not lost after the divorce, but rather become part of the bank of experiences that enable an individual to become a more mature, capable, and wise human being. Divorce, he asserts, is a process rather than a label. He lists four steps in the process:

1. Terror time, involving the initial separation and feelings that life is out of control

2. Mourning time, in which the past marriage is laid to rest in the same way the death of a loved one is mourned
3. Living in the present time, in which each new day is viewed as a challenge, with the best in life yet to come
4. Self-renewal time, the point at which it seems truly possible to survive happily, physically, and emotionally, as a single person

Many people have preconceived notions about when they should "get over" the emotional upheaval that follows a divorce. They have stern talks with themselves on specific dates: "All right, it's been a year now since the decree was entered. It's time to get over this. I'm going to be OK from here on out!" Despite such affirmations, the mourning process can't be rushed, nor is it possible to "get over" something as traumatic as divorce. A more realistic goal is to put the experience into perspective. Unless a person feels mired in one stage and is not moving forward at all, it's best to let it progress naturally. Comparing experiences with others who have been through a divorce can help.

The Family in Transition: Helping Children Cope with the Trauma of Divorce

Although all children suffer stress and anxiety when parents divorce, the experience does not always leave permanent psychological scars. In the book *Divorce Without Victims*, author Stuart Berger, M.D., confirms that two loving parents can help kids survive the trauma of divorce and that, in the process, both parent and child can grow.

The Unique World of a Child

Berger urges parents to realize that each child is a unique individual with his or her own personality and temperament. Because of the stages of child development, children live in a universe different from that inhabited by adults. Understanding the unique perspective of your son or daughter can help you to help the child get through the difficulties of divorce.

Young children two to six years old often have trouble distinguishing between thought and action and may believe that they cause all of the things around them to happen. Berger also believes they may feel an Oedipal rivalry with the same-sex parent and tend to be very egocentric. For this reason, young children need special, repeated reassurance that nothing they did caused the divorce.

Children who are six to twelve still have an exaggerated perception of their effect on the events around them and remain self-centered. This egocentrism persists through adolescence, when it is complicated by the natural rebellion of that age as teenagers don new roles and try new behaviors to discover their own personalities. Stability at home is especially important for kids who are testing the waters of the world outside, so divorce is very threatening to adolescents. Some mental health professionals think adolescents are more likely than any other age-group to suffer problems as a result of their parents' divorce.

Children of all ages often feel that they can take steps to get their parents back together, Berger says. Some even misbehave to encourage contact between the parents. Such fantasies often persist long past the time parents believe the children should have recognized that reconciliation won't happen. However, children tend to react differently to the breakup of a marriage that has been violent. For many, their first preference is to see harmony restored in the home, but departure of the violent parent is the next best alternative. Kids are usually relieved to see the constant terror and tension end.

Berger urges parents to try to avoid any extreme or contrived displays of emotion around children. Unnatural calm or cheerfulness may be confusing when the child knows something is very wrong in the home. It is especially hard for small children to see a parent fall apart or fly off the handle. Controlled expression of honest feelings may be taxing, but it is the best middle ground.

Explaining the Divorce to Children

Berger advises parents to tell their children about the divorce only when the decision is definite, and to tell them together if possible. This approach can be a powerful reinforcement to the child that although the parents are parting, they can still talk to each other and focus on the children. Berger also feels the entire family should be told together, as siblings can often support and help one another.

Berger and other experts stress that kids need constant reassurance that although the parents no longer love each other, both still love the children, and the divorce is not the children's fault. He suggests that parents state the real reason for the divorce, because children can perceive dishonesty, and besides, they may hear the truth elsewhere. Avoid lurid details, and keep the explanation simple and straightforward.

Sometimes children seem to react in peculiar ways to the news that parents will be divorced. Berger assures that such behaviors as disinterest, denial, and other seemingly bizarre reactions are no cause for alarm as long as they do not continue indefinitely. Kids will oftentimes be preoccupied with personal or trivial concerns, such as whether they will still have their own room or still have a birthday party that year. Berger and others who work with children point out that such concerns are not selfish, but rather an attempt to gain some control over the child's world when it is going through a frightening upheaval. Professionals stress the duty of addressing these concerns patiently, as well as dealing with what parents judge to be the more important issues.

Children need to be made aware of the changes that will occur in everyday life, why these changes are taking place, and how the changes will affect them. For example, many mothers who have been able to stay at home or to work part-time or flextime in order to spend more time with the children during the marriage will now be required to work full-time jobs. It is vital to honestly discuss the divorce process and what will happen with all children, including those as young as two. Youngsters usually know if they are being lied to or if information is being hidden from them. Hiding the truth can create anxiety about what is really happening and can cause children to lose faith in parents, which can be devastating.

The question of how much to tell is a stickler, all the more when misconduct by one parent is involved, but most experts advise giving accurate information that's appropriate to the age of the child. Author and counselor Diane Fassel advises parents to answer questions as they arise and to be forthright and not try to control the situation, no matter how sensitive the issues are at bottom. If one parent has abandoned the family, honesty is still the best policy. Berger reassures parents that it is OK to admit to children that they don't know the answer to a given question, such as where the absent parent has gone. The response should emphasize that the behavior of the parent is his or her own problem and was not caused by something the child did, and that the child was wanted and was the product of love.

When the Child's Home Is in Two Places

Some psychologists feel strongly that for a joint custody system to work well, parents must agree on certain consistent rules, especially when the child spends large blocks of time in both homes. Specific household rules may have to vary somewhat, but parents who are willing to put their own discomfort aside in the interest of the child can usually develop and impose a plan governing major expectations, responsibilities, and limitations. If serious problems arise with the child, it's best if the parents can present a clear and united front. Both parents need to remain legitimate authority figures. As always, if there are differences in the rules or expectations in the households, one parent should never belittle the other. Instead, the parent should explain to the child that that's simply how things work when you spend time in more than one home.

Counselor Kathryn Lang agrees that children need boundaries when spending time in two homes. "Kids tend to manipulate and divide the parents when they don't like something one is doing," she says. "Parents need to work together, so that the kids can't take advantage of the conflict between them. Parents need to make it clear that it's OK to have different rules in different homes. Kids simply need to be taught that just because the rules are different at one house, this is not a problem, it's just the way things are. This can actually help kids learn to be flexible."

Lang advises parents to look below the surface to determine the motive behind any major changes in children's behavior: "Parents are often worried when children say they don't want to go to the other parent's home. Often, the child may be trying to spare the parent's feelings, to be the emotional caretaker for that parent. Children frequently exhibit signs of depression, changes in academic performance, and physical aggression in school when their parents are divorcing. One determinant to watch for is how they are doing in their social life—how happy the child is in other settings."

Visitation, Shared Time, and Schedules

Another reason to make communication and cooperation between parents a constant goal is to allow for some flexibility in visitation schedules, particularly as the child gets older and engages in more activities. Even though the parenting plan filed with the court should be specific, it is better for the child if the parents can agree to minor modifications from time to time, especially for one-time occasions such as homecoming, a concert or ballet, or a sports competition.

It can be crushing for a child when a parent fails to arrive for a visit or is repeatedly late, or when the custodial parent sabotages the schedule of the visiting parent. Parents may slip into such habits, consciously or unconsciously, in order to irritate the other parent, but again, the child is the victim. Children may believe that the parent doesn't care about spending time with them or may feel guilty for "causing" an argument between the parents. If visitation schedules are disrupted by legitimate problems, the parent should call the child immediately, explain what happened, and make alternate plans.

It is common for teenagers to want to move back and forth between the homes of divorced parents. Most experts will tell you that it is advantageous to allow the teens to do so, unless there is a problem in one home. Teens have minds of their own and may run away or simply pick up and go to the other parent's house if their wishes are denied. Many parents negotiate a trial period for such changes before filing any official document memorializing the change with the court.

Avoiding the "Disneyland Syndrome." Experts in the field also emphasize the importance of allowing children to spend some unstructured time with the noncustodial parent. Many noncustodial parents feel bad about leaving the child and try to compensate by filling each visit with special activities and events. This "Disneyland Dad" syndrome can be detrimental for several reasons. First, it tends to feel artificial and may prevent the parent and child from focusing on each other. Second, many children today are run ragged by the demands of school, chores, sports, hobbies, and friendships; they may need a low-key weekend to relax and just hang out with the parent, with nothing planned. Third, children are sometimes hesitant to say what activities would truly please them if the parent constantly meets them with a detailed schedule.

It can be beneficial to ask the child if there is anything special he or she would like to do, and perhaps to include some of the child's friends in outings or activities. Small amounts of time, focused on the child and spent comfortably and creatively, seem to mean the most. Think back to moments you remember as special in your own childhood. Attention to the child is everything.

Psychologist Mel Krantzler alerts noncustodial parents to beware of falling victim to a belief that they are bad parents because they are not in their children's lives every day. No one should assume that there is one and only one way to be a good parent. Noncustodial parents can show children that they love and care for them by treating each child as a unique individual and simply devoting the time to learn about his or her life.

Custodial parents, too, often fall into the Disneyland syndrome by trying to buy and do everything for the children. Parents may push themselves beyond the sensible limit in trying to earn enough money to keep up the lifestyle they enjoyed before the divorce. This is not what kids need most. They need love, attention, and reassurance to a much greater degree. Other single parents can be a fount of ideas on how to cope, as well as provide practical assistance such as carpooling and shared babysitting.

Debunking the Gender Role-Model Myth. To address a myth that persists even today, divorce has nothing to do whatsoever with the sexual preferences a child will develop later in life. Whether a person will become homosexual, heterosexual, or bisexual is determined sometime between prebirth and the first two years of life. The lack of either a male or a female role model in the home has no relationship with homosexuality. Some sexual confusion is not uncommon during later childhood and adolescence as children struggle to figure out who they are in all aspects of life, but ultimate sexual preference is determined much earlier.

Diverse role models for a child are important, but gender is not as important as having a variety of good people from different walks of life and varied backgrounds to demonstrate to the child that all kinds of people can be successful and admirable. If you do not have a lot of other adults available to your children through social and neighborhood contacts, consider organizations such as Big Brothers and Big Sisters, the YWCA or YMCA, scouting, and other groups that can help your child interact with different adults on a positive level.

Common Behavior When Parents Divorce

All children react in some way to divorce, as does anyone whose life is touched by such a major change. Contrary to common belief, divorce does not guarantee that a child will have problems later in life. Divorce does not foreshadow long-term damage in the way that abuse, neglect, or severe hostility between parents often does.

Children often change their behavior during a divorce as part of their struggle to cope. These changes may occur at any time during the process, or after it is over. Some of the most common emotional reactions displayed are denial, grief, depression, anger, and regression to earlier behavior. These are the defense mechanisms that all human beings have and often use to make painful emotional states more endurable. Insecure behaviors such as clinging, refusal to go to school, and uncharacteristic shyness may also be manifested. This reflects the fear of desertion. Reassurance that the parents won't disappear, along with the imposition of gentle but sensible boundaries on the behavior, is usually the best treatment.

Young children may insist that an absent parent will return and refuse to listen to explanations that this will not happen. As with other emotional reactions, parents should generally let this behavior run its course and not try to force the issue unless it persists for more than a few months or interferes with the child's ability to enjoy life. If the state of denial continues, or the child seems depressed and can't participate in everyday activities, professional help may be necessary.

Children sometimes become angry with the custodial parent. This may reflect displacement of the anger regarding the situation of the divorce itself to the most available person. While you should certainly not permit dangerous or abusive behavior, it is important to try not to overreact or lose your temper, because this simply may make the problem worse. Children who behave this way often crave attention, and even negative attention may satisfy this need.

Children will often act out, or deliberately misbehave. Older children tend to be dramatic and sometimes self-destructive, such as an adolescent who begins or increases alcohol use, drug use, or sexual behavior. Professional help may be advisable, especially when the behavior is dangerous or illegal. Younger children generally act out through less harmful behavior, such as intentional disobedience, tantrums, verbal abuse, and refusal to cooperate. They may be testing the parent to see if they will still be loved even if they are "bad." Nondestructive tantrums in the home are best ignored until the child can be distracted with more positive activities. Misbehavior in public is often effectively stopped by telling the child that you will take him or her home immediately unless the behavior stops, following through whenever necessary, and explaining firmly to the child that he or she won't go out again unless the behavior improves. "Time-out," in which the misbehaving child is made to sit quietly in a boring place for about one minute per year of the child's age, is one of the most popular and effective forms of discipline. Remember also to reward positive and constructive behavior with praise and attention.

Parents are called on to exhibit the patience of saints at the very time when they are least able to cope with a rebellious, whiny, or angry child. Experts urge parents to strive to avoid reacting to petty misbehavior, as this only perpetuates the cycle. They also offer the reassurance that kids usually readjust and behavior problems disappear as the new situation stabilizes. For problems that persist longer than a year and a half or so, many sources of professional help aimed at children and families are available. The sooner overt conflict between the parents ends, the sooner most children begin to readjust.

Parents also contend with a restructuring of their own roles after divorce. For example, a mother who always left discipline up to the father may suddenly feel uncomfortable when she finds she must take on this responsibility. If you feel overwhelmed or uncertain in your new role as single parent, check into counseling, self-help groups, or parenting classes. Many are offered through local colleges, public agencies, social service groups, and private organizations. The national organizations listed in Appendix A can refer you to local chapters or other sources of help.

When the Adjustment Is Especially Difficult

In counselor Kathryn Lang's experience, boys often have a much harder time adjusting to divorce than girls. "Girls tend to be more verbal and to mature faster, socially and emotionally. They tend to do better. For both sexes, teens and young adults have the hardest time coping, harder than people expect. Parents worry more about the little ones, yet young children, five-year-olds for example, are really flexible. Plus, we tend to be more careful about children that age," she says.

"When young adults watch their parents divorce, they are horrified and really angry. They tend to be very protective of the parent who was left and think terrible things about the parent who did the leaving. Teens especially may get hostile in different ways. They don't have the ability to temper their anger as adults do, yet we expect them to be mature. Adolescent boys tend to have a really hard time, especially when the mother leaves," she adds.

Know When to Get Help. Lang advises parents of adolescents to watch for signs of anger, resentment, and depression, and to help their children seek counseling or therapy if needed. "Counseling can help normalize things for adolescents, help them realize that they are not alone and their feelings are normal," she explains.

Whether group or one-on-one therapy would be better depends on the individual. "Like people of other ages, some adolescents simply aren't comfortable in groups," says Lang. "Some just sob and sob and are too devastated to share their feelings with others. It helps them to hear from an individual counselor that this is typical. Sometimes we can almost give people a script for their lives because the patterns are so similar. They know the beginning of the drama, and we can offer them the rest. Recognizing that they will survive and recover is one of the biggest things that helps people of all ages."

Helping Children Heal

When parents divorce, each member of the family must go through a process of grieving, adapting, and learning to cope with the changes. Individuals may progress through this episode at different rates, and parents should realize that children may take more or less time to recover from the upheaval than expected.

Counselors who work with children after their parents' divorce often hear similar responses from kids when they ask what they wish their parents would do to make things easier. Following are among the most common requests:

- Recognize that kids love and need to be with both parents.
- Don't turn the kids into messengers or ask them to report on what goes on at the other parent's home.
- Don't say bad things about the other parent.
- If you have something angry to say to the other parent, don't do it around the kids.
- Don't make the children take sides.
- Don't make the kids feel that they are being disloyal if they have a good time with the other parent.
- Don't purposely forget to pack clothing or other items the children need when they are going to the other parent's home.

Psychologist Peter Favaro, in his book *Divorced Parents' Guide to Managing Custody and Visitation*, notes that while there is no harder time in parenting than moving children past suffering and into a more positive phase, this is when children rely most on parents. Remember that affection and communication are the number one priority for children, and you can provide an ample supply of these essentials without abdicating your other responsibilities, including your responsibility to yourself.

Parents also need to remember that the best thing they can give their children is a physically and emotionally healthy parent. As long as parents are in pain and not moving forward toward healing, children suffer too. Don't forget your own needs, including time on your own or with other adults. When your child is with the other parent, this can be a time to enjoy your freedom—but not the only time. You set a good example for your child if you maintain personal interests and recreation.

Favaro suggests that parents make an effort to collaborate on certain basic principles of good discipline and to maintain consistent, high expectations for their children (such as dedication to schoolwork), delivered with extra warmth and affection during this period of adjustment. Others counsel, however, that it is perfectly acceptable to have somewhat different rules and expectations in each home and that children will understand this if it is presented as normal. But while it is essential to maintain discipline, Favaro and other child development professionals advise avoiding two common forms of punishment that do more harm than good: spanking or any other form of hitting and withholding visitation with the other parent.

Children often worry about financial issues and other practical security matters, whether they express these concerns or not. Children who are left out of the process completely may become bewildered and reach the wrong conclusions, frequently blaming themselves for the divorce. Likewise, children who are told nothing about the circumstances that led to the parents' rift may deduce that they were at fault. One young man whose mother left the family commented that he was hurt by the way his parents quietly drifted away from each other and never seemed to express what was wrong. He felt that his parents had taken the "strictly business" aspect of their postdivorce relationship to an extreme, since neither ever discussed what had happened. As a result, he did not feel free to discuss his feelings about the situation with either parent.

Be empathetic. Put yourself in your child's shoes, perhaps by looking back on sorrows you endured in your own childhood. Remind yourself that you healed, and they will too. Try to prepare them for changes that you can foresee. For example, talk to them about dating before you become involved with another person who may hold a prominent place in your life. Explain that this is normal and that it is what parents do after a divorce. Share the cumbersome realities, such as tight finances, without expressing any insecurity or panic you may feel yourself. Set a good example for them as to ways in which unpleasant situations can be overcome.

Some parents lean on their children as emotional crutches. This can be bad for both parent and child. Parents need to tend to their own emotional needs through professional help or support from other adults. Never say to a child, "You're the man of the house now" or use similar expressions. While such remarks may seem innocuous or encouraging, children often take the message to heart and believe they are responsible for the welfare of the family. This may cause a child to take on more burdens, experience more anxiety, or feel accountable for the parent's happiness. It is a good idea to allow a child to take on additional, appropriate responsibilities, such as a few more chores or, for an older child, a part-time job to earn pocket money. But some children tend to worry too much anyway, and even casual comments can add to their burden.

Professionals stress that each parent should avoid criticizing the other in the presence of the child, with one exception: If the other parent has been abusive toward either the custodial parent or the children and could pose a danger to the family, the child must be made aware of the facts. In such situations, sole custody is often granted to the nonabusive parent, and no contact, or only supervised contact, with the abuser is allowed. These cases require careful handling by a parent who may have the difficult duty of explaining to the child why he or she cannot see the other parent. Fortunately, more and more sources of help for families in this type of crisis are becoming available, often in the form of group therapy offered by domestic violence shelters and other social service providers. It can be powerful reassurance for a child to know that he or she is not the only one who has suffered this type of trauma and that others have survived.

Helping Your Children Express Their Feelings. Therapists emphasize that children need to talk about their feelings of anger, sadness, worry, loneliness, resentment, guilt, and shame. "Children need help talking about each of these feelings more than one time," says Dino Thompson, director of the Northland Crisis Nursery and Center Against Domestic Violence, in Flagstaff, Arizona. "They need help exploring feelings, sorting them out from one another, getting labels on them, and having permission to feel that way. They also need to get the strong message that it is not OK to hurt yourself or others when you're angry or upset. Kids need help managing their feelings in order to feel better at some point."

Thompson recommends that parents acknowledge that it's normal to feel such emotions as anger—"the big mad," as she calls it—and says that parents should explain what behaviors are acceptable (such as shared physical activities) and not acceptable to work it off. She also recommends the use of "guessing statements" such as "I'm guessing that having Mom and Dad getting a divorce could feel really awful for you. You might be feeling [angry, sad, worried]." This can help children label feelings they can't identify for themselves and move toward feeling better as time passes. Thompson encourages parents to repeat such conversations often.

Maintain Continuity Through Routines and Rituals. Family rituals and familiar routines should be preserved as much as possible. New traditions often form naturally to replace the family customs that may be lost when a relationship ends. Constance Ahrons explains, "For a divorce to be a good divorce, family rituals around birthdays, holidays, dinnertimes, and vacations need to be redesigned to accommodate the new bi-nuclear family, and the loss of this portion of our lives must be balanced by its satisfactory reconstruction." Professionals caution that children should never be forced into a position of taking sides, such as choosing whether to spend Christmas or Hanukkah with one parent or the other; rather, the parents should make the decision, keeping the feelings of the children in mind. Some families preserve important traditions such as hanging up Christmas stockings in the home where the children lived before the divorce, and then establish a new ritual such as delivering food to homeless people at a local mission the next day.

Don't Let Your Kids Feel Caught in the Middle. Parents' feelings must sometimes take a backseat to their children's needs. Virtually all experts who have studied children of divorcing parents agree that excessive conflict between the parents is one of the most traumatic things children can face. This hostility is often the cause of ongoing or extensive psychological trouble after the divorce, as opposed to a reasonable recovery.

Kathryn Lang often counsels divorcing couples with children who cannot work out their anger and resentment or who make unrealistic demands. "Frequently, one of the two hasn't let go of the relationship, so that person tries to control the other. This party will set all kinds of rules, such as the ex can't bring anyone new around whom he or she is dating when the kids are visiting, or the child can't bring gifts from the other parent's home," she says. "In a typical case, couples need help in knowing when to let go and how to sort things out and reorganize their lives. Many need help in figuring out what is worth battling about and what is not."

Lang agrees that continued hostility between parents is intensely damaging to children, second only to abuse directed at the child. "Children are often forced into a situation of divided loyalties," she explains. "They love both parents and then hear the parents attack each other. It can ruin lives for years. Some parents still fight openly at their children's graduations and weddings. People can stay angry forever, with the kids caught in the middle. I've heard of more than one instance when battling parents have ruined a grown child's wedding day."

When counseling such couples, she tries to get them to look at the realities of their lives, noting, "When people divorcing are parents, 'till death do you part' becomes a given." The most important thing a child can have, during divorce or any other time, is unconditional love by both parents. Sensible rules, consistency, and an ongoing dialogue can go a long way in helping a child remain secure during the upheaval of a divorce. Remember, the parents are probably the most important role model a child will ever have. Do your best to set a good example, especially by listening to your child as well as talking to him or her.

Anything that creates a feeling of conflicting loyalties in children can be detrimental. This can include forcing a child to choose which parent to live with and questioning a child who has been to the other parent's home about that parent's habits, companions, and so forth. Almost everyone agrees that children should never be placed on the witness stand during a custody trial under any circumstances. In most courts, the child will talk either to the judge in the judge's chambers or to a court-appointed professional, such as a psychologist or social worker, in a less intimidating setting.

Parents who feel guilty about divorcing should remember that it is much worse for a child to be in a home filled with constant tension, strife, and conflict than to be in a peaceful environment with one parent. Likewise, anything parents can do to minimize the hostility during the divorce, such as avoiding custody battles, will promote normal recovery of the child.

8

Building a New Life

THERE'S AN OLD saying, "It's not over till it's over." In a divorce, a more accurate adage would be, "It's not over even when it's over." When parents divorce, ties will likely remain between them for the rest of their lives, or at least until the children are grown and on their own. But even in a divorce without children, in which all the financial, legal, and other tangible matters are resolved, emotional as well as practical baggage may be kept in storage.

Once a divorce is final, many people are surprised to have ambivalent feelings. Some may ricochet between elation and despair within the course of a single day. Even if you are thrilled to be out of an unhappy marriage, you may come to miss small, everyday things, such as dinner routines, regular contact with in-laws, a home you loved, security, and companionship.

Many professionals recommend that people experiencing such feelings look for the opportunities they present. For example, if you have been wanting to move, to redecorate, to take some time alone for introspection, to get a new job, to make new friends or reconnect with old ones, or to get involved with new hobbies or activities, this may be the ideal impetus to begin moving toward that goal. This is also the time to take stock of the healing that will begin.

The Divorce Is Final: Now What?

Experts advise caution in all areas of life immediately after a divorce. The exhaustion or exhilaration that many people experience can lead to bad decision making. It may be tempting to toss everything aside, move to a new state, and start a new life. This can be a wonderful adventure, but certain business must be taken care of first.

Relocating After Divorce

Moving is always stressful, and the stress level rises when the move is being made in response to a situation fraught with emotional upheaval. Whether you, your partner, or both of you will be moving, you will be assigned the task of creating a new home.

This work can be made easier in several ways. If you're alone when you're packing up your things, put on music—something new, without an emotional connection to the marriage—or a book on tape, to keep you from getting mired in memories or strung out by stress. You may want to ask a friend or family member to help you sort through your belongings. Many people turn the packing and sorting process, or the moving day itself, into a social event. Once you know what is staying and what is going, you can solicit friends to help you box and move everything that won't be transported by professional movers, and then treat them to food and drink in a casual housewarming party.

Packing and transporting usually takes at least a few days. For maximum efficiency, draw up a schedule with a definite date for accomplishing major elements. Many of the related tasks—especially the emotionally charged ones, such as dividing up photos—are best accomplished in stages. Many people favor starting with the simplistic chores and working up to the heftier ones. Details that can be accomplished even before the actual packing begins include accumulating labels, trash bags, boxes, packing materials, and marking pens. This is also the perfect occasion to weed out old clothing and other articles you no longer need and donate them to a thrift shop. If you're hiring professional movers, set up and confirm costs, date, and time. Send out cards or e-mails with changes in name, address, and telephone number to friends, neighbors, business associates, health care professionals and affiliates, religious institutions, credit card companies, membership organizations, health clubs, sports and social clubs, magazines and newspapers, catalogs, subscription services such as book and record clubs, insurance providers, and anyone else with whom you need to keep in contact. Some people also send a card or newsletter to a close circle briefly explaining the change in circumstances, which can be a comfortable way to break the news to those who need to know but don't need to be told in person.

Professionals such as Kathleen A. Kukor, president of Nest Builders, Inc., a company specializing in preparation before a household move and organization of the new home, are cropping up in more places. They can provide not only practical assistance but emotional support as well. Kukor says that people need to realize that healing takes time, and it helps to gradually begin making the new or changed home a special, individual place. She urges clients staying in the old house to buy items for the home that they never purchased before, redo wall coverings and other decorating details, and consider adding houseplants and maybe a pet to the family. Then again, don't be so eager to sweep away the past that you jettison things you may later wish you had saved. As a contributor to Margorie Engel's *Divorce Help Sourcebook*, Kukor advises, "At a time when you have to face so much change, surround yourself with your favorite and familiar things to give yourself some sense of continuity in your life."

Budget counselor and organizer Judy Lawrence adds that people can become overwhelmed by their possessions. "After a divorce, getting your things in place needs to be a priority," she says, "but do wait until the timing feels right. Some people need to put it off for a while until they feel ready to face it. There are so many other things going on, so much to assimilate and deal with. But when you are able to clear old things away, it gives you a great boost. Until you take care of your possessions, there is a subconscious nagging that drains your energy. One of my clients commented when we had finished a huge job—in her case it took a full week—that she felt as if fifty pounds had been lifted from her shoulders."

Lawrence advises those who feel ready to face the task but also feel cowed by it to line up someone to lend a hand—and lend an ear. "Call a relative, a friend, or a professional organizer," she suggests. "They can help you deal with the emotional aspects as well as the work." Choose someone with a good sense of empathy, who will assist you in making the decisions without trying to make them for you. Lawrence says that her background in counseling has been a boon in this facet of her work. "To help someone effectively, it's necessary to be able to tune in to people," she comments. "It's a job that has to be done by bits and pieces, and there will always be a big pile of stuff that only the person who owns it can decide on—whether to keep it and how to file it." Whatever route you decide to take, if you are still living out of boxes after six months, or still staring at empty closets and gaping reminders of your spouse's absence in the family home, it is time to spring into action. Your surroundings can have a profound effect on your emotional health.

Living alone after years of living with another can be a strenuous adjustment. Many people, especially men who leave the family home, are at a loss as to how to establish a new, comfortable dwelling. While keeping budgetary constraints in mind, resist the temptation to sign a lease on the least expensive place available. After all, you will want to bring friends and eventually dates to your home. Also, squalid surroundings can contribute to depression. If you have children, consider their need for some space to claim as their own, as well as the proximity to their school and other locations that they visit, such as a community center where they like to play basketball with friends.

In contrast, some people underestimate their financial responsibilities, more likely if the other spouse always paid the bills, and overcommit to a new space that's beyond their means. This adds to stress and the sense of being overburdened. Try to settle on a happy medium. Sprucing up need not be expensive. Some greenery, a few gallons of paint, and a couple of flea-market treasures can transform your abode into a new nest that is entirely your own, and many people take great pleasure in this ritual.

Entertaining can be a positive experience if it is not turned into a multifaceted ordeal. In other words, this is probably not the time to plan a sit-down formal dinner for two dozen people (unless this is truly your bliss). However, an informal buffet in which you prepare familiar favorite dishes, a potluck, or a cookout can be a venue for enjoying and renewing supportive friendships.

Setting Financial Goals

As you look to your future in the aftermath of a divorce, it is important to take care of certain matters that might have become overshadowed by the demands of simply getting through the day. List some of your immediate, short-term, and long-term goals, such as where you would like to be in the next six months, five years, and ten years. At the same time, consider where you don't want to be. This helps elicit problems and pitfalls you want to anticipate and avoid.

Also, list major life events that are likely or inevitable in the coming years that may require specific financial and other forethought. Examples are children reaching college age, your retirement, and your own educational goals. Compiling these lists can give you a realistic picture of what income you will need in the future and also help you make certain decisions, such as whether you may want to request support to continue your education.

Assess your work life, in terms of both your earning capacity and your personal satisfaction. You may need or want to consider a change of job, and this is an ideal time to explore your ambitions and your options. Drastic or impulsive change is inadvisable, but analysis, exploration, and planning are always positive steps.

Many people experience a wild sense of exhilaration after a divorce. They feel free, renewed, ready to take on anything the world has to throw their way. By all means, take advantage of this energy—but proceed with a modicum of caution before embarking upon irrevocable life changes. I once worked for a corporation that had, as one of its motivational mottoes, "Yard by yard it may be hard, but inch by inch it's a cinch." This is sound wisdom. Start taking those little steps toward the edge of the shore, but wait until you're fully confident in your abilities before you make a headlong dive into uncharted waters. Have a realistic image of your life as it is in the present before you make new commitments. Some transitions can be accomplished in five minutes, and some rightfully require five or more years to come to fruition. If you are struck with a sudden undeniable urge to paint the living room, go ahead—if you decide next week that you hate it, you'll be out no more than a few hours of work and the cost of a couple of cans of paint. In making decisions of more import, though, spontaneity can be your undoing. Do you really want to march into your boss's office and tell the old geezer what he can do with this penny-ante job? Maybe—but first give careful thought to the ramifications.

Postdivorce Career Issues

Kathy Potter, a career counselor who has also facilitated divorce support groups, rates career issues that come to the fore after a divorce as some of the most stubborn to address, for numerous reasons. "For women, even those who have good careers and were not dependent on their husband for income, the idea of being completely self-supporting can be very challenging psychologically," she explains. "Then there is the issue of reacting to the loss and coping with the grief. For those whose husbands just left, or those who left the marriage themselves before thinking things through, there is often a delayed reaction. It takes a while before the impact of the change hits, but when it does, a person's work life is inevitably affected."

Potter notes that any ending, even one that is broadly positive, such as leaving an abusive marriage, includes the loss of something, if only daily predictability and the presence of a life that is a known commodity. "There are three stages to any change," she says, "a beginning, a middle, and an end. The middle stage is the hardest place to be, because people are uncertain where they are headed; they're in limbo. Facing the unknown can create massive anxiety." This is also the stage at which grieving the loss is essential if it hasn't yet taken place. "It's really difficult to work on career issues, fix problems, and make sound decisions about changes until you have dealt with these emotional issues," Potter says.

Potter acknowledges that women more often face financial hardship after a divorce than men. She believes that it is generally wise for women to take the necessary steps to maximize their earning potential without delay, rather than, as others may propose, to hold off on seeking higher earnings so that they will get more support from the ex-spouse. "There are exceptions, of course," she states, "but usually, the best advice is to do what you need to do now, in order to get on with your life. If you're in doubt about a support issue, get the advice of a good attorney."

The life change that comes with a divorce frequently spawns a desire to rethink one's career. "Divorce forces people into some self-assessment," Potter says. "People may not be able to see things clearly, because so much is changing in their lives. In career counseling, we help them take off the blinders. Sometimes they see things just a bit differently, and sometimes they find a whole new world."

Discovering new aspirations is positive, of course, but Potter also advises against making extreme career changes soon after a divorce. "I would never tell someone to shelve a dream forever, but people do need to be practical first," she says. "Look at your short-term needs as well. For example, if you have a dream of becoming a ballet dancer, I would advise taking classes and continuing to work toward that goal, but keep working at your day job while you're at it."

The Importance of Time

A lot of divorced people become frustrated with their inability to put their former marriage behind them once and for all. Even those who have no continuing ties with their ex often are unable to shake uncomfortable feelings toward their former spouse and their marriage, no matter how hard they try to get on with a new life. Such feelings run the gamut from anger to care, resentment to concern, and love to hatred.

"In an era of instant everything, we expect ourselves to quickly heal and be rid of the ex forever," says Sid Buckman, an Arizona family therapist and divorce recovery specialist. "Even when we have children from the marriage, we expect ourselves not to have feelings toward our co-parenting partner. This is unrealistic, as it places us in the dilemma of telling ourselves not to feel when feelings are a natural part of our healing and becoming whole again. Feelings are not subject to our typical way of rationally responding to life. We may have been able to divorce ourselves from our former spouse with the stroke of a pen, but the feelings toward that person linger, and sometimes consume us, for many months to come."

Marriage involves constant interaction between two individuals who shared nearly all aspects of life over a period of years. The years of building bonds do not automatically disappear at the instant the divorce is final. Buckman explains that it takes time to let go of the feelings and memories and to change the behaviors learned as a part of the marriage. He adds, "It isn't necessary to rid yourself of all the feelings and memories from the past marriage. The best guide is your intuition, your sense of what is correct for you. Another guide is when your feelings impede your growth in life. If a year has passed and you discover you have not let go of many aspects of your marriage and divorce, this may indicate that you have unresolved feelings. It may not be easy to cleanse yourself of these murky emotions, but it is necessary if you are to have healthy relationships in your future."

Constance Ahrons reminds those suffering after a divorce that a grieving period is natural, but it is still a process, with stages and feelings to work through, and it will eventually end. She feels it is important for people to educate themselves about this process and accept that anger, emotional ups and downs, and pain are normal. As she explains, "People recover eventually, but there is a lot of upheaval, and it takes longer to get over a divorce than people think. For most, where the marriage has been of long duration, ten years or more, it takes at least two years."

Divorce is inevitably traumatic, even for a person who decides to leave a marriage of relatively short duration and with no children. "It takes a long time to get over it, even if you know it's the right thing, the best thing you could do for your life. You're messed up for a long time," says Laura Murphy, recalling the end of her three-year marriage. "You feel as if you've failed on some fundamental level, as if you failed as a human being." As one man succinctly remarked on the end of a six-month marriage, "It screws you up!"

"The good news is that eventually you do recover from the divorce completely," says Murphy, now divorced a dozen years and remarried. "Sometimes I literally forget that I was married before," she says with a laugh, adding, "but it took a long time to get here. My marriage was really bad at the end, and I lost perspective. I was so insecure when I came out of it that I was a different person. Now I don't know who that person was."

Even those who divorce under what appear to be the gentlest of circumstances may suffer more than they anticipate. "I really didn't expect this to be a big deal," says Elle Kovak, a research attorney. "My husband and I had been drifting apart for several years. We mutually agreed to a friendly parting and had no children and no major issues or disputes. Plus, I knew a fair amount about both the mechanics and the emotional aspects of divorce through my work. But a divorced friend advised me to expect the unexpected in terms of my emotional reactions, and boy, was she ever right. I had no idea how long the healing would take. Even now, although five years have passed and I'm in a wonderful new relationship, I still grapple with certain aspects of the past, still have things I'm sorting out with regard to this person who will always be a part of my family and of the history of my life."

Psychologists and sociologists who have studied the effects of life events on human emotions rank the stress of divorce as equal to the stress caused by the death of a child or spouse. Certain words are heard again and again by professionals working with people involved in a divorce: frustration, helplessness, anger, failure, hurt. In the words of Emily Couric, author of *The Divorce Lawyers*, "Sadness, disappointment, pain, and anger are the handmaidens of divorce, and their presence makes it difficult to behave with dignity."

For this reason, interaction with others who have been through and survived divorce can be invaluable in overcoming the initial pain as well as beginning the long-term healing. It can be especially helpful to talk to others who went through a divorce several years ago and know that perhaps the ultimate salve is the passage of time. The reassurance that the pain will pass as days go by is more meaningful if it comes from someone who has been in a similar situation. My mother, herself divorced, has often quoted the philosopher Friedrich Nietzsche, who said, "What doesn't kill me makes me stronger." In the context of the breakup of a marriage, the truth of these words resonates.

The Healing Process: One Woman's Experience

"My emotional state during my divorce was like being stuck in a nightmare. I felt lost, as though I was stumbling in the dark. I was terrified I would never find myself again," says Clayta Spear, a second-grade teacher who has now been divorced for ten years. "Actually," she concedes, "my divorce was a lot easier than most I've heard about. I really made an effort to keep it as simple as possible. I waited until I realized and accepted that there was no hope and that it was time to move on, so we could both have a life. By that time, I wanted to move away and leave the house where we had been living for ten years. Yet, it was hard to build up the courage to take the step."

On the surface, Spear's divorce indeed appeared simple. The couple had been married for eleven years and were childless. They owned a townhouse and a condominium, along with assorted personal property, but nothing that required complex division. Yet Spear hesitated before leaving, for a time she feels, in retrospect, was "about a year too long." As she reveals, "I didn't learn what was going on until the divorce was almost final."

She suspected that her husband was involved with another woman, but he refused to admit it. "The last year was just a matter of waiting. I encouraged him to see a psychologist before we made any decisions, and he did, for several months. But when I finally figured out what was up, I felt a deep sense of disappointment and betrayal. That was what created the nightmare. I think the hardest type of breakup is when one person feels rejected and betrayed by the other," she says.

At the same time her marriage was crumbling, her father was near death, and she was seeing a psychologist to help her through her grief. She continued to work with the psychologist on divorce issues, and he advised her to join a divorce support group. She reflects, "I wish I had joined a group then, but at that time, there weren't any in my own town, so I thought it would be too much effort. Also, I know now that I was too ashamed to join a group then and talk about my pain and feelings of rejection with strangers."

Eventually, Spear moved across the country, revitalized her career, and started building a satisfying new life. Even several years after her divorce, however, she realized that many of the issues that had arisen were not yet resolved. That's when inspiration appeared at her doorstep: "I got a flyer in the mail promoting a seminar on separation, divorce, and personal growth that would be held in the town where I was now living. It was an eleven-week program, and I recalled what my psychologist back in Massachusetts had recommended. I knew I had lots of feelings buried inside. I didn't even know it was anger. I was brought up in a New England family in which anger was not considered feminine, and any expression of anger was forbidden. Denial was the lifeblood of my family. Plus I always had the role of peacemaker. When I got divorced, I kept my anger suppressed, and it was still there."

She continues, "I was reluctant to join the group at first because, by that time, I had been divorced seven years, even though a volunteer who screened me before I signed up told me she thought it would be helpful to me and others in the group. Most of the people were newly separated or divorced. Some of them were still in relationships and trying to decide whether to leave. But the psychologist who ran the program wanted me to join, in part to show other people the importance of facing and dealing with the issues of a divorce, whether it be sooner or later. I was a living example that the pain and confusion doesn't go away until you are willing to confront it."

Spear found the seminar immensely helpful in both identifying her feelings and learning how they had naturally occurred because of the events that led to the end of her marriage. "My husband didn't treat me with respect or trust. He kept things from me and blamed all the problems we were having on me alone. As things deteriorated, he became emotionally abusive, telling me I was stupid and so on. I think a lot of this came from his own guilt," she explains. "For him to leave me for another woman was absolutely the last thing I expected, because his first wife had left him for another man. He was so insecure; he made me promise I'd never leave him. This made the betrayal doubly hard. I was even more surprised when he was so unfair to me in our settlement negotiations. It was easy to divide up the furniture and possessions, but we had a hard time with the money and some things that seemed small at the time—like his refusal to give me any of our photographs, and his insistence that a beautiful set of custom-made drapes I had chosen stay in the house. He wanted to impress his new girlfriend by bringing her to a showplace. It felt as if the drapes had become more important to him than I was. That was such a shock—it really hurt."

Although she had a successful career, Spear, no different from many other women, saw her marriage as the main focus in her life. "My childhood was bad, my parents were both alcoholics, and I never felt secure. So, it was very important for me to have security and stability in my home and through my marriage. When it ended, I lost the whole focus of my life. I was never suicidal, but I was in such terrible pain that I fully expected to die. All I could feel was rejection, shame, loss, and betrayal," she recalls.

Brightening, she adds, "I learned a lot in group therapy. Besides dealing with my own problems, I realized that although my husband had been divorced for seven years when we got married, he had not dealt with the baggage from his past relationship. Some of the problems in our marriage were a direct result of this. I think everyone needs some kind of therapy or support group when he or she is going through a divorce."

As in many other support groups, the seminar Spear attended included weekly sessions that combined structured activities with a chance for people to talk and share their thoughts informally. There were also social events that members could attend or not, as they chose. She notes, "Loneliness was a real problem for a lot of people, not so much for me because I had always been independent and had my career and friends, but it was still good to become a part of a social group with common issues."

The people in the group, who were at different stages of the breakup process, were able to learn from one another. "Days such as Christmas, the wedding anniversary, and other special times brought up a lot of emotions," says Spear. "People also reported how their moods and attitudes changed. Most found that their spirits and hopes really lifted between the beginning of the seminar period and the end."

After completing her seminar, Spear stayed on as a volunteer with a subsequent group. "The psychologist asked me to volunteer, and others in the group recommended me, so I was pleased to give it a try. It was really good for me to see how much I had learned and how far I had come. You also see the advantages and disadvantages in your own situation when you compare it with that of others," she says. "For instance, I had a much easier time than many people making the transition to single life because I'd always been independent and had other interests. My career as a teacher, strong friendships, and work with local drama groups had always been a part of my life. But the healing still takes a long time. I'd keep giving myself deadlines, thinking I should be over it by a certain period. But you never really get over it; it's always a part of your life. Those years are a component of your experience; you deal with it, and you go on. But you can't remove a block from the foundation that built your life. People have to realize that the marriage was a part of what made the life they have today. They should also realize that everyone is different, and everyone heals at different rates. I was my own worst and harshest critic. I would advise others to be patient with themselves and to realize that even after you do feel good, there will be things that will cause emotional upheaval. Going through this roller coaster of emotions is very upsetting, but typical."

The secondary purpose of the seminar group was to form new friendships, and some people went into the group seeking immediate contact with potential new mates. Spear relates, "The psychologist warned us about this at the outset. He recommended we not date anyone in the group until after the seminar was over. However, several people did date in both of the groups I worked with. These seemed to be troubled relationships, though, because the wounds were still raw from the marriage."

Spear says she garnered an unexpected bonus in the communication skills taught in the seminar: "This part really struck me, because of the weakness I've seen in my own relationships and as an educator. Communication skills are critical in all our interactions, but we are never taught the techniques. Children, parents and children, and men and women especially, all tend to communicate on a totally different level. In the school where I work, I'm pleased to say that we teach communication skills and effective dispute resolution techniques at the elementary level. We start training kids to be mediators at the third- to fifth-grade level so they can help others resolve their disputes without violence. It's a pilot program, and I'm pleased to see it catching on throughout the country."

The seminar Spear attended also featured sessions on accepting the grief process, managing anger, building self-esteem, learning to love and trust again, discovering new opportunities, intimacy, sexuality, and friendship. An optional session on helping children adjust to divorce was offered for participants who were parents. Spear gained new insights into her own experience and emotions, as well as those of other people. "The sexuality part was really interesting," she remarks. "There was such a broad range of reactions, from 'I never want anyone to touch me again,' to 'I'm ready to jump on anybody!' It was sad to see how many people had been so abused or put down by their former spouse that they felt unattractive and unlovable. But I know how that can happen. You get such a sense of failure. You know that you're intelligent and that you're attractive and lovable on an intellectual level, but on an emotional level, you remain convinced that you are not."

Despite the passing years, Spear struggled to let go of the past relationship and still felt an ongoing concern for her husband's well-being and happiness. "Even today, I still worry about him," she says, "but that's just the way I am about any friend. And I've learned it's OK to be this way. When you look at it logically, you wouldn't love someone if there were nothing about the person to love. That part doesn't go away. In the seminar, I learned that this is normal. The history you shared, with its bittersweet memories, is important."

She also acquired an enlightened perspective on the definitive labels we tend to place on relationships as a total success or a total failure. "Americans are so success oriented. We don't deal well with the realities of life. We expect absolute success or failure in relationships and don't recognize what's in between," she says. "We still believe that a marriage is supposed to be forever, and if it doesn't last, you've failed. It's shameful and devastating in our society to fail. Moving out of a marriage, for many reasons, is not a failure; it means you're taking another path in life. People need to support those who are divorcing, not reject them or place blame."

Although the seminar process helped her in innumerable ways, Spear cautions that people should not expect an immediate cure-all from this type of therapy. "I'm still afraid to trust, and to be vulnerable again to the risks in a relationship, because betrayal has been a pattern in my life," she admits, "but in the seminar, we covered a lot about our future and our goals, both actual planning of activities and imagining our dreams and our future life. I know

now that I will not marry again, but I am open to new relationships. I've done some casual dating, and I don't want to let the damage from my divorce make me bitter and unhappy. I've always been a survivor and a strong individual. I was independent from an early age. I taught with the Peace Corps and traveled around the world. This helped me to have the courage to start over after my divorce. I never dated much as a young woman and don't believe you have to have a man to be whole. It would be nice to have the love and understanding of a partner, but it's not something I require to have a happy and fulfilling life. I know now I can go on living a meaningful life just for myself."

Dating After Divorce

When to start dating after a separation or divorce is a subject of some controversy, among both professionals who work with those healing after a breakup and the people who have been there. Many strongly urge waiting until some specified time has passed. Others tell you to go with what feels natural and right. "I know it's probably not a good idea to be involved with another man so soon," said one woman who began dating another man almost immediately after breaking up with her husband, "but I really enjoy being with this person. Should I turn away from something good, someone special, just because others tell me the timing isn't right?" What it comes down to is that no rules are absolute in the untamed arena of human emotions.

During what some experts have labeled as the "walking wounded" stage immediately following a divorce, extreme views toward the opposite sex are not uncommon. Many people feel bitter, believing that all men or all women are alike, and they want nothing to do with the opposite sex ever again as long as they live. Others feel desperate to find another partner immediately so they won't have to be alone.

While both of these extremes are normal, actions taken in response to either can be detrimental. Those who feel they must find a new relationship immediately may believe that theirs is the healthier attitude, but it is actually the more dangerous. Desperation is a big turnoff to those who would be good partners. Too often, people who seek out new relationships immediately end up entangled with others whose problems are as great as or greater than their own.

Moreover, hostility tends to dissipate in a healthy person more quickly than dependence. According to psychologist Mel Krantzler, these extreme attitudes are mirror images and are both based on fear. He and many other professionals emphasize the importance of time alone to renew a sense of self-worth, let extreme feelings heal, and learn to be a whole and content person on your own. "People who go into a new relationship too soon after a divorce take the same problems with them," says counselor Kathryn Lang. "In the long run, it usually doesn't work well. Often, two dependent people get together, and you end up with two halves trying to be a whole."

Lang prescribes taking some time to heal and be alone before moving on to a new relationship. She speaks from experience: "For several years after I went through my divorce, I slept with only one pillow on the bed, to remind me that I had to learn to be a one before I could be a two. I realized that I'd never learned who I was before. I needed that time alone to discover my wants and needs, to figure out who I was." Lang waited ten years before she married again. "I was a lot more cautious the second time around," she says. "I would find myself taking inventory of a person when I went on a date, which people often tend to do on a subtle basis. Sometimes I wished we could just exchange lists of our characteristics and traits, what we were looking for, and information about our past, and be on with it," she jokes, "but I believe that it is important to know who you are and to be whole before you can have a healthy relationship."

Lang also believes that the period of time people need to fully heal after a divorce varies, but for many it may take up to five years. Krantzler warns that those who remarry too quickly—say, within two years—after a divorce are more likely to experience rifts in the subsequent marriage. Four out of five divorced people do remarry, and those who wait a reasonable amount of time before doing so have the best chance of success.

People who feel profound relief soon after their divorce may be tempted to start dating again sooner rather than later. However, Stephen Feher, Ph.D., cautions against jumping into another relationship before the dust has settled: "People feel fine, so they find another partner right away, but these rebound relationships hardly ever last. It's not conscious, but people often seek out someone else right away just to avoid facing the pain. They get very involved with the new person, yet later they will have to deal with their bad feelings about the end of the marriage. Inevitably, there will be pain."

After spending years in a marriage, people often reenter the dating scene with trepidation. Many wonder if the rules have changed. While innovations such as Internet dating have certainly made an impact on courtship in the twenty-first century, the fundamentals of human interaction are timeless. Liberal application of the Golden Rule, flexibility, frank communication, simple consideration, and respect for the other person are the ingredients for overcoming awkwardness. It takes a while for most people to make the transition from married to single, and detours are usually temporary.

Romance, as with other aspects of your transition back into single life, may not sail along as smoothly or quickly as you would like, but perseverance pays off. "I went through a frustrating phase where it seemed that the only men asking me out were perfectly nice guys, but they didn't spark my romantic interest in the least. At the same time, the men I did find intriguing were either unavailable or not interested, or took my phone number but never called," says Elle Kovak. "It was like high school all over again! I was beginning to wonder if I should lower my standards or just stop hoping. But one of my best friends kept preaching, 'Never settle!' I listened to her, and I'm so glad, because just when I was ready to give up, I met Larry—who was in exactly the same place as I was and having the same frustrations. That was three years ago, and we've been together ever since."

Many others describe similar experiences. It often seems that the powers that be wisely ignore our impatience and wait until we are genuinely ready before guiding us to the right person. "I didn't meet the right woman until I stopped looking," one man remarked. "I'd been divorced for almost ten years, and I'd been through enough. I just didn't want to bother with it anymore. Then a mutual friend introduced me to the woman who turned out to be the love of my life."

Author Erica Jong writes in her memoir *Fear of Fifty* that when she found herself single at the age of thirty-nine, with a child and an entirely new set of circumstances to face, this became the most critical period of her life—the period in which she became mistress of her own fate. Jong, who had spent nearly all of her adult life married, learned to change a tire, shovel snow, stack wood, and eventually build a peaceful relationship with the father of her child. She writes that she was able to achieve a marriage with a satisfying balance of power between equals only after she had come to a place where she was not afraid of being alone, in which she could treasure solitude and feel secure in her ability to provide for herself and her daughter. It was then that she was ready when she suddenly met a man she describes as "a soul mate and a friend."

Safe—and Sane—Sex

Those coming out of a long marriage may discover that the world of intimate relationships is a whole new frontier. Many people divorcing today are part of the baby boom generation and grew up in what has been called the "PPPP" (postpill, preplague) era, when it was possible to enjoy the freedom of sex without the fear of either unwanted pregnancy or life-threatening disease. Needless to say, things are notably different today. Be sure you know how to protect yourself if you have been in a monogamous relationship for many years and aren't familiar with the health precautions that are now essential. If you're feeling frisky, carry condoms—yes, women too—and don't be shy about using them. Most people consider this not only normal and acceptable today but also very smart.

It's also vitally important to practice emotionally safe sex as you reenter the lusty world of single life. This means respecting your partner and insisting that he or she respect you. Remember that regardless of your sexual proclivities, there is only one reason to have sex, ever, which is that you really want to enjoy sex with that partner. Anyone who expects sex as "payment" for a date or demands it after a certain number of evenings out is not worthy of your attention.

What About Sex with Your Ex? "No, no, no, *no*—do *not* date your ex!" That admonishment comes from Polly, a jeweler, who continued to enjoy an occasional tryst with her former husband for the first couple of years after they divorced, whenever her business took her to the state where he lived. She reminisces, "It seemed like a good idea at the time—easy, harmless, and fun. After all, Bob and I still liked each other, and neither of us was seeing anyone new. We were both lonesome and horny, and the sex was still great. But the intimacy postponed the detachment from each other and made the adjustment into single life more difficult—for both of us, I think."

Experts counsel that such relationships are especially risky for couples with children, who may be confused or latch onto a hope that their parents are headed for a reconciliation. But even for childless partners, prolonged intimacy can create unexpected problems. Polly was stunned at the confusion that surfaced during her first serious relationship after the divorce. Once her physical relationship with Bob finally ended, she was forced to confront new emotional territory as well. "Things were very comfortable with Bob until I got involved with Jack," she says. "That's when all the weird, conflicted feelings I still had for Bob came bubbling up, and I had to deal with them at the same time I was trying to build a new relationship. It really messed me up for a while, and it made things awkward between Bob and me. For the first time, we didn't know how to act with each other. Now we're friendly again. He'll always be family to me, but it took years to sort things out. I would advise anyone against continuing any type of romantic or sexual relationship with the ex, unless you really think you might get back together. If you're moving on, do it, and do it fast!"

Dating with Children

Divorced parents tend to feel awkward when they begin dating again, and they wonder how or whether to bring new partners around their children. Most experts advocate a casual approach and say that children need not be included in activities with the new partner until the relationship becomes at least somewhat serious. Many caution against making every new acquaintance a part of the child's life, because children often form swift emotional attachments and can become confused or hurt if the relationship doesn't last. By the same token, it's both unwise and dishonest to try to conceal essential facts about your life from either your children or your dating partners. Telling your partners about your children early on, and your children about those you date, makes the transition easier.

"I don't want my kids to get the idea that I have 'revolving-door' relationships, so I don't introduce every guy I go out with, although I do tell them if I'm seeing someone new," says a divorced mother of teenagers. "Especially since they're dating now themselves, I want to present a good picture of how healthy relationships should be handled."

It is also natural for children to be curious about sex. The consensus is that you should answer their questions honestly, within the context of your own sense of privacy. It is worse for children to have less information than more, as they tend to have vivid imaginations. Young children, especially, may misunderstand or be frightened by sights or sounds they can't identify.

When a dating relationship becomes serious, your children and your new partner should begin to spend time getting to know one another in a gradual and natural way. Stuart Berger, M.D., author of *Divorce Without Victims*, recommends that serious dating partners be introduced to children in settings where there is low pressure and little interaction required. An evening at home where strangers sit around the living room staring at each other can be uncomfortable all the way around. Berger recommends a group outing to a place such as a zoo, a movie, or some other recreational event, where all the children and adults can interact but have somewhere else to direct their attention and something besides themselves to talk about. He and other experts advise a parent's new partner not to overdo such gestures as gifts, which may be seen as bribes by the children. Blending a family is a long, often erratic process and, if forced, can cause insecurity, anxiety, and suspicion.

Berger also says that despite the earnest efforts of the parent and the new partner, children may remain intransigent and even profess hatred of someone they see as an intruder. Such reactions may be based not on a genuine dislike of the individual, but rather on a continued denial of the divorce or an ongoing reconciliation fantasy. He maintains that sacrificing an important relationship for the sake of the children is generally a mistake and notes that older children often are racked with guilt in later years if they believe the parent stayed single and suffered a lonely life on their behalf. Parents of children who reject a new partner must listen carefully to the children's objections, because occasionally there may be a legitimate concern. If there are indications of unkind or abusive behavior, then this of course demands action. In contrast, children who object to the new partner for disingenuous reasons can often come up with only inconsequential complaints, such as deriding the person's appearance, petty habits, or unfavorable comparison in the child's eyes with the absent parent. Berger and other experts reassure parents that kids nearly always soften their stance eventually and establish a relationship with the new partner that is at least civil, although it may take a year or even longer.

Remarriage and Stepfamilies

According to sociologist Constance Ahrons, approximately 85 percent of divorced men and 75 percent of divorced women marry again within three years. These numbers demonstrate that most divorced people are not left bitter toward the institution of marriage and retain the requisite hope and optimism to try again. While any remarriage hits bumps and roadblocks along the way, the obstructions have a way of multiplying when children and parents must form blended families or stepfamilies.

Like many professionals in the field of family therapy, Ahrons asserts that the language we use to refer to family members can be potent. For instance, she deplores the phrase "broken home" because of its negative connotation. There is, without question, a lack of appropriate terminology for many modern relationships. Children asked by teachers to tell the class about their families often have to spend ten or fifteen minutes describing not only stepparents, stepbrothers, and stepsisters, but also half siblings, stepparent's brothers and sisters, adults who function as grandparents but are not related by blood, or mates with whom their parents cohabit. Not only is the shortage of positive nomenclature confusing, but degrading and prejudicial phrases such as "living in sin" and "illegitimate children" still persist.

Roles among these new family members also may be uncomfortable and suffer from a lack of guiding norms. One duty of

Ahrons and other family therapists is to dash unrealistic expectations of the ideal "Brady Bunch" instant family. Caring relationships take time to evolve, and expectations of immediate love between stepparents and stepchildren can lead to disappointment and ill will. Ahrons quotes Emily and John Visher, founders of the Stepfamily Association of America: "If the stepfamily relationships are allowed to develop as seems comfortable to the individuals involved, then caring between steprelatives has the opportunity to develop."

Blending Your New Family

The approach that gets the most votes is to let kinship relationships develop naturally according to the feelings of the people involved. Patience and the passage of time are the main ingredients. "I had never had children of my own, so when my partner's teenage daughter moved in with us, I was really anxious," says Elle Kovak. "I wanted everything to be perfect, but money was tight, and our apartment was short on space. The physical arrangement was hard for me, and there were times I wasn't very gracious about the inconvenience. I'd find myself snapping or getting bitchy sometimes, and then I felt just awful. But Larry and his daughter didn't see my outbursts as such a big deal—they aren't such perfectionists as I am," she says with a laugh. "They had their moments too, and we all came to realize that occasional friction is just a part of the family condition. We all love each other and do the best we can, and that's what's important."

Although it is important for the authority of the new adult in the family to be established and for household rules to be consistently enforced, change should be minimized and ultimatums avoided. Direct orders to the children, such as to do chores, complete homework, or go to bed, should generally come from the biological parent, at least during the adjustment period. However, while most authorities agree that expressions of direct authority and any type of discipline are the province of the biological parent, a stepparent must have the power to enforce rules in the other parent's absence and should support the biological parent if there is a conflict.

A stepparent who has no biological children is charged with learning a whole new set of skills that may be completely unfamiliar. Experts advise taking some time to read books and learn about children, their development, and their behavior. A stepparent who moves in with a set of strict new household rules is courting disaster. At the same time, a stepparent should never be expected to give up all personal privacy or preferences. It is altogether reasonable to insist, for example, that the children not borrow or bother the stepparent's personal possessions without asking first. The adults must compromise, reach an agreement on boundaries and ground rules that both will honor, and back each other up (which, of course, may take time and much trial and error).

Stepparents should never try to be the same as a biological parent, but rather should develop an individual role in the child's life. A stepfamily won't necessarily function in the same way as a biologically related family, and that is perfectly all right. Stepfamilies need to remember and respect the fact that children of divorced parents still have another family, too. Parents who try to force the children to accept a stepparent as a replacement for the biological parent are putting a terrible burden on the child. For example, children should not be forced to call the stepparent Mom or Dad, but instead should be allowed to use the person's first name or an alternate name that is comfortable to everyone.

Stuart Berger advises parents and stepparents to be sensitive to small issues that may underpin a child's sense of stability. Simple rituals and routines, such as having a particular blanket or toy every night, may seem trivial, but a child thrives on predictability and security. Stepparents often have to be extremely patient, persistent, and loving toward a child. This may be a lot to ask, especially when the child seems to be critical and rejecting. Youngsters are often confused about how to treat the stepparent. They may worry that loving and accepting a stepparent means abandoning the biological parent.

As noted previously, one of the most common hindrances that stepfamilies must bypass is unrealistic expectations. These new relationships are complex, involving everything from rearranging deep emotional ties to the logistics of more people sharing a bathroom. As Berger says, "Stepparenting is not for the timid at heart."

Building a stepfamily requires patience, flexibility, love, determination, and a constant sense of humor. Perfect harmony all the time is not a realistic expectation. Stepfamilies tend to deal with all of the problems visited on biological families, and then some. Bonding does not have the force of history and biology behind it. Nevertheless, as the many successful stepfamilies prove, great love and wonderful relationships can and do blossom over time.

"Especially since I've never had my own children and don't plan to, having a stepdaughter has been a real blessing," says Elle Kovak. "She's a lot like I was at her age, and we can discuss things she may not be comfortable bringing up with her parents, because they never had some of these experiences or interests or concerns—but I did. Plus, I really enjoy having her around. We have a lot of fun together. But I don't see myself in a mother role at all; I feel more like a big sister or a mentor. I always encourage her to maintain a close bond with her mom—that's so important, something no one can replace."

Berger advises new stepparents to look for common ground and shared interests with their stepchildren. He reminds the family to laugh and relax and keep things in perspective. While the time required for a new family to become bonded varies widely, one to three years may pass before the family feels entirely comfortable together.

These intervening years may be trying. It is characteristic for children to idealize the absent parent even if that parent has abused, abandoned, or never been close to the child. Biological parents must reject this tempting opportunity to criticize the other parent. It's entirely possible that the children are fully aware of the parent's shortcomings and are lavishing this constant praise to appease their guilt over what is in fact a growing fondness for the stepparent.

For the child's well-being, the noncustodial parent should strive to promote adjustment to the new situation. It is distressing for children when that parent is hostile toward a stepparent. All the adults on both sides need to reassure the child that the new development is positive and will bring more love and richness, not less.

Stepparents, especially those without children of their own, also need to remind themselves that children are not thoughtful, considerate, or grateful by nature. It is equally vital for a stepparent to acknowledge the special bond between the biological parent and child and allow them some time alone. Children may fear that a parent who remarries will transfer to the stepparent the affection formerly reserved only for the child. Biological parents need to reassure the child that they have plenty of love to go around and make some special efforts to convince the child that he or she is still a very important part of their life.

Meanwhile, the biological parent is dealing with the intricacies of acclimating to life with a new spouse. The two need to attend to their own relationship—for example, by taking a traditional honeymoon away from the children, and through communication and consideration for each other's needs. Everyone in the family, especially the new stepparent, should have some personal space, if at all possible. This is helpful to stepbrothers and stepsisters as well if virtual strangers must now share a room. Even in a large home, everyone is apt to feel crowded, both emotionally and physically, until the settling-in period has passed.

Berger and other experts warn that clashes between newly minted siblings are especially common when the children are close in age. Berger advises parents to let the kids try to reach their own solutions to problems. Of course, they should not be allowed to brawl or act in ways that are hostile or destructive, but petty squabbles are best ignored and usually resolve themselves.

Constance Ahrons recommends looking to other cultural systems to learn new ways of coping with the changes in the family structure today. She points out that African American families have developed more flexible kinship structures over the centuries, in what social scientists refer to as a "pedi-focal" family system. In this type of system, child rearing is a task of the community, and all the adults who are a part of the child's world may contribute to the child's well-being. Taking part in the upbringing of a child is considered a privilege, not a burden. This philosophy and practice is echoed in many other cultures around the world. It is seen in the Israeli kibbutz and in other settings, where people believe that it truly does take a village to raise a child.

One of the best ways to build a feeling of family is to participate in enjoyable activities together and to create new family rituals—shared pleasures that will become a part of the history of the new family. These should be balanced with special times alone between the biological parent and child. Something as mundane as a day trip to a park can be a memorable way to create a bond between the family, as can a move to a new home that the family works together to decorate, or the addition of a pet to the household. Adding a new child into the family is a more complicated matter. The ideal here, many believe, is to wait until the new family has achieved some stability before increasing the number.

Teens Speak: How to Ease the Adjustment to Stepfamily Life. In an article in *Parade* magazine, several teenagers who had experienced the trials of adjusting to life in a stepfamily shared their insights on how to make the experience better. Many of their ideas paralleled the advice of the experts. For example, several talked about the importance of a personal space to call their own, such as a bedroom where they can find privacy and be as messy as they like. Others emphasized the importance of direct access to the biological parent and personal time together. Some discussed the importance of communication between all members of the family, in which the stepparent and stepchild listen to each other. All emphasized compromise and sharing by family members, and drawing appropriate lines so that mean or rude behavior is not allowed. Open and clear communication about rules, with agreement between the parents, was also noted as essential. Some of the teens emphasized the positive aspects of the stepfamily, such as finally getting a big brother or sister they'd always wished for. One young woman said she resented having to share her room at first, but eventually she and her stepsister became as close as biological siblings.

Resources for Blended Families. Social scientists estimate that at least half of all Americans alive today will find themselves in some form of stepfamily relationship during their lifetime. As blended families are becoming more common in American society, both attitudes toward and services for such families are improving. More family counselors are creating targeted programs and therapies to help blended families improve communication and build good relationships.

Today, stepparents also can receive a good deal of support from others. Some family counselors and support groups specialize in helping stepfamilies cope and interact to the greatest advantage. Stepfamily coaches can help families create a plan of action to blend more harmoniously. Stepparent support groups have helped members educate themselves and band together to encourage state legislatures to pass new laws protecting their rights, and for judges to be more enlightened in the way they look at stepparents and their ties to their stepchildren. National organizations, such as the Stepfamily Association of America, provide information and support, and many have local branches (see Appendix A).

Certain family members may need individual therapy or another type of group therapy. For example, play therapy can help young kids communicate and express their feelings in a way that is comfortable and familiar to them. Local mental health associations, medical associations, clinics, nonprofit organizations, Parents Without Partners, religious institutions, and social service agencies are all potential sources of services for stepfamilies.

Legal Aspects of Blending Families. The legal relationships between members of stepfamilies may be confusing. Stepparents are frequently considered "legal strangers" even to children for whom they provide daily care. In many states, a stepparent is not recognized as having any legal relationship with a stepchild—which can cause real problems in some situations, such as when a child needs emergency medical care and the natural parent is unavailable. Stepfamilies should be sure that powers of attorney, school records, medical forms, and other documents are properly completed and filed so that authority can be shared or transferred as the family wishes.

Traditionally, if blended families broke apart, stepparents were generally not recognized as having any special right to continue a relationship with stepchildren under the law. Today, all fifty states have either statutes or binding case law dealing with custody, visitation, and support by stepparents. It is becoming more common for courts to facilitate a continued relationship between stepparents and stepchildren, if it will be beneficial to the child.

In a few rare cases, custody may even be granted to a stepparent rather than the biological parent. As a rule, this decision is indicated when there is a strong showing that this arrangement would be far better for the child, especially if the couple married when the child was young, the child has never known a father or mother other than the stepparent, and the marriage was of long duration with a close bond between stepparent and child. As more courts place emphasis on the key determination in child custody cases—the best interest of the child—the primacy of biological ties is giving way to the individual circumstances of the child and the adults with whom he or she has formed valued relationships.

Innovations in the Divorce and Family Recovery Fields

As the divorce rate rises, new options to deal with divorce and try to reverse the trend are being implemented. One of the most innovative is a satellite-broadcast, interactive television program designed to educate teenagers about divorce, child custody, and conflict resolution between couples. This program, with the goal of lessening the frequency of divorce, was the brainchild of Lynne Z. Gold-Biken, an author and family law attorney. Students, generally high school seniors in psychology classes, learn relationship skills by working in pairs to set budgets, fight fair, and meet other challenges that couples face. Local family lawyers visit classes to discuss the divorce system and field questions.

The schools participating are linked by satellite dish, television, and telephone. Gold-Biken appears with a family therapist on a live spot to answer questions, discuss issues raised in previous programs, and work with student actors who portray young couples caught up in various dilemmas. Callers from the schools can ask questions. Students then continue with exercises presented in the programs, such as fair fighting. While teaching relationship skills and divorce law together may seem peculiar, Gold-Biken believes the two combine well. The students learn what it takes to make relationships work, and what they can expect to encounter if they don't.

Education for adults has expanded remarkably in recent years as well. For example, Santa Fe Community College, in Santa Fe, New Mexico, serves a progressive yet relatively small community and offers an impressive array of credited and noncredited classes of interest to people experiencing divorce. Included are practical training classes such as computer technology, job hunting skills, financial planning for women, starting a business, art training, and photography, along with personal growth classes such as peer counseling, coping with anxiety, overcoming fear, health care, setting personal boundaries, and healing old hurts.

Women in Transition

A Santa Fe Community College program called "Women in Transition" provides free workshops for single mothers and other women undergoing personal, financial, or employment difficulties as a result of divorce, widowhood, or other changed circumstances. The workshops assist women in meeting the challenges of transition, developing goals, establishing a positive self-image, and preparing to reenter the workforce.

The curriculum is unique in its approach. "There are other programs to help displaced homemakers learn job skills, but the ones I am familiar with are not organized like ours," says Anita Shields, director of the Women's Resource Center at Santa Fe Community College. "Many focus on job hunting, résumé writing, and interview techniques. We deal with self-esteem and building healthy relationships first."

"Women in Transition" has expanded since its inception to serve a broader group of participants. "When we started the program in 1985, we focused on displaced homemakers—women who had been in the home and out of the workforce. We have evolved since then to serve a wider range of people. Most of the women attending the program do have limited education and are struggling with financial problems, and many come from abusive situations. But everyone facing a transition into single life after marriage experiences trauma and grief, even women with successful careers and financial stability. We teach that the grief process doesn't happen overnight," she says.

After completing the twenty-four-hour program, which is scheduled flexibly on weekdays, weekends, and evenings to meet the participants' needs, each woman is assisted in taking the next step that is right for her. "The help we give them varies according to each individual's needs," Shields remarks. "Some go on to take specific courses at the community college, some go to job training programs, and others get free career counseling from Student Services. The women also share an incredible amount of information and ideas among themselves."

The camaraderie that occurs in the group is one of the program's most significant aspects. "There is so much support and encouragement among the members of every group—sometimes I think I could leave these thirty or forty women in a room by themselves, and they would end up in the same place as at the end of the class," she says. "So many people think they are the only one going through this. When they find out they are not alone, it is such a relief. A lot of long-lasting relationships and small support groups form after the program."

Some women are inspired to maintain ties with the program, as well. "The first day of each new workshop, women who have been through the program come back and do testimonials. It has changed lives," Shields states. The view of life as a continuing work in progress is a core component of the program. "These women always emphasize where they are in their own journey, and not that they have 'made it' " she explained.

Words of Wisdom from Those Looking Back

Ernest Hemingway wrote, "The world breaks everyone and afterward many are strong at the broken places." Divorce is different for everyone who experiences it. However, in the words of people who have been through a divorce and now look back years later, certain insights invariably are heard over and over.

Contrary to the myth that many people leave marriages impulsively and then live to regret it, few people divorce in haste. In fact, one of the most common sentiments is a wish that the couple had taken steps to end the marriage earlier. "I wish I hadn't hung around so long hoping it would get better," one man reflects. "I'm a romantic by nature, so I always believed that if you love someone, everything had to work out in the end. But some people just aren't meant to stay together, and I can see that now."

Not as surprising is the conclusion that the more civilized the parting, the better the relationship between the former partners is likely to be. "My first wife and I were only twenty when we got married. We were just too young to know what we were doing," one man declares. "We figured out that we made a mistake, but there was no hostility. We both agreed to part, we did all of the paperwork on the agreement ourselves, and we've remained good friends. In fact, when my second wife learned she was pregnant, my ex was the first person she told!"

Further, it's a mistake to think of divorce as a panacea that solves every problem and ends a frustrating old life in favor of a sparkling, exciting, instant rebirth. People sometimes report still feeling married even though a divorce is over, both because of the necessity of continued contact with the former spouse, and because they sometimes remain mired in old habits that they expected to break as soon as the final decree was issued. Creating a new reality and identity can stump the best of us. People are sometimes incredulous to find that they are still unhappy, even though their spouse, deemed to be the sole precipitate of their unhappiness, is no longer there to blame. As Mel Krantzler states, "Freedom means taking personal responsibility for one's own behavior, which is the difficult but necessary demand that divorce imposes on every man or woman who separates from a spouse."

One divorced woman observes, "Many people do learn something from previous divorces. Unfortunately, we frequently focus on what's wrong with the other person. Blaming someone else relieves an individual of owning up to responsibility for any part in the failed relationship equation. The real learning process comes from taking personal responsibility for what contributions the individual made to the failure of the relationship, and then not repeating those mistakes in the next relationship. I finally realized that at age thirty-five and went on a quest to discover how I was sabotaging my own life and why."

Therapists who work with people recovering from a divorce often make the case that it is truly possible to view a glass as either half empty or half full, and the way a person looks back on the divorce and forward to the life ahead can make a dramatic difference in his or her future. Most people eventually reflect on former marriages with mixed emotions, including regret, nostalgia, and a bittersweet wisdom born of survival and growth. While the loss of identity and status as a married person can be a blow, it also opens the door to discovery of a new identity as a unique individual. In his outstanding book *Callings: Finding and Following an Authentic Life*, author and teacher Gregg Levoy advises, "Rather than asking 'Who am I?' we might ask, 'In how many ways can I be myself?' Rather than asking 'What is my place in the world?' the question might be better put, 'In how many ways can I experience a sense of belonging to the world?'"

Budget counselor and professional organizer Judy Lawrence, along with Jane Blustein and S. J. Sanchez, coauthored *Daily Riches: A Journal of Gratitude and Awareness*. Lawrence believes that the time after a divorce is a time to actively seek silver linings. "It may not be possible at first," she says, "but with healing, most people can look back and be grateful for something that came out of the whole experience."

Lawrence constantly encounters people who found a part of themselves they would not have discovered without going through the divorce. "It brings a gift of perspective," she explains. "Through the pain comes transformation. For those who can be flexible enough to shift their thinking, divorce can crack open old beliefs and reveal new thoughts, people, circles, and experiences." Most people who have been through one or more divorces do bring the acquired knowledge of themselves and the nature of their relationship to new involvements. Mel Krantzler, speaking of his second marriage to a woman who also was divorced, says, "We have learned from our past, not repeated it."

Appendix A

National Organizations

MANY OF THESE organizations maintain international websites. I have listed some, but websites tend to change often. A search using the group's name will take you to the current site.

Academy of Family Mediators
5 Militia Drive
Lexington, MA 02173
(781) 674-2663
This organization promotes mediation as an alternative to the adversarial system and publishes various periodicals, audiotapes, and videotapes.

Ackerman Institute for Family Therapy
149 E. Seventy-Eighth Street
New York, NY 10021
(212) 879-4900
E-mail: ackerman@ackerman.org
Various clinical, educational, professional, and research programs, including a library and speakers' bureau.

Alcoholics Anonymous World Services
475 Riverside Drive
New York, NY 10163
(212) 870-3400
alcoholics-anonymous.org

Alternative Dispute Resolution Committee of the
ABA Family Law Division
740 Fifteenth Street NW
Washington, DC 20005-1009
(202) 662-1690
abanet.org
This group of lawyers, a division of the American Bar Association, supports family mediation and arbitration. It conducts various educational programs.

American Academy of Matrimonial Lawyers
150 N. Michigan Avenue, Suite 2040
Chicago, IL 60601
(312) 263-6477
This organization is composed of attorneys specializing in the field of family law. It provides various publications, including lists of members.

American Association of Marriage and Family Therapy
Research and Education
112 S. Alfred Street
Alexandria, VA 22314-3061
(703) 838-9809 or (800) 347-AMFT (347-2638)
aamft.org
Provides referrals to marriage and family therapists in local areas and publishes a consumer's guide to marriage and family therapy.

American Association of Retired Persons (AARP)
601 E Street NW
Washington, DC 20049-0001
(202) 434-2277 or (800) 687-2277
aarp.org

Publishes *Divorce After Fifty: Challenges and Choices* and provides a broad range of information on related issues, including a brochure on the visitation rights of grandparents.

American Bar Association/Section on Dispute Resolution
740 15th Street NW
Washington, DC 20005-1009
(202) 662-1680
abanet.org
E-mail: dispute@abanet.org
This division of the American Bar Association provides information, services, a library, and numerous publications.

American Bar Association/Section on Family Law
750 N. Lake Shore Drive
Chicago, IL 60611
(312) 988-5000 or (800) 621-6159
abanet.org
National association of attorneys practicing in the family law field. Numerous publications.

American Divorce Association of Men (ADAM)
(248) 356-ADAM (2326)
mens-divorce.com
This organization promotes reform in the divorce laws and encourages counseling, mediation, education, and related services. It maintains lawyer referral lists and publishes a periodic newsletter.

American Family Therapy Academy, Inc.
1608 Twentieth Street NW, Fourth Floor
Washington, DC 20009
(202) 438-8001
afta.org

American Institute of Stress
124 Park Avenue
Yonkers, NY 10703
(914) 963-1200 or (800) 247-RELAX (73529)
stress.org

Professionals from various disciplines provide information, workshops, and consultation for individuals, institutions, and organizations.

American Self-Help Group Clearinghouse

Northwest Covenant Medical Center
Denville, NJ 07834-2995
(201) 625-7101
mentalhelp.net/selfhelp
Publishes a sourcebook.

American Society of Appraisers

555 Herndon Parkway, Suite 125
Herndon, VA 20170
(703) 478-2228 or (800) ASA-BALU (272-2258)
appraisers.org
This society is composed of professional appraisers of all types of property. It offers consumer information materials and produces numerous publications.

Annual Credit Report

(877) 322-8228
TDD: (877) 730-4104
annualcreditreport.com
Provides a free copy of credit reports from Equifax, Experian, and Transunion credit reporting agencies online, with appropriate identifying information. May be used free of charge once a year. Other services and information available.

Association for Children for Enforcement of Support, Inc.

ACES National
P.O. Box 7842
Fredricksburg, VA 22404
(888) 310-2237
childsupport-aces.org
This organization is composed of parents seeking enforcement of child support awards. It advocates improved enforcement and

sponsors education, research, and a speakers' bureau. Various publications.

Association of Family and Conciliation Courts
6526 Grand Teton Plaza
Madison, WI 53719
(606) 664-3750
afccnet.org
This organization is composed of judges, attorneys, mediators, counselors, family court personnel, teachers, and others concerned with the resolution of family disputes and the effect on children. It publishes a newsletter, a directory, a journal, and other documents.

The Beginning Experience
1657 Commerce Drive
South Bend, IN 46628
(574) 283-0279 or (886) 610-8877
beginningexperience.org
Catholic support programs for divorced adults and children of divorced parents.

Big Brothers/Big Sisters of America
230 N. Thirteenth Street
Philadelphia, PA 19107
(215) 567-7000
bbbsa.org
National program with many local chapters to provide children from one-parent homes with adult volunteers to act as friend, mentor, and role model.

C. Henry Kempe National Center for the Prevention and Treatment of Child Abuse and Neglect
1825 Marion Street
Denver, CO 80218
(303) 864-5300
kempecenter.org
This organization is associated with a similar international society.

Center for Dispute Settlement
1666 Connecticut Avenue NW, Suite 501
Washington, DC 20009
(202) 265-9572
cdsusa.org
This organization promotes and evaluates mediation and similar programs, offers consulting and training, and manages a complaint center.

Center for Law and Social Policy
1015 Fifteenth Street NW, Suite 400
Washington, DC 20005
(202) 906-8000
clasp.org
This public-interest law firm works toward strengthening policy for low-income families and making improvements in family law policy. It publishes *Family Matters*, a newsletter, as well as publications on various issues, including opportunities for AFDC recipients, parental cooperation, and child support.

Child Abuse Listening Mediation (CALM)
1236 Chapala
Santa Barbara, CA 93101
(805) 965-2376
This is a program designed to prevent and treat child sexual, physical, and emotional abuse, offering intervention, referrals to other organizations and resources, and volunteer and emergency assistance. It also maintains a twenty-four-hour bilingual listening service at (805) 569-2255. Various publications.

Child Find of America
P.O. Box 277
New Paltz, NY 12561-0277
(914) 255-1848 or (800) I-AM-LOST (426-5678)
childfindofamerica.org
This organization works to prevent child abduction and locate missing children. It conducts mediation and counseling programs for parents involved in, contemplating, or worried about child

abduction and produces various videos, children's games, publications, and other tools for information and education. Call (800) A-WAY-OUT (292-9688) for mediation information. Children who have been abducted and people who can identify missing children can call (800) I-AM-LOST.

Children's Divorce Center
88 Bradley Road
Woodbridge, CT 06525
(203) 387-8887

Services, information, and publications for individuals and professionals to help children and parents deal with divorce and remarriage.

Children's Rights Council
6200 Editors Park Drive, Suite 103
Hyattsville, MD 20782
(301) 559-3120
gocrc.com

This organization supports joint custody, harmony between divorced parents, and mediation and conducts various programs and services to achieve these goals. Maintains computer databases, resource and information lists, and numerous publications for those working to promote the rights of children.

Consumer Information Center
Eighth and F Street NW, Room G-142
Washington, DC 20405
(202) 501-1794 or (888) 878-3256

General information of interest to consumers. Free publications, including those on credit and divorce.

Dads Against Discrimination
P.O. Box 8525
Portland, OR 97207
(503) 222-1111
peak.org/~jedwards/dads.htm

Information and services for divorced fathers, publications, and referrals.

Debtors Anonymous
P.O. Box 920888
Needham, MA 02492-0009
(781) 453-2743
Coordinates self-help groups and publishes various materials.

Depressives Anonymous: Recovery from Depression
329 E. Sixty-Second Street
New York, NY 10021
(212) 689-2600
Publishes brochures, pamphlets, and a newsletter.

Divorce Care
220 S. Allen Road
P.O. Box 1739
Wake Forest, NC 27588
(800) 489-7778
divorcecare.com
Network of divorce support groups.

Divorce Magazine
2255B Queen Street East, Suite 1179
Toronto, ON M4E 1G3
Canada
(416) 368-8853
divorcemagazine.com

Divorce Support
5020 W. School Street
Chicago, IL 60641
(773) 286-4541
divorcesupport.about.com
Support and assistance for members, as well as an information network.

Divorced Parents X-Change
P.O. Box 1127
Athens, OH 45701-1127
(614) 664-3030

Domestic Violence Hotlines
For battered women:
National Domestic Violence Hotline
(800) 799-7233 or (800) 787-3224 (TTY)

For battered men:
Battered Men's Helpline
(888) 743-5754

Elisabeth Kubler-Ross Center
S. Route 616
Headwaters, VA 24442
(703) 396-3441
　　This network serves families and individuals in personal crisis, including divorce, sponsors programs, conducts a lecture series, and produces various publications.

Equality in Marriage Institute
250 W. Fifty-Seventh Street, Suite 2404
New York, NY 10107
(212) 489-5590
equalityinmarriage.org
　　This organization collects information on divorce and promotes marriage as an emotional, legal, and financial partnership of equals. It provides resources and support to men and women before, during, and after marriage.

Ex-Partners of Servicemen for Equality (EXPOSE)
P.O. Box 11191
Alexandria, VA 22312
(703) 941-5844
ex-pose.org

This group of former military spouses maintains a hotline, (703) 255-2917, and publishes a newsletter as well as a booklet entitled *A Guide for Military Separation or Divorce*.

Families and Work Institute
267 Fifth Avenue, Floor 2
New York, NY 10016
(212) 465-2044
familiesandwork.org
Research, education, publications, and seminars on balancing work and family responsibilities. Involved in "The Fatherhood Project" to support various options for men in child rearing. Call (212) 268-4846.

Families Anonymous
P.O. Box 3475
Culver City, CA 90231-3475
(800) 736-9805
Group with many local chapters for people who care about those with drug or alcohol problems or who deal with substance abuse in the family.

Family Resources Database
(763) 781-9331 or (888) 781-9331
ncfr.org
Provides references to literature and information on programs and services offered by other organizations.

Family Support America
200 S. Michigan Avenue, Suite 1600
Chicago, IL 60604
(312) 341-0900
familysupportamerica.com
Network of nationwide family support organizations of various types. Offers numerous services and publications.

Fathers for Equal Rights, Inc.
701 Commera Street, Suite 302
Dallas, TX 75202
(214) 953-2233
    This group publishes a directory of fathers' rights organizations, publishes self-help packages, provides attorney referrals, and maintains an extensive website.

Fathers Rights and Equality Exchange (FREE)
3140 De La Cruz Boulevard, Suite 200
Santa Clara, CA 95054-2444
(415) 853-6877
dadsrights.org
    Advocates in areas related to noncustodial fathers. Educational programs, information, referrals, and free newsletter.

Financial Planning Association
4100 Mississippi Avenue, Suite 400
Denver, CO 80246-3053
(800) 322-4237
    Provides names of financial planners and analysts who have met rigorous requirements for membership.

Find the Children
11811 W. Olympic Boulevard
Los Angeles, CA 90064-1113
(310) 314-3213 or (888) 477-6721 (for information directly related to a missing child)
findthechildren.com
    Services, education, and assistance to families and law enforcement personnel working to locate missing children. Also provides referrals and publishes a directory of missing children with pictures.

Foundation for Grandparenting
108 Farnham Road
Ojai, CA 93023
grandparenting.org

Information, reading list, publications, classes, and speakers' bureau dedicated to increasing public awareness of the importance of grandparents in children's lives.

Grandparents Anonymous
1924 Beverly
Sylvan Lake, MI 48320
(312) 682-8384

Assists grandparents who have been denied visitation with grandchildren. Publishes a periodic newsletter.

Grandparents' Rights Organization
100 W. Long Lake Road, Suite 250
Bloomfield Hills, MI 48304
(248) 646-7191 or 646-7177

Education and advocacy to assist grandparents who have been denied visitation with grandchildren.

Institute for Divorce Financial Analysts
24901 Northwestern Highway, Suite 710
Southfield, MI 48075
(800) 875-1760 or (989) 631-3605
institutedfa.com

Information, website, referrals to member analysts.

Institute of Business Appraisers
P.O. Box 17410
Plantation, FL 33318
(954) 584-1144

This organization supports education, legislation, and certification of appraisers. It provides information on business valuation. Various publications.

Internal Revenue Service
Employee Plans Technical and Actuarial Division
1111 Constitution Avenue
Washington, DC 20224

(202) 622-6074 or (800) 829-1040

irs.gov

Information on publications explaining tax laws and consequences in many areas directly or indirectly related to divorce.

International Association for Marriage and Family Counselors

Dr. Robert Smith, Executive Director

Texas A&M University

College of Education

6300 Ocean Drive

Corpus Christi, TX 78412

(361) 825-2307

Produces various publications, promotes excellence in the field, offers therapist credentialing, and collaborates with national Academy for Certified Family Therapists.

Joint Custody Association

10606 Wilkins Avenue

Los Angeles, CA 90024

(310) 475-5352

jointcustody.org

Provides information on joint custody and the law surrounding it.

Legal Momentum Advancing Women's Rights

395 Hudson Street

New York, NY 10013

(212) 925-6635

A division of NOW, this organization produces resource kits on divorce and child custody. Sponsors a national judicial education program to fight gender bias in the courtroom.

Men/Fathers Hotline

807 Brazos, Suite 315

Austin, TX 78701

(512) 472-3237

Crisis line for men and fathers, and referrals to other organizations.

Military OneSource
Within United States: (800) 342-9647
Overseas: (800) 3429-6477 or collect (484) 530-5906
militaryonesource.com
Crisis counseling, information, and assistance for military families on virtually all topics, including legal information on divorce, visitation, child custody, and support.

Mothers Without Custody
P.O. Box 36
Woodstock, IL 60098
(800) 457-MWOC (6862)
Network through which mothers without primary custody of their children can share experiences. Send a self-addressed, business-size envelope with two 39-cent stamps for information.

Ms. Foundation for Women
120 Wall Street, Thirty-Third Floor
New York, NY 10005
(212) 742-2300
Funds and assists women's self-help organizing efforts. Pursues change in social policy and law to end discrimination.

National Action for Former Military Wives
2090 N. Atlantic Avenue, No. PH2
Cocoa Beach, FL 32931-5010
(407) 783-2101
This group works to promote legislation that supports benefits for former military spouses. Publishes a newsletter.

National Association of Enrolled Agents
1120 Connecticut Avenue, Suite 460
Washington, DC 20036-3922
(202) 822-6232
naea.org
Provides names of accountants qualified to practice before the IRS.

National Association for Family Child Care
5202 Pinemont Drive
Salt Lake City, UT 84123
(800) 359-3817
 Promotes family day care services in private homes, operates an accreditation program for family day care providers, and advocates and promotes high-quality standards for family and other day care providers.

National Association of Child Care
Resource and Referral Agencies
3101 Wilson Boulevard, Suite 350
Arlington, VA 22201
(703) 341-4100
 Information and resources for parents, including special military programs.

National Association of Professional Organizers
(847) 375-4746
napo.net
 Provides home organization services, tips, and local referrals.

National Association of Retired Federal Employees
606 N. Washington Street
Alexandria, VA 22314
(703) 838-7760
narfe.org
 Information on pension rights and other retirement benefits, and referrals to local chapters.

National Center for Missing and Exploited Children
Charles B. Wang International Children's Building
699 Prince Street
Alexandria, VA 22314-3175
(703) 274-3900, hotline: (800) 843-5678, for people who are hearing impaired: (800) 826-7653
missingkids.com
 Provides assistance and a clearinghouse of information for parents and law enforcement. Merged with The Adam Walsh Child

Resource Center to work toward legislative changes to better protect children, advocate child safety, and conduct prevention and awareness programs. Publications, website, and toll-free hotlines to exchange information on sightings of children.

National Child Care Association
2025 M Street NW, Suite 800
Washington, DC 20036-3309
(202) 367-1133 or (800) 543-7161
nccanet.org
    Information for parents and child care professionals, including referrals to centers.

National Child Support Enforcement Association
Hall of States
444 N. Capital NW, Suite 414
Washington, DC 20001-1512
(202) 624-8828
ncsea/org

National Clearinghouse on Child Abuse and Neglect Information
1250 Maryland Avenue SW, Eighth Floor
Washington, DC 20024
(703) 385-7565 or (800) 394-3366

National Coalition Against Domestic Violence
1120 Lincoln Street, Suite 1603
Denver, CO 80203
(303) 839-1852
ncadv.org
    Various publications; several categories of membership. Referrals to local coalitions.

National Coalition of Free Men
P.O. Box 582023
Minneapolis, MN 55458-2023
(888) 223-1280

Advocate for legal rights of men in various legal fields, including custody. Support for divorcing fathers. Speakers' bureau, library, and publications.

National Congress for Fathers and Children
9454 Wilshire Boulevard
Beverly Hills, CA 90212
(310) 247-6051
ncfc.net

This coalition is dedicated to promoting and preserving father-child relationships. It maintains a website with information for fathers and produces various publications.

National Council on Child Abuse and Family Violence
1025 Connecticut Avenue NW, Suite 1000
Washington, DC 20036
(202) 429-6695 or (800) 222-2000

Information, publications. Call toll-free number for referrals to local services.

National Council on Family Relations
3989 Central Avenue NE, Suite 550
Minneapolis, MN 55421
(763) 781-9331 or (888) 781-9331
ncfr.org

Education, tips for families, website, and publications.

National Court Appointed Special Advocates Association
100 W. Harrison Street, North Tower, No. 500
Seattle, WA 98119
(800) 628-3233

This organization, composed of juvenile court judges, attorneys, and advocates, supports programs that provide court-appointed special advocates for abused or neglected children. Produces various publications.

National Domestic Violence Hotline
(800) 799-7233 (SAFE)
TDD: (800) 787-3224

This hotline is staffed twenty-four hours a day by trained counselors who can provide crisis assistance and information on help available in the caller's area.

National Foundation for Consumer Credit
8611 Second Avenue, Suite 100
Silver Spring, MD 20910
(301) 589-5600
nfcc.org
Membership organization for Consumer Credit Counseling Services and other nonprofit credit organizations. Sponsors credit counseling services and distributes various publications. Call (800) 388-2227 for a directory of local affiliates.

National Military Family Association
2500 N. Van Dorn Street, Suite 102
Alexandria, VA 22302-1601
(703) 931-6632
nmfa.org

National Network for Women's Employment: Womenwork!
1625 K Street NW, Suite 300
Washington, DC 20006
(202) 467-6346
womenwork.org
Information on displaced homemakers, women's employment, and women in transition.

National Organization for Women (NOW)
1100 High Street NW, Third Floor
Washington, DC 20005
(202) 628-8669

National Organization of Single Mothers
P.O. Box 68
Midland, NC 28107-0068
(704) 888-5437
singlemothers.org
Provides resources, information, a website, and publications.

National Women's Law Center
11 DuPont Circle NW, Suite 800
Washington, DC 20036
(202) 588-5180
nwlc.org
This organization works to advance women's legal rights in areas such as child support enforcement and family law.

Nationwide Patrol
P.O. Box 2629
Wilkes-Barre, PA 18703
(717) 825-9684
This group of volunteers assists parents trying to locate a missing child by distributing flyers, organizing search efforts, and offering fingerprinting and other services. Works to increase public awareness, sponsors programs, and publishes a national directory.

North American Conference of Separated and Divorced Catholics
P.O. Box 360
Richland, OR 97870
(906) 482-0494
Helps develop regional groups of divorced Catholics. Organizes workshops, retreats, and training programs and distributes resource materials.

Office of Children's Issues
Overseas Citizens' Services
U.S. State Department, Bureau of Consular Affairs
(202) 736-9090 or (888) 407-4747
From overseas: (202) 501-4444
Provides information and assistance in cases of international child abduction.

Older Women's League (OWL)
3300 N. Fairfax Drive, Suite 218
Arlington, VA 22201
(703) 812-7990, Ext. 14

Provides information to older women facing divorce and related issues, such as health insurance rights.

Operation Lookout
(800) LOOKOUT (766-5688)
operationlookout.org
National and international organization to help find missing children.

Parents Anonymous
675 W. Foothill Boulevard, Suite 220
Claremont, CA 91711-3416
(909) 621-6184
parentsanonymous.org
Works for prevention and treatment of child abuse. Sponsors support groups for parents who have abused or fear they could abuse their children. Local chapters throughout the nation.

Parents United International, Inc.
615 Fifteenth Street
Modesto, CA 95354-2510
(209) 572-3446
This organization supports families in which child sexual abuse has occurred and acts as an umbrella group for related organizations.

Parents Without Partners
16505 S. Dixie Highway, Suite 510
Boca Raton, FL 33432
(561) 391-8833
parentswithoutpartners.org
Support and social group for single parents and children, with local chapters. Referrals, resource lists, and numerous publications.

Pension Rights Center
1350 Connecticut Avenue NW, Suite 206
Washington, DC 20036
(202) 296-3776

The purpose of this public-interest group is to protect and promote pension rights and work toward solving the nation's retirement income problems. It operates a lawyer referral service and assists with complex pension issues. Produces various publications.

Rainbows
2100 Golf Road, Suite 370
Rolling Meadows, IL 60008-4231
(800) 266-3206
rainbows.org
This international organization provides training and curricula for peer support groups aimed at those who have suffered a loss due to a divorce or other reasons. Publications and newsletter.

Single Parent Resource Center
31 E. 28th Street, Second Floor
New York, NY 10016-7923
(212) 951-7030, Ext. 231
National group working to establish a network of regional single-parent organizations. Publishes a newsletter and provides callers with referrals to services and support groups.

Stepfamily Association of America, Inc.
650 J Street, Suite 205
Lincoln, NE 68508
(402) 477-STEP (7837) or (800) 735-0329
saafamilies.org
Local chapters, numerous publications, and educational resources.

Stepfamily Foundation
333 West End Avenue
New York, NY 10023
(212) 877-3244 or (800) SKY-STEP (759-7837)
Provides information and counseling for stepfamilies and training for professionals who work with them. Telephone counseling service and many publications.

Suicide Hotline
National Hopeline Network
(800) 784-2433

U.S. Department of Health and Human Services
Administration for Children and Families
Office of Child Support Enforcement
370 L'Enfant Promenade SW, Fourth Floor
Washington, DC 20447
(202) 401-9373
acf.dhhs.gov/programs/cse
  This agency helps states develop, operate, and improve child support enforcement programs according to federal regulations. Its services include the Federal Parent Locator Service, which helps locate parents who are not paying child support or those who have kidnapped children. Provides handbooks, fact sheets, and a website with links to state websites.

Women in Transition
21 S. Twelfth Street, Sixth Floor
Philadelphia, PA 19107
(215) 564-5301
  This group provides various services, including training for women facing problems such as abuse, unpaid child support, and issues related to divorce. It maintains a twenty-four-hour telephone crisis line for counseling, information, and referrals at (215) 922-7500.

Women in Transition/Women's Resource Center
Santa Fe Community College
P.O. Box 4187
Santa Fe, NM 87502
(505) 428-1736
  Provides workshops for divorced and widowed women and for single mothers to help build self-esteem and prepare to reenter the workforce.

Women's Institute for Financial Education (WIFE)
P.O. Box 910014
San Diego, CA 92191
(858) 792-0524
wife.org
  Holds classes and seminars to educate groups on financial issues surrounding divorce, how to prepare for divorce, the legal process, what to expect, mediation, and coping emotionally. Publications.

Women's Law Project
National Partnership for Women and Families
125 S. Ninth Street, Suite 401
Philadelphia, PA 19107
(215) 928-9801
womenslawproject.org
  Nonprofit feminist law firm that conducts class-action and test case litigation in family law and, among other activities, publishes books on child support and custody.

Women's Legal Defense Fund
1875 Connecticut Avenue NW, Suite 710
Washington, DC 20009
(202) 986-2600
  This organization, composed of attorneys and others, seeks to secure equal rights for women through litigation, advocacy, legal counseling, and education.

Womenwork! The National Network for Women's Employment
1625 K Street NW, Suite 300
Washington, DC 20006
(202) 467-6346
  Provides and helps develop programs and services for displaced homemakers. Publishes a directory of programs and provides information and flyers.

Appendix B

State Laws

ALL STATES NOW have some form of no-fault divorce. In addition, many provide for divorce after a period of separation or on various "traditional grounds"—adultery, cruelty, desertion, insanity, addiction, or nonsupport. Several states (Arkansas, Arizona, and Louisiana, as of 2006) have special laws establishing a form of marriage known as "covenant marriage," in which different laws and requirements apply if the couple divorces.

Be aware that the laws governing divorce are changing rapidly. Be sure you get up-to-date legal information before embarking on any family law matter in which you plan to represent yourself. Each state has a bar association that can provide information, guidance, and referrals. Some also offer publications, recorded messages, educational programs, and various other services to the public. These programs tend to change, so it is best to call or visit the website and inquire about what is available. Websites change frequently as well, so a search using the name of the bar association is generally the best way to find the current site, or you may link to each state bar site from the American Bar Association website at abanet.org. Websites for each state's child support enforcement program may be linked directly from the Federal Office of Child Support Enforcement website at acf.dhhs.gov/programs/cse.

Local bar associations, law schools, bar foundations, courts, legal aid groups, and other organizations also provide services at the local level in some areas. Contact your state bar or family court for information.

Alabama
Statutes: 30-2-1 through 12
30-2-30 to 54
30-3-1 through 99 (child custody)
Alabama Bureau of Child Support: (334) 242-9300
Alabama State Bar: (205) 334-269-1515

Alaska
Statutes: 24.24, 25.24.050, 25.24.080, 25.24.120,
25.24.130, 25.24.200, 25.25.101
25.30.010 (child custody)
Child Support Enforcement Division: (907)
269-6829 or (800) 478-3300
Alaska State Bar: (907) 272-7469

Arizona
Community Property State
Covenant Marriage State
Statutes: Uniform Marriage and Divorce Act
25-311 et seq.
25-431 et seq.
Arizona Child Support Enforcement
Administration: (800) 882-4151
Arizona State Bar: (602) 252-4804

Arkansas
Covenant Marriage State
Statutes: 9-12-301 et seq.
9-13-101 et seq. (child custody)
Arkansas Office of Child Support
Enforcement: (501) 683-7933
Arkansas Bar Association: (501) 375-4606

California
Community Property State
Statutes: Fam. Code 2310 et seq.
Fam. Code 3401 et seq. (child custody)
Fam. Code 3900 et seq.
See also other sections of the Family Code generally.
Community property, Civ. C. 5107 et seq.
California Rules of Court prescribe specific procedures and forms.
Cal.R.Ct. 1-201 et seq.
California Department of Child Support Services:
(916) 464-5000 or (866) 249-0773
State Bar of California: (415) 561-8200

Colorado
Statutes: 14-10-105 et seq.
Uniform Marriage and Divorce Act
14-10-123 et seq. (child custody)
See also 19-1-117 et seq.
Colorado Division of Child Support
Enforcement: (303) 866-4300
Colorado Bar Association: (303) 860-1115 or (800) 332-6736

Connecticut
Statutes: Title 466
46b-56, 46b-59 (child custody)
Connecticut Child Support Division: (860) 723-1002
Connecticut Bar Association: (860) 223-4400
Connecticut Self-Help/Mutual Support
Network: (203) 789-7645

Delaware
Statutes: Title 13-1503 et seq.
13-721 et seq. (child custody)
Delaware Division of Child Support
Enforcement: (302) 577-7171
Delaware State Bar Association: (302) 658-5279

District of Columbia
Statutes: 16-901 et seq.
16-911 et seq., 16-914 (child custody)
District of Columbia Child Support
Enforcement: (202) 442-9900
District of Columbia Bar: (202) 737-4700
Free Divorce Clinic: (202) 737-4700, Ext. 292

Florida
Statutes: Chapter 61, in particular,
61.021, 61.031, 61.052, 61.19
61.13 et seq. (child custody)
Florida Office of Child Support Enforcement:
(904) 922-9564 or (800) 622-KIDS (5437)
Florida Bar: (850) 561-5600

Georgia
Statutes: 19-5-1 et seq.
19-9-1 et seq. (child custody)
See also 19-7-1 et seq.
Georgia Office of Child Support Recovery:
(404) 657-3784 or (800) 227-7993
State Bar of Georgia: (800) 334-6865

Hawaii
Statutes: HRS 580
571-46 (child custody), 571, 576, 580-47
Hawaii Child Support Enforcement Agency:
(808) 692-8265 or (888) 317-9081
Hawaii State Bar Association: (808) 537-1868

Idaho
Community Property State
Statutes: 32-603, 32-698, 32-610, 32-616, 32-901
32-717 et seq. (child custody)
32-1008
Idaho Bureau of Child Support Enforcement: (800) 356-9868
Idaho State Bar: (208) 334-4500

Illinois
Statutes: 750 ILCS 5/401 et seq.
750 ILCS 5/601 et seq. (child custody)
Illinois Child Support Enforcement Division: (800) 447-4278
Illinois State Bar Association: (217) 525-1760

Indiana
Statutes: IC 31-1-11.5-1 et seq.
IC 31-1-11.5-20C et seq. (child custody)
Indiana Child Support Enforcement Division: (317) 232-3447
Indiana State Bar Association: (317) 233-5437 or
(800) 840-8757

Iowa
Statutes: 598.1 et seq.
Iowa Child Support Recovery Unit: (888) 229-9223
Iowa State Bar Association: (515) 243-3179

Kansas
Statutes: 60-1601 et seq., 38-129
60-1610 et seq. (child custody)
Kansas Child Support Enforcement Program: (913) 296-3237
Kansas State Bar Association: (785) 234-5696
Kansas Self-Help Network: (316) 978-3843 or (800) 445-0116

Kentucky
Statutes: KRS C. 403, 465
Kentucky Division of Child Support
Enforcement: (502) 564-2285
Kentucky Bar Association: (502) 564-3795

Louisiana
Community Property State
Covenant Marriage State
Statutes: L.R.S.A. Sections 9:301 et seq.
9:331 et seq. (child custody)
Louisiana Support Enforcement Services: (504)
342-4780, Hotline (800) 256-4650
Louisiana State Bar Association: (504) 566-1600

Maine
Statutes: Title 19 Sections 661 through 752
19 752 (child custody)
T. 19, 801-825
Maine Division of Support Enforcement
and Recovery: (207) 287-2886
Maine State Bar Association: (207) 622-7523

Maryland
Statutes: Family Law Articles 7-103 et seq.
9-102, Fam. 5-203 (child custody). See
also Maryland Rules 570-577.
Maryland Child Support Enforcement
Administration: (800) 332-6347
Maryland State Bar Association, Inc.: (410) 685-7878

Massachusetts
Statutes: c.208, 209, 119
208.28 et seq. (child custody)
Mass.R.Don.Rel.P.
Massachusetts Child Support Enforcement
Unit: (800) 332-2733
Massachusetts Bar Association: (617) 338-0500

Michigan
Statutes: MCLA Sections 552 et seq.;
MSA Sections 25.81 et seq.
Rules 721 to 731
MCLA Section 552, MSA Sections 25 et seq. (child custody)
Michigan Office of Child Support: (517) 373-7570 or
(866) 540-0008
State Bar of Michigan: (517) 346-6327
Michigan Self-Help Clearinghouse: (517) 484-0827 or
(800) 777-5556

Minnesota
Statutes: C. 518 et seq., 257022
518.17, 518.551 (child custody)

Minnesota Office of Child Support: (612) 297-5846
Minnesota State Bar Association: (612) 333-1183 or
(800) 882-MSBA (6722)
First Call for Help: (612) 224-1133

Mississippi
Statutes: 93-5-1 et seq. See also 93-11-3; 93-23-1 et seq.
93-16-1, 93-5-23, 93-5-24 (child custody)
Mississippi Division of Child Support
Enforcement: (866) 388-2836
Mississippi State Bar: (601) 948-4471

Missouri
Statutes: C. 452
452.375 (child custody)
Missouri Division of Child Support
Enforcement: (573) 751-4224
Missouri Bar Association: (537) 635-4128
Missouri Self-Help Clearinghouse: (314) 773-1399

Montana
Statutes: 40-4-101 through 40-4-221
40-7-101 et seq., 40-4-211 et seq. (child custody)
Montana Child Support Enforcement Division:
(800) 346-KIDS (5437), (800) 346-5437, or (406) 444-9855
State Bar of Montana: (406) 442-7660
Lawyer Referral Service (406) 449-6577

Nebraska
Statutes: 42-341 through 42-823
42-357, 42-364 (child custody)
Nebraska Child Support Enforcement Office:
(402) 441-8715 or (877) 631-9973
Nebraska State Bar Association: (402) 475-7091
or (800) 927-0117—Pamphlets available.
Nebraska Self-Help Information Services: (402) 476-9668

Nevada
Community Property State
Statutes: 125.010 et seq.
125-134, 125-140 (child custody)
Nevada Child Support Enforcement Program: (775) 684-0500
State Bar of Nevada: (702) 382-2200

New Hampshire
Statutes: C. 458 et seq.
458.16-20 (child custody)
New Hampshire Office of Child Support
Enforcement Services: (603) 271-4427
New Hampshire Bar Association: (603) 224-6942

New Jersey
Statutes: Title 2A, c.34
Title 2A, c.3423; Title 9, c.2; Rule 5:8 (child custody)
New Jersey Child Support and Paternity
Programs: (877) NJKIDS1 (655-4371)
New Jersey State Bar Association: (732) 249-5000
New Jersey Self-Help Clearinghouse: (201) 625-9565 or
(800) 367-6274

New Mexico
Community Property State
Statutes: 40-4-1 et seq.
40-4-7 et seq., 40-10-1 et seq. (child custody)
New Mexico Child Support Enforcement
Bureau: (505) 827-7200
State Bar of New Mexico: (505) 797-6000; for
lawyer referral service, (800) 867-6228

New York
Statutes: D.R.L. 170, 200-240
DAL 240 (child custody)
New York Office of Child Support
Enforcement: (518) 474-9081

New York State Bar Association: (518) 463-3200;
for lawyer referral service, (800) 342-3661

North Carolina
Statutes: c.50
50-13.1 et seq., 50A-1 et seq., 50-30 to 50-39 (child custody)
North Carolina Child Support Enforcement
Office: (919) 733-3055
North Carolina Bar Association: (919) 677-0561 or
(800) 662-7407
North Carolina State Bar: (919) 828-4620

North Dakota
Statutes: 14-05-03 et seq., 14-09-05.1, 14-08.1-01
14-05-22-24 (child custody)
North Dakota Child Support Enforcement
Agency: (701) 328-3582
State Bar Association of North Dakota: (701) 255-1404

Ohio
Statutes: c.3105R.C. et seq.
3109 et seq., Ch 3115, (child custody)
Ohio Office of Child Support Enforcement: (614) 752-6561
Ohio State Bar Association: (614) 487-2050

Oklahoma
Statutes: Title 43-101, et seq.
43-107 et seq. (child custody)
Oklahoma Child Support Enforcement Unit: (800) 522-2922
Oklahoma Bar Association: (405) 416-7000

Oregon
Statutes: c.107
107.105, 107.137, 107.159, 109.121, 109.700 (child custody)
Oregon Child Support Enforcement Agency: (503) 986-6090

Oregon State Bar: (503) 620-0222 or (800) 452-8260; for
lawyer referral service, other information, and
pamphlets: (503) 684-3763 or (800) 684-3763
Oregon Recovery Services Section: (503) 378-5439
Northwest Regional Self-Help Clearinghouse: (503) 222-5555

Pennsylvania
Statutes: Title 23* 3101 through 23* 3707, Pa. Rules
of Civil Procedure 400 et seq. and 1920 et seq.
23* 5301 et seq. (child custody)
Pennsylvania Bureau of Child Support
Enforcement: (877) 727-7238
Pennsylvania Bar Association: (717) 238-6715 or
(800) 932-0311

Rhode Island
Statutes: 15-5-1 through 15-5-28
15-5-16 et seq. (child custody)
Rhode Island Bureau of Family Support: (401) 222-2847
Rhode Island Bar Association: (401) 421-5720

South Carolina
Statutes: 20-3-10 through 20-3-440, 20-7-420
20-3-160, 21-21-10 et seq., 20-7-100 (child custody)
South Carolina Child Support Enforcement
Division: (800) 768-5858
South Carolina Bar: (803) 799-6653 or (800) 868-2284;
for lawyer referral service, (803) 799-7100

South Dakota
Statutes: 25-4-2 et seq.
25-4-45 to 56 (child custody)
South Dakota Office of Child Support
Enforcement: (605) 773-3641
State Bar of South Dakota: (605) 224-7554 or (800) 952-2333

Tennessee
Statutes: 36-4-101 et seq.
36-6-101 et seq. (child custody)
Tennessee Child Support Services: (800) 838-6911
Tennessee Bar Association: (615) 383-7421 or (800) 899-6993

Texas
Community Property State
Statutes: Fam. C. Ch.3
Fam. c.152-157 (child custody)
Texas Child Support Enforcement Division: (512) 460-6000
State Bar of Texas: (512) 463-1463 or (800) 204-2222

Utah
Statutes: 30-3-1 et seq., 30-5-2
30-3-10 (child custody)
Utah Office of Recovery Services: (801) 536-8500
Utah State Bar: (801) 531-9077 or (800) 257-9156

Vermont
Statutes: Title 15-551, 15-554, 15-562, 15-
563, 15-592, 15-631, 15-1101
15-291, 15-296, 15-292, 15-664 (A), 15-
656-661 (child custody)
Vermont Office of Child Support Services: (800) 786-3214
Vermont Bar Association: (802) 223-2020

Virginia
Statutes: 20-91 et seq.
20-103, 20-107.2, 20-108, 20-109.1, 20-124.2
(child custody)
Virginia Division of Support Enforcement
Program: (804) 726-7000 or (800) 552-3431
Virginia State Bar: (804) 775-0551; for lawyer referral
service, (800) 552-7977 or (804) 648-4041

E-mail: vsb@usb.org—publications and pamphlets available
Self-Help Clearinghouse of Greater Washington
(northern Virginia): (703) 941-5465

Washington
Community Property State
Statutes: 26.09.010 et seq.
26.09.050 et seq. (child custody)
Washington Office of Support Enforcement:
(306) 664-5200 or (800) 442-KIDS (5437)
Washington State Bar Association: (206) 727-8200—
programs and publications available

West Virginia
Statutes: 48-2 et seq.
48-2-13 et seq. (child custody)
West Virginia Child Advocate Office: (304) 558-3780
West Virginia Bar Association: (304) 522-2652
West Virginia State Bar: (304) 558-7993

Wisconsin
Community Property State
Statutes: 767001 et seq.
76723, 76724, 767325 (child custody)
Wisconsin Bureau of Child Support: (608) 267-0924 or
(800) 362-8096 (statewide), (800) 728-7788 (nationwide)
State Bar of Wisconsin: (608) 257-3838; for lawyer
referral service, (800) 362-9082 or (608) 257-4666—
pamphlets and videotapes available

Wyoming
Statutes: 20-2-101 et seq.
20-2-13, 20-2-113 et. seq., see also 20-4;
20-6; 20-7 (child custody)
Wyoming Child Support Enforcement Section: (307) 777-6948
Wyoming State Bar: (307) 632-9061

Resources and Suggested Readings

Ackerman, Mark J., and Andrew W. Kane. *Psychological Experts in Divorce, Personal Injury, and Other Civil Action*. Somerset, NJ: John Wiley & Sons, 1993.

Ahrons, Constance R. *The Good Divorce*. New York: HarperCollins, 1994.

———. *Seven Golden Rules of Good Divorce*. New York: HarperCollins, 2006.

———. *We're Still Family: What Grown Children Have to Say About Their Parents' Divorce*. New York: HarperCollins, 2005.

American Association of Retired Persons. *Divorce After Fifty: Challenges and Choices*. Washington, DC: AARP, 1987.

Anderson, Keith, and Roy MacSkimming. *On Your Own Again: The Down-to-Earth Guide to Getting Through a Divorce or Separation and Getting On with Your Life*. New York: St. Martin's Press, 1992.

Astle, Matthew. "An Ounce of Prevention: Marital Counseling Laws as an Anti-Divorce Measure." 38 *Family Law Quarterly* 733 (Fall 2004).

Bartholet, Elizabeth. *Family Bonds: Adoption and the Politics of Parenting*. New York: Houghton Mifflin, 1993.

Bauer, Jill. *From "I Do" to "I'll Sue": An Irreverent Compendium for Survivors of Divorce*. New York: Plume/Meridian, 1993.

Belli, Melvin, and Mel Krantzler. *The Complete Guide for Men and Women Divorcing*. New York: St. Martin's Press, 1990.

———. *Divorcing*. New York: St. Martin's Press, 1988.

Berger, Stuart. *Divorce Without Victims*. Boston: Houghton Mifflin, 1983.

Berner, R. Thomas. *Parents Whose Parents Were Divorced*. Binghamton, NY: Hawthorne Press, 1992.

Berry, Dawn Bradley. *The Divorce Recovery Sourcebook*. Los Angeles: Lowell House, 1998.

————. *The Domestic Violence Sourcebook* (3rd ed.). Los Angeles: Lowell House, 2000.

————. *Equal Compensation for Women: A Guide to Getting What You're Worth in Salary, Benefits, and Respect.* Los Angeles: Lowell House, 1994.

————. *The Estate Planning Sourcebook.* Los Angeles: Lowell House, 1999.

————. "Let Freedom Ring!" *Healing Your Life After Divorce*, June 1991.

Beyer, Roberta, and Kent Winchester. *Juggling Act: Handling Divorce Without Dropping the Ball: A Survival Guide for Parents and Kids.* Minneapolis: Free Spirit Publishing, 2001.

————. *Speaking of Divorce: How to Talk With Your Kids and Help Them Cope.* Minneapolis: Free Spirit Publishing, 2001.

Blackstone-Ford, Jann, and Sharyl Jupe. *Ex-Etiquette for Parents: Good Behavior After a Divorce or Separation.* Chicago: Chicago Review Books, 2004.

————. *What in the World Do You Do When Your Parents Divorce?* Minneapolis: Free Spirit Publishing, 2001.

Blau, Melinda. *Families Apart.* New York: Putnam, 1993.

————. "What Every Woman Must Know About Divorce." *McCall's*, June 1994, p. 90.

Blume, Judy. *Letters to Judy: What Your Kids Wish They Could Tell You.* New York: Today Reader Service, 1987.

Blustein, Jane, Judy Lawrence, and S. J. Sanchez. *Daily Riches: A Journal of Gratitude and Awareness.* Deerfield Beach, FL: Health Communications, 1998.

Bradford, Laura. "The Counterrevolution: A Critique of Recent Proposals to Reform No-Fault Divorce Laws." 49 *Stanford Law Review*, February 1997, p. 607.

Brandt, Elizabeth Barker. "Valuation, Allocation and Distribution of Retirement Plans at Divorce: Where Are We?" 35 *Family Law Quarterly* 469 (Fall 2001).

Brown, Laurene Krasney, and Marc Brown. *Dinosaurs Divorce.* Boston: Little, Brown, 1988. (A book for kids.)

Brown, Ronald L., and Michael J. Albano. *Bankruptcy Issues in Matrimonial Cases: A Practice Guide.* Englewood Cliffs, NJ: Prentice Hall Law and Business, 1992.

Browne, Marlene. *Boomer's Guide to Divorce (and a New Life).* New York: Alpha Books, 2004.

Bruch, Carol S. "Parental Alienation Syndrome and Parental Alienation: Getting It Wrong in Child Custody Cases." 35 *Family Law Quarterly* 527 (Fall 2001).

Buckman, Sid. "Ghosts from Your Past." *Healing Your Life After Divorce*, June 1991.

Burns, Bob. *Through the Whirlwind: A Proven Path to Recovery from the Devastation of Divorce*. Nashville: Oliver-Nelson Books, 1989.

Carlson, Linda. *Everything You Need to Know About Your Parents' Divorce*. New York: Rosen Publishing, 1992.

Carpenter, Krista. "Child Support Payments Increase by 27 Percent." *Albuquerque Tribune*, January 9, 1998, p. A7.

———. "Why Mothers Are Still Losing: An Analysis of Gender Bias in Child Custody Determinations." *Detroit College of Law at Michigan State University Law Review*, Spring 1996, p. 33.

Chiriboga, David, and Linda S. Catron. *Divorce: Crisis, Challenge or Relief?* New York: New York University Press, 1991.

Chused, Richard H. *Private Acts in Public Places*. Philadelphia: University of Pennsylvania Press, 1994.

Clapp, Genevieve. *Divorce and New Beginnings*. New York: John Wiley & Sons, 2000.

Clementson, Lynette. "Distant Relations." *San Diego Union-Tribune*, April 15, 2006, Sec. D, p.1.

Coleman, Gerald D. *Divorce and Remarriage in the Catholic Church*. Mahwah, NJ: Paulist Press, 1988.

Commerce Clearinghouse Staff. *Divorce and Taxes*. Chicago: Commerce Clearinghouse, 1992.

Couric, Emily. *The Divorce Lawyers*. New York: St. Martin's Press, 1992.

Crown, Bonnie. *D-I-V-O-R-C-E-S Spell Discover: A Kit to Help Children Express Their Feelings About Divorce*. Pimbrough Pines, FL: Courageous Kids, 1992.

Crumbley, D. Larry, and Nicholas G. Apostolou. *The Handbook of Financial Planning for Divorce and Separation*. New York: John Wiley & Sons, 1990 (Cum. Suppl., 1993).

Curtis, M. Carol. "Rites of Passage—Rituals of Release." *Healing Your Life After Divorce*, June 1991, p. 2.

Dahlquist, Robert. "Family Law Mediation: Problems and Possibilities." *North County Lawyer*, January 2006, p. 1.

DeAngelis, Sidney M. *You're Entitled! A Divorce Lawyer Talks to Women*. Chicago: Contemporary Books, 1989.

Depner, Charlene E., and Charles H. Bray. *Non-Residential Parenting: New Vistas in Family Living*. Newbury Park, CA: Sage Publications, 1993.

DiFonzo, J. Herbie. "Alternatives to Marital Fault: Legislative and Judicial Experiments in Cultural Change." 34 *Idaho Law Review* 1, 1997.

Donahue, William A. *Communication, Marital Dispute and Divorce Mediation*. Hillsdale, NJ: Lawrence Erlbaum Associates, 1991.

Dorf, Paul A., and Russell G. Alion Jr. "Louisiana Marriages—Your Choice of Marriage!" *Lawatch Online* (ardhs.com/pubs/marriage.htm), May 20, 1998.

Dubin, Murray. "Teens Get Early Shot at Marriage Skills." Knight-Ridder Newspapers/*Albuquerque Journal*, November 11, 1994, p. B10.

Emerick-Cayton, Tim. *Divorcing with Dignity: Mediation—the Sensible Alternative.* Louisville: Westminster/John Knox Press, 1993.

Engel, Margorie L. *Divorce Help Sourcebook.* Detroit: Visible Ink Press, 1994.

———. *Weddings for Complicated Families.* Boston: Mount Ivy Press, 1993.

Engel, Margorie L., and Diana D. Gould. *The Divorce Decisions Workbook: A Planning and Action Guide.* New York: McGraw-Hill, 1992.

Enright, Elizabeth. "A House Divided." *AARP Magazine*, July and August 2004.

Evans, Joshua Shane. *How to Go to Visitation Without Throwing Up.* Livingston, TX: Pale Horse Publishers, 2002. (A book for kids.)

Ewald, George R. *Jesus and Divorce: A Biblical Guide for Ministry to Divorced Persons.* Stockdale, PA: Harold Press, 1991.

Ferguson, Bill. *How to Heal a Painful Relationship and If Necessary, How to Part as Friends.* Houston: Return to the Heart, 1999.

Fintushel, Noel, and Nancy Hillard. *A Grief Out of Season: When Your Parents Divorce in Your Adult Years.* Boston: Little, Brown, 1991.

Flosi, James V. *Lives Upside Down: Surviving Divorce.* Anaheim: ACTA Publications, 1993.

Forer, Lois G. *What Every Woman Needs to Know Before (and After) She Gets Involved with Men and Money.* New York: MacMillan/Rawson Associates, 1994.

Gardner, Richard A., M.D. *The Boys and Girls Book About Divorce.* Northvale, NJ: Arenson, Jason, 1992.

———. *The Boys and Girls Book About One-Parent Families.* Cresskill, NJ: Creative Therapeutics, 1983.

Genasci, Lisa. "Working Mothers: Courts Often Hold Them to Higher Standards in Custody Battles, Legal Experts Say." *Albuquerque Journal*, January 23, 1995, p. E8.

Golabuk, Phillip. *Recovering from a Broken Heart.* New York: Harper and Row, 1989.

Gold, Lois. *Between Love and Hate: A Guide to Civilized Divorce.* New York: Plenum Publishing, 1992.

Gold-Biken, Lynn Z., and Steven Kolodny. *The Divorce Trial Manual: From Initial Interview to Closing Argument.* Chicago: American Bar Association, 2004.

Gottlieb, Dorothy Weiss, Inez Bellow Gottlieb, and Marjorie A. Slavin. *What to Do When Your Son or Daughter Divorces: A New Guide of Hope and Help for Parents of Adult Children.* New York: Bantam Books, 1988.

Gottfried, Sarah. "Virtual Visitations: The Wave of the Future in Communication Between Children and Non-Custodial Parents in Relocation Cases." 36 *Family Law Quarterly* 475 (Fall 2002).

Greif, Geoffrey. *The Daddy Track and the Single Father.* New York: Lexington Books, 1990.

Greif, Geoffrey L., and Rebecca L. Hegar. *When Parents Kidnap: The Families Behind the Headlines.* New York: Free Press, 1992.

Grizzard, Lewis. *Lewis Grizzard's Advice to the Newlywed . . . and the Newly Divorced: I Can't Remember the Names of My Ex-Wives: I Just Call Them Plaintiff.* Marietta, GA: Long Street Press, 1989.

Gumz, Edward. *Professionals and Their Work in Family Divorce Court.* Springfield, IL: Charles C. Thomas Publishers, 1987.

Hardie, Dee, and Tom Hardie. "Grandparenting." *Albuquerque Journal*, February 26, 1995, p. C9.

Hendrix, Lorraine. *Caught in the Crossfire: The Impact of Divorce on Young People.* Summit, NJ: PIA Press, 1991.

Hirschfield, Mary. *The Adult Children of Divorce Workbook.* Los Angeles: Jeremy P. Tarcher, 1992.

Hyde, Margaret O., and Elizabeth Held Forsyth. *Parents Divided, Parents Multiplied.* Louisville: Westminster/John Knox Press, 1989.

Ives, Sally B., David Fassler, and Michele Lash. *The Divorce Workbook: A Guide for Kids and Families.* Burlington, VT: Waterfront Books, 1992.

Johansen, Frances. *The Financial Guide to Divorce.* Irvine, CA: United Resources Press, 1991.

Johnson, Colleen Leahy. *Ex-Familia: Grandparents, Parents and Children Adjust to Divorce.* New Brunswick, NJ: Rutgers University Press, 1988.

Jones, Thomas F. *The Single Again Handbook.* Nashville: Oliver Nelson Books, 1993.

Jong, Erica. *Fear of Fifty: A Midlife Memoir.* New York: HarperCollins, 1994.

———. *Megan's Two Houses.* New York: Dovekids, 1996.

Kaith, Pat M. *The Unmarried in Later Life.* New York: Praeger Publishers, 1989.

Kamm, Phyllis. *Remarriage in the Middle Years and Beyond.* San Leandro, CA: Bristol Publishing Enterprises, 1991.

Kass, Anne. "Don't Give Children a Sophie's Choice." *Albuquerque Tribune*, October 8, 1989.

———. "A Word from the Bench: Dispelling a Few Myths About Divorce Court." *New Mexico Verdict* 1, no. 4, August/September 1994, p. 16.

Kiley, John Cantwell. *Self Rescue.* Los Angeles: Lowell House, 1992.

Krantzler, Mel. *Creative Divorce.* Chicago: Signet NAL, 1974.

Krantzler, Pat, and Mel Krantzler. *The New Creative Divorce.* Cincinnati: Adams Media, 1998.

Krementz, Jill. *How It Feels When Parents Divorce*. New York: Alfred A. Knopf, 1988.

Kuczynski, Alex. "The Thirty-Seven-Year Itch." *New York Times*, August 8, 2004, Sec.9, p. 1.

Larkin, Twila B. "Guidelines for Alimony: The New Mexico Experiment." 38 *Family Law Quarterly* 29 (Spring 2004).

Larson, Hal, and Susan Larson. *Suddenly Single: A Lifeline for Anyone Who Has Lost a Love*. San Francisco: Halo Books, 1990.

Lawrence, Judy. *The Budget Kit*. Chicago: Dearborn Financial, 1992.

———. "Children, Divorce and Budgets." *New Mexico Verdict* 1, no. 4, August/September 1994, p. 5.

———. *Common Cent$: The Complete Money Management Workbook*. Albuquerque: Lawrence & Co., 1989.

"Lawyering à la Carte." *San Diego County Bar Association Bar Report*, February 22, 2006, p. 15.

Lebowitz, Marcia L. *I Think Divorce Stinks*. Woodbridge, CT: CDC Press, 1989.

Leonard, Frances. *Money and the Mature Woman*. Reading, MA: Addison-Wesley, 1993.

Leonard, Robin, and Steven Elias. *Family Law Dictionary*. Berkeley: Nolo Press, 1990.

Levoy, Gregg. *Callings: Finding and Following an Authentic Life*. New York: Harmony Books, 1997.

Lewin, Elizabeth S. *Financial Fitness Through Divorce*. New York: Facts on File, 1988.

Lowe, Peggy. "McDonald's Meets L.A. Law at Chain of Drive-Up Legal Stops." *Albuquerque Journal*, December 20, 1992, p. D7.

Maccoby, Eleanor. *Dividing the Child*. Cambridge: Harvard University Press, 1992.

McMillan, Terry. *Waiting to Exhale*. New York: Viking Penguin, 1992.

Margulies, Sam. *Getting Divorced Without Ruining Your Life*. New York: Simon & Schuster, 1992.

Marston, Stephanie. *The Divorced Parent: Success Strategies for Raising Your Children After Separation*. New York: William Morrow, 1994.

Mayle, Peter. *Why Are We Getting a Divorce?* New York: Harmony Books, 1988. (A book for kids.)

Miller, Mary Jane. *Upside Down*. New York: Puffin Books, 1994. (A book for kids.)

Mills, Eithne, and Keith Akers. "Who Gets the Cats . . . You or Me?" 36 *Family Law Quarterly* 283 (Summer 2002).

Minton, Lynn. "Fresh Voices: Getting Along with Stepparents: Teenagers Talk Frankly." *Parade*, February 26, 1995, pp. 24–25.

Moss, Anne E. *Your Pension Rights at Divorce: What Women Need to Know.* Washington, DC: Pension Rights Center, 1994.

Murphy, Patricia A. *Making the Connections: Women, Work and Abuse.* Winter Park, FL: GR Press, 1993.

———. *Making the Connections Workbook: A Career and Life Planning Guide for Women Abuse Survivors.* Winter Park, FL: GR Press, 1995.

National Center for Women in Retirement Research. *Women and Divorce: Turning Your Life Around.* Brooklyn: Long Island University Press, 1993.

Nelson, Jane, L. Lott, and H. Glenn. *Positive Discipline A–Z: 1,001 Solutions to Everyday Parenting Problems.* Rocklin, CA: Prima Publishing, 1993.

NiCarthy, Ginny. *Getting Free: You Can End the Abuse and Take Back Your Life.* Seattle: Seal Press, 1986.

Nichols, J. Randall. *Ending Marriage, Keeping Faith: A New Guide Through the Spiritual Journey of Divorce.* New York: Crossroad Publishing, 1993.

O'Dell, Larry. "Lesbian's Mother Wins Custody of Grandchild." *Albuquerque Journal*, April 22, 1995, p. C4.

Pitzele, Sefra K. *Surviving Divorce: Daily Affirmations.* Deerfield Beach, FL: Health Communications, 1991.

Pruett, Kyle D. *The Nurturing Father: Journey Toward the Complete Man.* New York: Warner Books, 1987.

Quello, Dan. *Safely Through the Storm.* Eugene, OR: Harvest House Publishers, 1992. (A book for kids.)

Reidy, Thomas J., Richard M. Silver, and Alan Carlson. "Child Custody Decisions: A Survey of Judges." *Family Law Quarterly* 23, no. 1 (Spring 1989).

Reske, Henry J. "Domestic Retaliations: Escalating Violence in Family Courts." *ABA Journal*, July 1993, p. 48.

Reynolds, Randy. *Divorce Recovery: Putting Yourself Back Together Again.* Grand Rapids, MI: Zondervan Publishing, 1992.

Robertson, Christina. *A Woman's Guide to Divorce and Decision Making: A Supportive Workbook for Women Facing the Process of Divorce.* New York: Fireside/Simon & Schuster, 1989.

Robinson, Margaret. *Family Transformation During Divorce and Remarriage.* New York: Routledge Chapman & Hall, 1993.

Rosenberg, Maxine B. *Living with a Single Parent.* New York: MacMillan/ Bradbury Press, 1992. (A book for kids.)

———. *Talking About Stepfamilies.* New York: MacMillan/Bradbury Press, 1990.

Rosenberg, Stephen M., and Ann Z. Peterson. *Every Woman's Guide to Financial Security.* Atlanta: Capital Publishing, 1994.

Rosenstock, Harvey A., Judith D. Rosenstock, and Janet Weiner. *Journey Through Divorce: Five Stages Toward Recovery.* New York: Human Sciences Press, 1988.

Rotruck, Sandra E. "Where Are We Going with Alimony?" *New Mexico Bar Bulletin*, November 21, 2005, p. 12.

Russo, Francine. "Can the Government Prevent Divorce?" *Atlantic Monthly*, October 1997, p. 28.

Schilling, Edwin, and Carol Ann Wilson. *Survival Manual for Men in Divorce.* Boulder, CO: Quantum Press, 1992.

Schoichet, Barbara. *The New Single Woman: Discovering a Life of Her Own.* Los Angeles: Lowell House, 1994.

Shami, Nailah. *Taking the High Road: How to Cope With Your Ex-husband, Maintain Your Sanity, and Raise Your Child in Peace.* New York: Penguin Group, 1999.

Shapiro, Robert B. *Separate Houses: A Practical Guide for Divorced Parents.* New York: Fireside/Simon & Schuster, 1989.

Shefts, Kimberly R. "Virtual Visitations: The Next Generation of Options for Parent-Child Communications." 36 *Family Law Quarterly* 303 (Summer 2002).

Splinter, John P. *The Complete Divorce Recovery Handbook.* Grand Rapids, MI: Zondervan Publishing, 1992.

Stinson, Kandi M. *Adolescence, Family, and Friends: Social Support After Parents Divorce or Remarriage.* New York: Praeger Publications, 1991.

Strater, Carole Sanderson. *Finding Your Place After Divorce: Help and Hope for Women Who Are Starting Again.* Wheaton, IL: Harold Shaw Publishers, 1992.

Sugarbaker, Geneva. *Nice Women Get Divorced: The Conflicts and Challenges for Traditional Women.* Minneapolis: Deaconess Press, 1992.

Sumrow, Kathie. "Tax Boomerang: Are Your Clients' Divorce Settlements at Risk?" 35 *Family Law Quarterly* 567 (Winter 2002).

Sullivan, Maria. *The Parent/Child Manual on Divorce.* New York: Tor Books, 1988.

Tangvald, Christine Harder. *Mom and Dad Don't Live Together Anymore.* Elgin, IL: Chariot Books, 1988.

Teyber, Edward. *Helping Children Cope with Divorce.* New York: Lexington Books, 1992.

Thompson, Dino. "Working Off the Big Mad." *Healing Your Life After Divorce*, June 1991.

Thrash, Sara A. *Dear God, I'm Divorced!: Dialogues with God.* Grand Rapids, MI: Baker Book House, 1991.

Trafford, Abigail. *Crazy Time.* New York: Harper Perennial, 1992.

Trump, Ivana. *The Best Is Yet to Come.* New York: Pocket Books, 1995.

Ungar, Alan B. *Financial Self-Confidence for the Suddenly Single: A Woman's Guide.* Los Angeles: Lowell House, 1993.

Vigeveno, H. S., and Anne Clire. *No One Gets Divorced Alone: How Divorce Affects Moms, Dads, Kids, and Grandparents.* Ventura, CA: Regal Books, 1987.

Wallerstein, Judith S., and Sandra Blakeslee. *Second Chances: Men, Women and Children a Decade After Divorce.* New York: Ticknor & Fields, 1989.

Wallman, Lester, and Sharon McDonnel. *Cupid, Couples, and Contracts: A Guide to Living Together, Prenuptial Agreements, and Divorce.* New York: Master Media, 1994.

Walther, Anne N. *Divorce Hangover.* New York: Pocket Books/Simon & Schuster, 1991.

Watson, Jane Werner, Robert E. Switzer, and J. Cotter Hershberg. *Sometimes a Family Has to Split Up.* New York: Crown Publishing, 1988.

Watson, Rita E. *The Art of Decision Making: Twenty Winning Strategies for Women.* Los Angeles: Lowell House, 1994.

Weitzman, Lenore J. *The Divorce Revolution.* New York: Free Press, 1985.

Wilson, Patricia. *Beyond the Crocodiles: Reflections on Being Divorced and Being Christian.* Nashville: Upper Room, 1990.

Woodhouse, Violet, and Victoria Felton-Collins. *Divorce and Money.* Berkeley: Nolo Press, 1993.

———. "Woman's Work." *People*, December 22, 1997, p. 72.

Zipp, Alan S. "Divorce Valuation of Business Interest: A Capitalization of Earnings Approach." *Family Law Quarterly* 23, no. 1 (Spring 1989).

Recommended Websites

Bonus Families: bonusfamilies.com

Collaborative Law: collaborativedivorce.com; divorcehq.com/collabor ative.html; divorcenet.com/collaborative; nocourtdivorce.com

Divorce Central: divorcecentral.com

Divorce Coaching: divorcecoach.net

Divorce and Bankruptcy: divorceinfo.com/bkrcybankruptcy.htm

Divorce Net: divorcenet.com

Divorce Source: divorcesource.com; divorcesupport/about.com

Divorce Support: divorcesupport.com

Federal Office of Child Support Enforcement: acf.dhhs.gov/programs/ cse

Long-Distance Families: longdistancefamilies.com

Men's Resource Network: themencenter.com

Military Divorce On-Line: militarydivorceonline

Military OneSource: militaryonesource.com

Nolo: nolo.com

Nolo began as a publisher of self-help legal books and has expanded to provide other law-related information and services. The excellent website provides both legal and practical advice.

Stepfamily Association of America: saafamilies.org
Unbundled Legal Services: unbundledlaw.com

Credits

GRATEFUL ACKNOWLEDGMENT IS made for permission to reprint portions of the following:

"Dispelling Myths About Custody Matters," by Anne Kass. Reprinted with permission of *The New Mexico Verdict* and Anne Kass, copyright © 1994. All rights reserved.

Divorce Help Source Book, by Marjorie Engel. Copyright © 1994 by Marjorie L. Engel. Published by Visible Ink Press. All rights reserved.

The Divorce Lawyers, by Emily Couric. Copyright © 1992 by Emily Couric. St. Martin's Press, Inc., New York, NY. All rights reserved.

The Divorce Revolution: The Unexpected Social and Economic Consequences for Women and Children in America, by Dr. Lenore J. Weitzman. Copyright © 1985. Published by The Free Press, an imprint of Simon & Schuster, Inc. All rights reserved.

Divorce Without Victims, by Stuart Berger, M.D. Copyright © 1983 by Stuart Berger. Published by Houghton Mifflin Company. All rights reserved.

Divorcing, by Melvin Belli Sr. and Mel Krantzler, Ph.D. Copyright © 1988 by Melvin Belli Sr. and Mel Krantzler. St. Martin's Press, Inc., New York, NY. All rights reserved.

"Domestic Retaliations: Escalating Violence in Family Courts," by Henry J. Reske. Copyright © 1993, *ABA Journal*. Reprinted by permission of the *ABA Journal*. All rights reserved.

"Don't Give Children a Sophie's Choice," by Anne Kass. Copyright © 1989 by Anne Kass. Reprinted with permission of Anne Kass and the *Albuquerque Tribune*. All rights reserved.

Fear of Fifty, by Erica Jong. Copyright © 1994 by Erica Mann Jong. Published by HarperCollins Publishers, Inc. All rights reserved.

Index